AF477895

Judith-Ann Walker
DEVELOPMENT ADMINISTRATION IN THE CARIBBEAN
Independent Jamaica and Trinidad & Tobago

Saskia Wieringa
SEXUAL POLITICS IN INDONESIA

Institute of Social Studies, The Hague
Series Standing Order ISBN 0–333–71477–6
(outside North America only)

You can receive future titles in this series as they are published by placing a standing order. Please contact your bookseller or, in case of difficulty, write to us at the address below with your name and address, the title of the series and the ISBN quoted above.

Customer Services Department, Macmillan Distribution Ltd, Houndmills, Basingstoke, Hampshire RG21 6XS, England

Development Administration in the Caribbean

Independent Jamaica and Trinidad & Tobago

Judith-Ann Walker

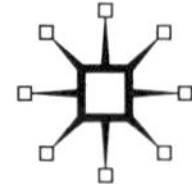

First published 2002 by
PALGRAVE MACMILLAN
Houndmills, Basingstoke, Hampshire RG21 6XS and
175 Fifth Avenue, New York, N. Y. 10010
Companies and representatives throughout the world

PALGRAVE MACMILLAN is the global academic imprint of the Palgrave Macmillan division of St. Martin's Press, LLC and of Palgrave Macmillan Ltd. Macmillan® is a registered trademark in the United States, United Kingdom and other countries. Palgrave is a registered trademark in the European Union and other countries.

ISBN 0–333–98719–5

This book is printed on paper suitable for recycling and made from fully managed and sustained forest sources.

A catalogue record for this book is available from the British Library.

Library of Congress Cataloging–in–Publication Data
Walker, Judith Ann.
    Development administration in the Caribbean: independent Jamaica and Trinidad and Tobago
        p. cm. — (Institute of Social Studies (Series))
    Includes bibliographical references and index.
    ISBN 0–333–98719–5 (cloth)
        1. Jamaica—Economic policy. 2. Trinidad and Tobago–
Economic policy. 3. Public administration—Jamaica. 4. Public administration—Trinidad and Tobago. 5. Economic development–
–Management—Case studies. I. Title. II. Series.

HC154 .W35 2002
338.97292—dc21

                                                              2001058218

10   9   8   7   6   5   4   3   2   1
11   10   09   08   07   06   05   04   03   02

Printed and bound in Great Britain by
Antony Rowe Ltd, Chippenham and Eastbourne

For Veronica Victoria

Contents

List of Tables

Acknowledgements

Several individuals and institutions contributed to the completion of this work. I wish to thank the Institute of Social Studies, which supported the Doctoral research from which this book derives. The Institute of Social and economic research, St Augustine; the libraries of the University of West Indies (Mona, St Augustine and Cave Hill), and the Caribbean Centre for Development Administration have all kindly facilitated the fieldwork of this study. The support of the Jamaican and T&T High Commissions in Nigeria where this work was finally completed must also be acknowledged.

I wish to thank the many scholars at the ISS who commented on various drafts of this work. I am especially grateful to Professor J.W. Bjorkman and Dr. V.V. Moharir for their support and criticism. There are many others, too numerous to mention, who have contributed in some way to the completion of this work. To them I extend my sincerest thanks.

Finally, I am eternally grateful to Yahaya, Aisha, Hana and Zoe for putting up with me as I yielded to the temptation of consulting one more reference or conducting one last interview.

Acronyms and Abbreviations

CAG	Comparative Administration Group
Caricad	Caribbean Centre for Development Administration
CB	Central Bank of Trinidad and Tobago
CEO	Chief Education Officer
CSA	Civil Service Association
CSO	Central Statistical Office
CTU	Central Training Unit
GDP	Gross Domestic Product
GNP	Gross National Product
GOJ	Government of Jamaica
GOTT	Government of Trinidad and Tobago
HATT	Housewives' Association of Trinidad and Tobago
JIDC	Jamaica Industrial Development Corporation
JLP	Jamaica Labour Party
JTA	Jamaica Teachers Association
IDB	Inter-American Development Bank
IDC	Industrial development corporation
IMF	International Monetary Fund
ISS	Institute of Social Studies
MOE	Ministry of Education
MOI	Ministry of Industry
NAR	National Alliance for Reconstruction
NJAC	National Joint Action Committee
NPA	National Planning Agency
O&M	Organization and Management Division
OPEC	Organization of Petroleum Exporting Countries
PNM	People's National Movement
PNP	People's National Party
PSA	Public Service Association
QRC	Queens Royal College
Servol	Service Volunteered for All
STATIN	Statistical Institute of Jamaica

THA	Tobago House of Assembly
T&T	Trinidad & Tobago
T&TIDC	Trinidad & Tobago Industrial Development Corporation
TRINTOMAR	Trinidad and Tobago Marine Petroleum Company
TRINTOC	Trinidad and Tobago Oil Company
TRINTOPEC	Trinidad and Tobago Petroleum Company
USAID	United States Agency for International Development
WHO	World Health Organization

Development Administration and Development Bureaucracies: Failure of Theory and Practice

1

Introduction

This is a study in Development Administration. Perhaps better said, this is a study of the failure of theory building in development administration and the failure of development bureaucracies in independent Jamaica and Trinidad & Tobago (T&T). Both of these events occurred in the 1970s. Within the fraternity of development administrationists led by the Comparative Administration Group (CAG), the 1970s marked a watershed. This was the time when most scholars lost confidence in the discipline, and the flow of publications dried up to be replaced by introspective critiques which indicted the discipline as Western, reductionist, state-centric and anti-democratic. The deadlock in development administration had arrived.

The central problematic of development administration remains that of devising explanations and prescriptions on the attributes of public bureaucracies which result in the achievement of development goals in different systems. However, since the 1970s this problematic has only been addressed *en passé* by scholars and institutions as they confront important questions within economics, planning, political economy and other sub-disciplines in development studies. In the 1970s, development administration concerns were addressed largely from the standpoint of political economy within a change model. In the 1980s and 1990s, the World Bank has dominated theorization on what now passes for development administration.

The 1970s crisis in development administration was not just another case of paradigmatic fatigue by over-zealous theoreticians. To be sure, the crisis was precipitated by the failure of development bureaucracies and the invalidation of the state-led model of development in the real world of debt burden and poverty overload. In Jamaica and T&T, the crisis of development bureaucracies was heralded by revolutionary uprisings on the streets of Kingston and Port-of-Spain. The state-led model of development was cursed, bureaucracy was condemned for its conspiratorial role with international capital, and bureaucrats were painted as status quo-oriented oppressors.

Not surprisingly, the 'new' development administration that emerged in the 1970s also failed to provide convincing answers to the question of the bureaucratic attributes necessary to effect development, now viewed as change. This was of course due to the theoretical problems involved in defining development as change and the fractured nature of the discipline, the latter undermining attempts to fashion clear causal relations between bureaucratic attributes and goal attainment.

In the late 1970s, development administration experienced yet another crisis as the emphasis on participation, decentralization and bureaucratic politics was overtaken by a return to the growth models of the 1950s and 1960s and the ascendance of the World Bank as the chief ideologue in this area. The Bank suggested bureaucratic attributes for restarting the engine of growth in Third World countries that harked back to development administration positions of the 1950s and 1960s. Where the Bank addressed issues of social development and change, themes from the 1970s were also invoked.

The development experiences of Jamaica and Trinidad & Tobago mirrored the ups and downs in development administration in the period from the early 1970s to 1990s. By the early 1980s, the development policies designed to redress discrimination against 'the underclasses' were hastily abandoned. The governments in Kingston and Port-of-Spain returned to growth programmes of the 1960s, but this time under the tutelage of the IMF and the World Bank. This period of groping for growth was to persist into the late 1990s. The 1990s witnessed miraculous policy zigzags, as parties that had pursued socialist policies in the 1970s became advocates of the free market and economic growth.

Objective

The objective of this study is to determine the attributes of development bureaucracies that lead to the achievement of development goals.

In this way, the study is located in the original mission statement of early development administrationists in the CAG. This was an ambitious mission statement that aimed to establish causal relations based on methodological rigour and comparative studies at both macro and micro levels: findings were to have universal applicability. It was upon this foundation that the science of public administration was to be built. A somewhat rigorous methodology is adopted in this study, wherein an explanatory framework is developed and tested in a longitudinal comparative research design to explain goal realization by development bureaucracies at both macro and micro levels. In this way, the study aims to advance the discipline of development administration by distilling explanations of bureaucratic performance from the long history of development administration, from Fred Riggs to the World Bank. The one important change made to the methodology of early development administrationists is that the study builds up an explanatory framework based on associations rather than causality.

The explanatory abilities of the framework of association are subject to two lines of examination. The first is at the level of a longitudinal comparative study of development bureaucracies in Jamaica and T&T over the period roughly equal to the first 30 years of independent nationhood, 1960–90. This study was conducted over a four-year period commencing in 1991 as partial fulfilment of the Doctorate of Philosophy programme at the Institute of Social Studies in The Hague. The findings constitute the basis upon which the second line of examination is conducted, spanning the contemporary period from 1990 to 1998.

The Failure of Theory

This work takes two problems as its point of departure: the theoretical inadequacy of Development Administration, and the inability of development bureaucracies to realize development goals. The theoretical problem stems from the failure of Development Administration to explain the performance of public bureaucracy as it undertakes development goals. Development Administration had its roots in an era characterized by big government, central planning and the promise of state-led development. The impetus of the discipline can be traced to Robert Dahl's 1947 essay, 'The Science of Public Administration: Three Problems.' In this essay, Dahl called into question the state of Public Administration, indicting it for its failure to develop a comparative framework.

The debates, discussions and advances in Public Administration in the post-World War II era have been mainly a reaction to Dahl's 1947 challenge. The emergence of the newly independent nations, advances in the field of comparative politics, and the abundance of development research funding, coupled with problems in the American Aid programme, meant that Dahl's challenge did not fall on deaf ears. The Americans, who then dominated the discipline with articles of faith from Woodrow Wilson and Ernst Freund, were confronted with different systems that defied easy explanation.

Consequently, in the quest for a science of Public Administration, the American Political Science Association established an *ad hoc* committee on comparative administration in 1953. A year earlier, the Public Administration Clearing House had sponsored a conference on Comparative Administration at Princeton University. As a result of the 1952 conference, a subcommittee was formed with the following terms of reference:

> (1) Review and assess the existing state of knowledge of the field, (2) identify major research needs, (3) suggest means of stimulating new types of studies and (4) develop criteria of relevance and prepare a general research guide for such studies. (Gable 1975: 4)

The subcommittee published its report in 1953. By 1954, two of the major contributors to the 1953 report, Wallace Sayre and Herbert Kaufman, together with Fred Riggs, formed a Working Group on Comparative Administration (CAG). The Working Group developed a proposal for comparative research in administration entitled 'Research design for a pilot study in Comparative Public Administration.' In 1959, Fred Riggs assumed chairmanship of the group. When Ford Foundation grants were secured by the CAG in 1962, the Group directed its research exclusively towards establishing causal relations between public bureaucracy and development. Because it was felt that public bureaucracy in all countries—in the First, Second and Third Worlds—formulated and implemented development goals, it was theoretically possible to justify the quest for scientific principles, albeit in such a narrow area of specialization. The Third World offered the greatest potential for determining causal relations between public organizations and development goals, because the *raison d'être* of public bureaucracies in the newly emergent countries was purely developmental. Hence, the association of Development Administration with the newly emerging 'Third World'.

The developing world, and therefore Development Administration, also presented a superior laboratory for developing a science of Public Administration because of the availability of funding, the virgin appeal of developing areas and an anthropologically-driven compulsion of American scholars to conceptualize 'the other.' Writing on a similar experience in comparative politics, Colin Leys once said: 'We have possibly learned more about politics from studies of underdeveloped countries than from studies in developing ones in recent years' (1969: 10).

Thus, an opportunity was presented to advance Public Administration, which up to that time had remained the soft underbelly of Political Science. However, differing theoretical, methodological and ideological orientations amongst scholars resulted in a lack of consensus on the scientific principles that 'cause' public bureaucracy to 'maximize' development goals.

The failure of Development Administration to develop a comprehensive and comparative paradigm on how such organizations realize development goals has created in a gap into which economists, planners and political scientists have entered. Currently, neo-liberal development institutions such as the World Bank dominate the behavioural and normative agenda in Development Administration. The neo-liberal political economy of development theorizes the appropriate role, size and structure of public bureaucracy as it undertakes economic growth goals. This study argues that neo-liberal contributions are inadequate, ahistorical and lack real input from Public or Development Administration.

More than 40 years have passed since Dahl raised his challenge to develop a science of Comparative Public Administration. Development administrationists of the 1950s and 1960s attempted to do this in the narrow sub-field of Development Administration. The failure of the development administration effort has further set back the discipline and, in the words of Henry (1989), public administration remains in a 'quandary.' More polemically, Hood equates the state of the discipline with that of Britain after World War II, 'having lost an empire and not yet found a role' (1990: 107). Though scholars from other disciplines have tried to fill the gap in Development Administration, they too have failed to come up with convincing, holistic explanations grounded in empirical research. A comparative paradigm to make sense of how public bureaucracies undertake development goals is still as elusive today as it was in 1947, though, as Peters (1990) notes, it remains imperative as ever. In this regard, a recent contribution from one of public and development administration's foremost gurus, Fred Riggs, warrants extensive quotation:

> The globalization of our world compels us to rethink the context of what we call 'Public Administration.' We can no longer afford to base our theories on the truly exceptional American experience and to limit 'Comparative Public Administration' to the study of 'foreign' governments.
>
> In a global world system, we need to develop frameworks and theories for the study of public administration that are truly universal in scope—they will be based on a comprehensive ecological understanding of the place of public administration in all governments, historical as well as contemporary. Such a framework will ... be nomothetic, focusing on explanatory theories that account for the continuously changing properties and problems faced by governments as they seek to implement public policies. Its normative guidelines will be anchored in empirical knowledge of the institutions and dynamics of any society in which they are employed. (1991: 473)

It is this gap in the theoretical literature that this study takes as its point of departure.

The Failure of Development Bureaucracy in Jamaica and Trinidad & Tobago

The empirical problem this study focuses upon stems from the extreme pessimism, teleology and ahistoricism accompanying the charge of state and bureaucratic failure in Jamaica and T&T. In the late 1960s to the early 1970s, the streets of Jamaica and T&T resonated to the cries of political dissenters demanding a change to neo-colonial economic and social structures. By April 1970, T&T had suffered an army mutiny and a 'Black-Power Revolution,' and the houses of Members of Parliament and top businessmen had become targets for firebombs. In Jamaica, university students and lecturers clashed with state security forces over the banning of University Lecturer Walter Rodney, from Jamaica; arson, looting and property destruction followed these riots. Around the same time, a less violent but perhaps more virulent form of resistance was taking shape in the Rastafarian movement (Gray 1983 and C. Parris 1976).

The 1980s witnessed a new charge of state and bureaucratic failure in Jamaica and T&T. On this occasion, however, the critique came largely from the right. It was led by the 'neo-Ricardian' economists on the St Augustine Campus of the University of the West Indies, independent economists 'rethinking Caribbean development,' and international development institutions such as the World Bank and the International Monetary Fund.

By the 1980s, the old dependency economists had left the St Augustine campus of the University of the West Indies. Indeed, by 1981, Lloyd Best, one of the leading dependency economists, was no longer at the Department of Economics. Although the new generation of economists were students of the old dependency economists, they addressed themselves squarely to the question of growth, albeit under conditions of dependent development within a capitalist framework. These economists no longer found it useful to discuss the problems of Caribbean development in terms of metropolitan extraction and the predatory role of the multinational corporation. They were more concerned with deriving lessons from and, indeed, reifying the Newly Industrializing Countries (NICs). In addition, the implosion of the Grenadian revolution in 1983 left the St Augustine-based economists even more weary of the radical path to economic development, though many of them had laboured in service of the revolution in its early days.

It is against this background that a somewhat conservative wind swept through the St Augustine campus in the 1980s, and economists at the Department of Economics launched a formidable critique of macroeconomic management in the Caribbean in general, and in T&T under the Peoples National Movement (PNM) in particular. The critique of T&T had serious implications for the role and size of the state and its administrative apparatus. In this regard, the analysis of the St Augustine economist T.M.A. Farrell is particularly noteworthy because of its language of pessimism and high-drama. Farrell declared: 'The region is rapidly being Haitianized. If we don't change direction soon, we are doomed' (1986: 21). He argued further:

> That we have failed, and are failing, to achieve the economic transformation of the region is by now quite clear. There are some on the naive left who would doubtless blame our failures on imperialism and/or on wicked foreign corporations... To my mind, three things are clear. One

is that we have failed. The second is that it is our decisions at governmental level that are primarily to blame. The third is that our failure is in the final analysis our responsibility. (Farrell 1986: 7)

Similarly, during the 1980s, international development institutions such as the International Monetary Fund (IMF), the United Nations Industrial Development Organization (UNIDO), the Inter-American Development Bank (IDB) and the World Bank indicted overdeveloped public bureaucracies in T&T for their inability to support the government's structural adjustment programme. The 1988 World Bank Country Economic Report on Trinidad & Tobago described the T&T Industrial Development Corporation as:

> ... slow to exchange its traditionally strong nationalistic and technology-oriented role as the promoter of local manufacturing production for that of the commercially oriented, outward-looking seeker of foreign investment and export markets that is now urgently required. (World Bank 1988: 19)

Similar charges were made in the 1988 UNIDO Report on the Industrial Sector and the 1991 IDB Private Investment Diagnostic Study.

Critics of state and bureaucratic performance in Jamaica in the 1980s took their point of departure from what they perceived as the failure of the Manley socialist experiment. Critics ignored the phenomenal social transformation that had taken place in the 1970s in the face of the nation's balance-of-payments crisis, its staggering unemployment rate and huge public sector deficit. Accordingly, the developmental performance of state and public institutions was judged mainly in terms of economic growth and not in terms of change. Thus the term 'Jamaica Disease' was coined in the 1980s within international development circles to describe the phenomenon of burgeoning and inefficient public developmental agencies. To be sure, under Manley, official statistics recorded 'public administration's contribution to GDP' as having increased from 8 per cent in 1971 to 14 per cent in 1980 (Appendix Table A1.1). Accordingly, the percentage of the work force employed in public administration increased from 11 per cent in 1970 to 14 per cent in 1980 (Appendix Table A1.2a & b). By 1980, a conservative estimate revealed that Jamaica had 249 public enterprises (Adams et al. 1993), many of which duplicated functions and operated at a loss.

Furthermore, the 1980s and early 1990s also witnessed a proliferation of works by independent economists reflecting on the 'crisis' of state-led development in the English-speaking Caribbean. These studies took as their point of departure the negative growth rates of the 1970s and 1980s, the persistence of structural unemployment, and the new reality of pernicious balance-of-payments deficits. Their titles testify to the pessimism of this period—*Crisis in the Caribbean* (Ambursley & Cohen 1983), *Development in Suspense* (Beckford & Girvan 1989), *The Poor and the Powerless* (Thomas 1988), *Rethinking Development* (Girvan et al. 1991), and *Rethinking Caribbean Development* (Schuyler & Veltmeyer 1988).

Taken together, the critiques of the 1970s and the 1980s paint a Naipaulian picture of the state and public bureaucracy in Jamaica and T&T where nothing is created and all development interventions end in failure. This study takes this bleak vision of failure as its point of departure.

Methodology, Assumptions and the Framework of Association

Methodology

The study employs the ends–means methodology derived from Development Administration. In Development Administration, development goals are the ends of development and public bureaucracy is the means of development. As applied in this study, the methodology hinges on three questions:

1. What were the 'actual' and 'dominant' goals of development?
2. To what extent have they been realized?
3. What attributes of public bureaucracy were associated with goal realization?

The research focuses on two types of ends or goals of development:

1. the end of economic growth, and
2. the end of change: economic and social change.

As an end/goal of development, economic growth is fundamentally about quantitative increases in a society's stocks of goods and services; it 'does not necessarily lead to changes in economic structure' (Lesson & Nixon 1988: 56). Braibanti and Spengler (1961) define economic growth as 'the diversion of a nation's scarce resources and productive powers to the augmentation of its stock of productive wealth and to the progressive enlargement of its gross and net national product of goods and services' (quoted in Heady 1979: 84). Although 'augmentation' of a nation's stock of productive wealth, i.e., economic growth, is often associated with changes in the techniques and structures of production, the *raison d'être* of such changes is inevitably the quest for a quantitative addition and not change as an end in itself. Consequently, while Gable sees economic growth as a type of social change, he concludes that 'growth is the process of producing the same kinds of ends. Growth involves nothing more than a quantitative change or expansion' (1975: 65). Gross Domestic Product (GDP) is the indicator of economic growth used in this study.

Where the state has a central role in stimulating economic growth—by directing, facilitating or undertaking economic initiatives—its administrative apparatus can be considered a factor of production. Inputs from administration are required at each stage of the policy cycle: formulation, implementation and evaluation; all attributes contributing to efficient outputs from public bureaucracy are associated with goal realization.

Because change is subjectively defined within Development Studies, the concept takes on different meanings according to the orientation of the writer. Consequently, while change can be defined as structural disruption followed by a qualitative improvement, scholars take different views on the intensity of the disruption and the nature of the improvement. Thus change can mean modernization (McClelland 1964) or transformation to socialism (Thomas 1974). Within Development Studies, change is defined in contra-distinction to growth.

This study views 'economic change' as a process whereby the existing neo-colonial economic order is disrupted and replaced by production structures which constitute a qualitative improvement over the old order. The old order was one of staple domination, low value-added and foreign ownership of productive enterprises. Thus the new and improved status quo aims at:

1. diversification away from dominance by an export staple with low value-added, and
2. transfer of foreign ownership to local interests in this and other sectors. (This is essentially an issue of economic nationalism.)

These were the issues raised by dependency economists in the early 1970s. These were also the issues around which radical social movements rallied in the late 1960s.

Despite differing perspectives on social change in Development Studies, the origins of this discussion within the neo-populist (Kitching 1989) and dependency (Allahar 1989) literature of the 1970s has made the question of underclass empowerment central to the understanding of this concept. Consequently, this study views social change as a dynamic process whereby groups, subordinated under the existing status quo, achieve mobility in the social structure. The study focuses on women and argues that, at independence, this group, along with others including workers, peasants and the descendants of African slaves and Indian indentured labourers, was effectively an underclass. Social change is measured in terms of occupational mobility. Because women's occupational mobility is, in itself, linked to women's educational attainment (King & Hill 1993), the question of social change for women will be discussed exclusively in terms of education policy and the education bureaucracy.

Assumptions

The study assumes that 'growth' and 'change' are inherently different goals of development, and that different patterns of bureaucratic attributes are associated with their realization. This assumption is based on a well-established distinction in the literature between different types of policy goals and associated differences in political and bureaucratic configurations. Indeed, this perspective can be traced to Lowi's pioneering 1964 work which distinguished three areas of policy or governmental activities.

A second assumption of this study is that public bureaucracies are partially open systems; that is to say, they act upon and are acted upon by their external environment. Thus, bureaucratic attributes associated with goal realization should be located both within the internal organization and in the organization's external environment. However, not all aspects of the public bureaucracy's environment exert the same degree of influence on the organization's ability to support development goals. Moreover, not all aspects of the environment can be considered within the finite framework of such a study. Consequently, we assume further that, in matters concerning development goals, public bureaucracy's 'policy' and 'political' environments have the greatest impact on its performance. In the language of organizational theorists, the policy and political environments constitute the organization's immediate 'task environment.' This assumption draws upon advances in organizational theory and organizational dimensions of public administration (Heady 1979, Jun 1976, Henry 1989, Hassard & Parker 1994).

Framework of association

Having selected the ends–means methodology and specified internal and external loci for identifying variables of association, the next step is to construct a framework for exploring associations between bureaucratic attributes and the realization of economic growth goals and change goals. In doing so, however, we are confronted with the disparate, partial and weak explanations of bureaucratic performance in the literature addressing this question. Because we aim to fill gaps in existing explanations, we propose to construct a framework of association that is comprehensive and comparative. Such a framework should view development as both growth and change, locate explanators in both the internal and external organization, and be based on cross-national experiences and be applicable to different countries.

Against this background, an eclectic approach is taken to the disparate literature dealing with development administration. The literature is reviewed and variables of association are selected based on two factors: convergence or recurring themes and their comparative merit. Because of the long history of development administration theory, the extent to which the same factors recur and/or converge recommends them for selection. The extent to which the same factors are thrown up from different systems (the developing world, Eastern bloc countries and Western democracies) also recommends them for selection. Variables are selected and placed within the framework based on their location within the internal organization and in the political and policy environments. They are also selected and placed based on whether they address the issue of development as economic growth or as change.

The Most Similar Systems Research Design

The Most Similar Systems Research Design is employed to collect, organize and analyse data and to operationalize the ends–means methodology of the study. The comparative or Most Similar Systems Design has its origins in John Stuart Mill's method of 'concomitant variation.' Mill argued that:

> ... if an instance in which the phenomenon under investigation occurs
> and in which it does not occur have every circumstance in common

save one, that one occurring only in the former, the circumstance in which alone the two instances differ is the effect, or the cause, or an indispensable part of the cause of the problem. (Quoted in Meckstroth 1975: 133)

The Most Similar Systems Research Design is operationalized by selecting a dependent variable for explanation in systems that are as generally similar as possible. Covariation between dependent and independent variables is established in theory. Differences in the dependent variable in similar systems are then determined. Differences should covary with the independent variable according to the relationship established in theory. To the extent that the covariation explains differences, we can say that the theoretical assumptions on which dependent and independent variables are based are confirmed. The advantage of the Most Similar Systems Research Design is based on the premise that 'systems as similar as possible with respect to as many features as possible constitute the optimal samples for comparative inquiry' (Przeworski & Teune 1970: 32). Resemblance between this research design and conventional 'area studies' has been noted by Przeworski and Teune.

Lijphart sees this comparative research design as 'a research methodology for testing hypothesized empirical relationships among variables' (1975: 164). Similarly, Meckstroth demonstrates how this design can be employed for positivist research by detailing its various steps:

(1) on the basis of some rational, theoretical argument, two or more attributes are hypothesized to covary under specified conditions; (2) the specified conditions are established according to the canons of the comparative method; (3) the hypothesized covariation fails to materialize; and (4) this failure is not due to errors of observation or errors in the 'auxiliary theory of measurement' itself ... Under these conditions, it follows that the proposition is false, as initially stated. And so, following Popper's usage ... we shall employ the term 'corroborated', rather than 'established,' for a proposition that withstands serious effort at falsification through this procedure. (1975: 136)

He notes further that the design is limited by the rigor of the positivist research methodology. Theoretical propositions can either be 'corroborated' or 'disproved' but never established, and empirical propositions generated by the inquiry have limited application to other similar areas and cases.

Because this study neither attempts to corroborate nor disprove causality within a positivist framework, the Most Similar Systems Research Design is merely employed as a heuristic device for organizing data to answer the research question and to operationalize the ends-means methodology of the research.

The design suggests that, given general similarities between the selected case countries, differences in the dependent variable—realization of development goals—should be associated with differences in attributes of the independent variable—public bureaucracy. Since the attributes of public bureaucracy will be presented in the framework of association, the realization of growth and change goals should covary with the framework.

Jamaica and Trinidad & Tobago: Most Similar Systems in the English-speaking Caribbean

The English-speaking or Commonwealth Caribbean consists of 13 states from Trinidad & Tobago and Guyana in the South to Jamaica and Belize in the North. It is a complex grouping defying convenient attempts at classification based on political system, constitutional status, and level of economic and social development, size or location. Appendix Table A1.3 presents a profile of the countries of this region.

Though not without its limitations, the More Developed Country (MDC)/Less Developed Country (LDC) classification generally applied to the region (World Bank 1978) provides a useful starting point for discussing similarities. Within the grouping of MDCs, Jamaica and T&T have emerged as the most developed economies in the post-independence era. Compared to the two other MDCs, Guyana and Barbados, industry is more developed in Jamaica and T&T and constitutes a more significant share of these countries' GDP (World Development Report 1987 & 1990). It must be noted, however, that while Barbados has lost the comparative edge in economic development, it has more than compensated in the level of social development it offers its citizens (*The Courier*, September/October 1990).

Moreover, with the first and second largest populations of the region (Appendix Table A1.4), politicians in Jamaica and T&T, more so than those of Barbados or Guyana, have had to deal with developmental problems from a relatively large population with high expectations, hence the social insurgency both countries faced in the early 1970s (Parris 1976). The post-independence political history of both countries has not been uneventful, what with the 1990 coup in T&T, and the spectre of political violence hanging over Jamaica's general and even local elections. However, these countries stand mid-way between the endemic political volatility of Guyana and the political tranquillity of the ideal-typical British colony, Barbados.

Jamaica and T&T were also the first countries of the Commonwealth Caribbean to achieve political independence in 1962; Barbados and Guyana, the two other MDCs, only became independent in 1966. Therefore they have also had the distinction of the longest experience of state-directed development interventions in the region. From the early 1960s to the present, social and economic development policy in both countries have been formulated, implemented and evaluated by the state and the public bureaucracy. Indeed, this phenomenon has its roots in colonial development policy following the labour unrest of the late 1930s. At that time, the colonial government 'took out insurance against disorder' (Post 1978) in the jewels of the British West Indian colonies—Jamaica and Trinidad & Tobago—by according to the state a central role in new development initiatives. Decolonization, preparation for self-government and the creation of a developmentalist state, therefore, got off to an earlier start in these two colonies (Lewis 1968).

In the post-colonial era, the state after independence came to be viewed as the embodiment of development. The existence of an underdeveloped non-governmental sector, coupled with the state's new role as guarantor of external development loans, made this institution even more central to the process of development. While it is true to say that the developmentalist state in Jamaica, T&T and in other countries of the English-speaking Caribbean is a colonial construct (Thomas 1984), the absence of alternative institutions has earned the state legitimacy, both from internal forces and external actors. Consequently, the post-independence history of development in these two countries is a history of the promise of development through the state and public bureaucracy. Based on the above, it can be concluded that, in general terms, Jamaica and T&T are the most similar countries in the English-speaking Caribbean.

The Empirical Inquiry

The research question is explored in a comparative study of development bureaucracy in independent Jamaica and Trinidad & Tobago. The empirical inquiry sets out to discern differences in the realization of growth and change goals, and tries to determine whether differences are associated with bureaucratic attributes contained in the framework. This is done at the macro and micro levels. At the macro level, the association between goal realization and the attributes of public bureaucracies will be explored in terms of sections of the aggregate public sector. At the micro level this relationship is explored in two case studies of development bureaucracies: the Industrial Development Corporation (IDC), and the Ministry of Education. In the IDC study, associations between differences in goal realization (growth and change goals) and organizational and environmental attributes are explored. The Ministry of Education case study is used exclusively to consider the goal of social change for women. Associations are explored between differences in the degree of occupational change for women and attributes of the Ministry of Education in Jamaica and T&T.

Chapter Summary

Chapter 2 discerns differences in the dependent variable—growth and change goal realization—between the two countries over the research period (1960–90). This period is subdivided into the decades of the 1960s, 1970s and 1980s for purposes of collecting and analysing data in a manageable time-series. Chapter 3 reviews the literature that associates development goals and public bureaucracy. Variables of association are selected and a framework is constructed accordingly. The next chapter (Chapter 4) explores associations between the realization of the economic growth goal and bureaucratic attributes at both macro and micro levels. Chapter 5 explores associations between the realization of the economic change goal and public bureaucracy. Again, this is done at both macro and micro levels. Chapter 6 considers associations between the realization of social change for women and attributes of the Ministry of Education. Chapter 7 presents the findings, applies them to the decade of the 1990s, and considers the implications for the theory and practice of development administration in the 21st century.

2 Development Goals and their Realization in Jamaica and Trinidad & Tobago

Introduction

This chapter compares the extent to which Jamaica and Trinidad & Tobago achieved development goals during the 1960s, 1970s and 1980s. Their development plans, annual budgets, *ad hoc* policy statements and actual policy choices constitute the focal point for identifying their respective goals. While it is recognized that governments can simultaneously pursue multiple and sometimes conflicting development goals, the chapter aims to establish the dominant development goal or goals in the designated decades.

This analysis is based on the assumption that, given the centrality of the state in the process of development in Jamaica and T&T, gains or losses can be attributed to state action or inaction. Consequently, we are not too concerned with unintended outcomes in the development process, such as T&T's oil boom in the 1970s, as this is fundamentally a study in the ends and means of development.

This chapter occupies an important place in the Most Similar Systems Research Design as it seeks to identify differences in the dependent variable for explanation, 'goal realization.' Two types of goals are focused upon—economic growth and change, in particular, economic and social change.

Economic Growth: Goals and their Realization

A central theme in the discussion on economic growth in the English-speaking Caribbean is that of increasing productive capacity to solve the region's chronic unemployment problem. This theme runs through the works of Lewis (one of the earliest advocates of industrialization), the 'neo-Ricardians' on the St Augustine Campus in the 1980s and policymakers in the 1990s. To what extent was economic growth a development goal in the 1960s, 1970s and 1980s? How was this goal to be achieved, and to what extent was it achieved? These are the questions of economic goals and realization.

It is important to situate the development goals of the 1960s in Jamaica against the background of rural poverty and a skewed income distribution which accompanied the unprecedented economic growth rates of the 1950s (Ahiram 1966). Thus, the main planning document of the 1960s—The First Five Year 1963–68 Independence Plan—affirmed the government's commitment to redressing inequalities through social and community programmes for rural areas.

The previous plan—the 1957–67 National Plan for Jamaica—prepared by the People's National Party (PNP) government of Norman Manley, prioritized economic growth as the goal of development. In 1962 the Norman Manley government lost the general election to the Jamaica Labour Party (JLP). The chronic unemployment problem inherited by the new government, coupled with the swing of the rural vote against the PNP, left it with no choice but to institute redistributive policies, especially for the rural poor. To compound this situation, emigration from Jamaica to the United Kingdom dipped from 37,615 in 1961 to a mere 3,248 in 1963 due to UK restrictions (Jefferson 1972: 23). An 8 per cent population growth rate was also projected over the planning period.

Against this background, the 1963–68 First Five Year Development Plan of the JLP promised redistribution through social and community services. The plan promised to address rural poverty, since this problem was especially recognized, and to reduce migration to overcrowded towns. Indeed, the 1963–68 Plan went so far as to eschew economic growth by stating that:

> There will be less than full concentration on economic growth … it is believed that such a balance between overall economic growth and immediate improvement in levels of living for the people will result in the stabilisation of development gains through the minimisation of discontent which is a deterrent to development … the long-term projects will follow as investment in education, technical training, agricultural techniques, marketing and specific economic projects. (GOJ First Five-year Plan 1962: 51)

However, if the JLP is judged on the actual policies implemented over the 1962–72 period in which it constituted the government, rather than on the 1963–68 Plan, it will be clear that the 1960s were dominated by the goal of economic growth, not of redistribution and social change. This point is borne out by a close look at actual versus proposed expenditure (Table 2.1).

Table 2.1   *Proposed versus actual capital expenditure for the 1963–68 planning period as a percentage of total capital expenditure*

Allocation	Proposed %	Actual %
Agriculture	33	18
Communication, works	17	24
Local government	16	16
Trade & industry	6	10
Finance & development	5	18
Education	7	6
Public health	4	2
Housing & social welfare	12	5
Other	—	1
Total	100	100

Source: Girvan 1971: 121.

Further evidence of the JLP's actual commitment to economic growth is found in budget speeches of the period. These portray a JLP government adamantly committed to economic growth. With Edward Seaga as Minister of Finance, the government was even prepared to do battle with the local private sector in its attempts to mobilize revenue domestically for economic growth. Moreover, the JLP government engaged in an orgy of self-congratulation in its Annual Budget Speeches as its 'prudent financial management' strategies were applauded by the World Bank.

Despite the JLP's efforts to convince Jamaican voters of its economic management skills, the People's National Party won the 1972 general elections. During Michael Manley's two consecutive terms in office—1972–76 and 1976–80—Jamaica's developmental focus shifted to change. This period also saw an interregnum in medium- to long-term planning in Jamaica: development goals were contained in annual budget speeches, *ad hoc* policy documents and political addresses. However, in response to Jamaica's financial crisis in the late 1970s, the Manley government saw the need to restart the engine of economic growth. Thus, the government tried to set growth targets and strategies in its 1977 Emergency Production Plan. This plan was set aside as the government's growth programme was soon superseded by IMF agreements in its twilight years in office. The fact that the first July 1977 agreement bore limited conditionalities, coupled with the PNP's fundamental adherence to the goals of change, means that the 1970s can best be described as a decade of change in Jamaica. The mechanics of this change are discussed below.

With the JLP's return to office in 1980, the entire question of economic growth was raised as a precondition for Jamaica's economic recovery. Seaga criticized the Manley government for wanting to socialize poverty rather than create wealth. Seaga outlined a programme of economic recovery anchored firmly on growth. This was to be achieved through what he called 'the structural adjustment of the economy.'

The 'structural adjustment' of the Jamaican economy meant a radical programme of economic change to precipitate growth and create a hundred thousand jobs over three years (GOJ Annual Budget Speech 1981). These jobs were to be created in the private sector given the government's commitment to reducing the public sector work force. In this regard, Seaga sought to diversify the productive base of the economy into seven non-traditional export areas with high value-added. This was essentially a model of growth through far-reaching economic change, funded by foreign bilateral and multilateral lending agencies. The mechanics of this model were contained in the government's New Industrial Plan. Seaga's 'special relationship' with US President Ronald Reagan was to provide the security and stability for potential investors in Jamaica.

During the 1980s, the Seaga government seemed unrelenting in its commitment to economic growth. In response to critics concerned about the social costs to Jamaica's vulnerable populace, the government retorted that 'It takes Cash to Care.' Despite Seaga's celebrated 'Adjustment at a More Human Pace' speech to the IMF-World Bank joint annual meeting in Seoul in 1985, the pursuit of growth continued to dominate Seaga's public policy agenda, even on the eve of the 1989 general elections. This can be seen from the government's Medium

Term Economic Programme, entitled 'Going for Growth,' and from the contents of the 1988–89 Annual Budget. In the 1988–89 budget, the JLP government led by Seaga congratulated itself on the record achievement of 5 per cent growth for 1988. It stated that this was 'the highest in 16 years' (GOJ Annual Budget Speech 1988: i). Michael Manley's PNP was returned to office in February 1989 on a platform that promised to 'Put People First' and to 'Care.'

In T&T, the experience of the 1960s revealed a preoccupation with economic growth for the alleviation of unemployment: 'Operation Jobs' was the subtitle of the industrialization programme. Indeed, the fact that the 1960s People's National Movement (PNM) government of Eric Williams did not inherit a boom economy, as the JLP did in Jamaica, made the lure of growth an even more attractive prospect in T&T. Unemployment and rapid population growth were seen as the biggest problems facing the small island state. The context of these problems was a small dependent economy heavily reliant on petroleum, and to a lesser extent sugar and asphalt exports. The 1958–62 First Five Year Development Plan (The Peoples' Charter) and the 1964–68 Second Five Year Plan proposed to solve these problems through government support of a private sector-led development programme in manufacturing and tourism. Government set itself the task of providing the physical and legal infrastructure required for economic growth.

While the JLP government of the 1960s covertly pursued growth and paid lip service to redistribution and social change, the PNM's plans of the 1960s were more candid about the government's concern with promoting economic growth. This was so, despite the fact that the Second Five Year Plan (1964–68) stressed human resource development; the ultimate aim of human resource development was to support economic growth. Consequently, the expenditure priorities of the 1964–68 plan placed infrastructural expansion first, with an allocation of over 45 per cent of total expenditure. Social expenditure in education, health, housing and community development combined were allocated only 22 per cent of total projected expenditure. In contrast, the 1963–68 Jamaica Independence Plan allocated 39 per cent of total expenditure to economic services, and 47 per cent to social and community services (Girvan 1971: 115).

With the civil unrest of the late 1960s leading to the 1970 'February Revolution,' the PNM was confronted with the need to change neo-colonial economic and social structures. The oil boom of the 1970s provided the revenue to fund these changes, whose nature and extent are discussed in the following section. Suffice it to say that, during the 1970s, the PNM saw no need to strategize for growth. Rather, the issue of the day was how to use surplus resources in pursuit of change.

It was not until the 1980s that growth was re-established as the primary goal of development in T&T. This was precipitated by declining oil production and falling oil revenues, the latter due to a 14 per cent fall in the world market oil prices in 1983. The effect on the country's economy was a 6 per cent fall in GDP between 1980 and 1986, the most dramatic decline in GDP of upper middle-income countries in the 1980s (World Development Report 1988). In this context, economic growth remained an elusive goal for the PNM government of Chambers (1981–86) and the successor National Alliance for Reconstruction (NAR) government of Robinson (1986–91).

The Draft Development Plan 1983–86, subtitled 'Imperatives of Adjustment,' spelt out the growth goals of the PNM government. The plan proposed to put T&T back on a course of economic growth by diversification into heavy and light industries and services. Because of the substantial investments already made in the heavy diversification programme during the 1970s, it was this sector that was expected to lead the way in recovery and growth in the following decades. Investments in steel, petrochemicals and natural gas were expected to generate foreign exchange earnings, provide direct foreign investment and create new jobs. However, it was in the area of light manufacturing that the PNM government envisaged the creation of new jobs. Thus, increased manufacturing output, especially for the non-regional export market, became a goal of the PNM (GOTT Annual Budget Speech, 1986). In light of this, the Industrial Development Corporation was to be reorganized and strengthened along the lines suggested by the 1985 Scotland Committee report, a new Export Development Corporation (EDC) was created in 1984, and the services of a Trade Facilitation Advisor were contracted through the United Nations Development Programme (UNDP).

The Robinson/NAR government took office in 1986, at a time of economic crisis in T&T. The country's total debt stood at US$1,062 million, and total debt as a percentage of GDP was 31 per cent; both figures were the highest in the post-independence history of the country (CB Handbook of Key Economic Statistics 1955–1985, 1989: 60–61).

While the 1987 budget simply aimed to cut expenditure and, in the words of the new Prime Minister, to 'escape the debt trap and dependence on the IMF,' subsequent NAR budgets outlined a programme and strategies for economic growth. In addition, the whole issue of growth targets, plans and strategies attained a new status when the government decided to approach the Fund for a line of credit in 1988. In this regard, three planning documents were prepared by the NAR government in 1988—the Draft Medium Term Macro Planning Framework 1989–95, the Draft Medium Term Programme 1989–91 and the Public Sector Investment Programme 1990. Growth through economic diversification was the central tenet of these documents. As the 1989–95 Medium Term Macro Planning Framework puts it: 'the aim of this restructuring is the achievement of greater autonomy, self-reliance, a more diversified and efficient production base that possesses the resilience that is needed to give us reasonable assurance of sustained growth' (GOTT 1988: i).

In its short time in office during the 1980s, the NAR government continued the PNM's focus on light and heavy export industry as a strategy for recovery and growth. Thus, the 1980s were characterized by the pursuit of economic growth, albeit through a strategy of economic change.

How successful were governments in Jamaica and T&T in realizing the growth goals they set for themselves in the 1960s and 1980s? Tables 2.2, 2.3, and 2.4 provide the basis for answering this question.

Table 2.2 suggests only slight differences in the economic growth record of the two case countries. Indeed, overall, both economies grew by an average of 1.9 per cent over the 1960–90 period. Because this study is fundamentally concerned with explaining goal realization, findings of high or low economic growth are only meaningful in so far as economic growth was the dominant development goal of the period. The findings presented above must be interpreted in this light.

Consequently, the two periods in which economic growth was stressed as the dominant goal of development in both countries, the 1960s and 1980s, reveal that achievements were marginally better in Jamaica, suggesting greater goal realization. The only period in which significant economic growth was achieved in T&T, the 1970s, was the period in which the government was committed to change, and not growth. Moreover, because T&T was not an OPEC member, the government in Port-of-Spain cannot even be credited with having orchestrated the phenomenal increase in growth caused by the 1974 oil boom.

Table 2.2   Average annual growth in GDP at constant 1985 prices in Jamaica and T&T, 1960–90

Country	1960–69	1970–79	1980–89	Total average
Jamaica	4.7	0.5	0.7	1.9
T&T	3.3	4.6	-2.1	1.9

Notes: Figures are in constant 1985 prices. No pre-1967 data exist for T&T; consequently, the years 1967, 1968, and 1969 are taken as representative of the 1960–69 period for both countries.

Sources: IMF International Financial Statistics, Institute of Social Studies National Accounts Database.

Table 2.3   Average annual employment rate in Jamaica and T&T in the 1960s, 1970s & 1980s

Country	1960–69	1970–79	1980–89
Jamaica	85	78	82 *
T&T	85	87	84

*   This figure captures the years for which data were available: 1980, 1981, 1984, 1988 and 1989.*

Sources: Jamaica data compiled from Boyd 1988: 9; Jefferson 1972; NPA, Economic and Social Survey of Jamaica, several years; STATIN, Statistical Abstracts. T&T data compiled from CB, Handbook of Key Economic Statistics 1955–85.

However, there are important differences in the pattern and cost of growth between these two countries which are worth noting. While T&T had two decades of strong and sustained growth in the 1960s and 1970s followed by a period of sharp decline in the 1980s, the Jamaican economy experienced a boom in the 1960s followed by two periods of less than modest economic growth. As regards the cost of this growth, growth in Jamaica during the 1960s was more heavily financed by public debt from external borrowing than in T&T, while in the 1980s both countries engaged in substantial deficit financing.

Table 2.4   Total population and size of labour force in Jamaica and T&T, 1960–90

	1960	1970	1980	1989
Jamaica				
Total population	1 600 000	1 993 500*	2 143 200	2 392 300
Labour force	606 823	820 000*	1 022 800	1 062 900
T&T				
Total population	827 957	970 900	1 081 700	1 213 182
Labour force	348 200	363 600	430 000	469 100

* These figures are for the year 1974.

Sources: Jamaica data compiled from STATIN, Statistical Abstracts 1976; and NPA, Economic and Social Survey of Jamaica 1981 and 1989. T&T data compiled from CSO, Annual Statistical Digest 1966 and 1989; CB, Handbook of Key Economic Statistics 1955–85; and CSO, Social Indicators 1975.

In the 1960s, Jamaica's public debt increased five-fold, from J$46 million at the end of 1958 to J$222 million at the end of 1969 (Jefferson 1972: 236). Indeed, Jefferson (ibid.: 235) shows further that 13.4 per cent (J$128.8 million) of Jamaica's total expenditure in the 1960s was from deficit financing. In T&T, public debt as a percentage of total expenditure for the period 1960–66 stood at only 7.0 per cent (Annual Statistical Digest 1966; CSO 1967: 118).

The Seaga government of the 1980s inherited a substantial external public debt from the Manley government (US$1,867 total external long-/medium-term debt) (Levitt 1991: 2–3). However, the orgy of deficit financing into which the new government entered made the cost of growth in the 1980s a lifelong burden to future generations of wage-earners in Jamaica. Between 1980 and 1988, Jamaica's total debt service to exports averaged 32 per cent. However, between 1989 and 1992, this figure declined to 29 per cent (World Debt Tables, Institute of Social Studies Data Base 1993).

In T&T, substantial surpluses saved in long-term development funds in the boom years of the 1970s provided a cushion in the lean post-1983 years. T&T therefore 'ended the second boom in a sound financial position: by the end of 1981 reserves were US$3.4 billion and medium and long-term debt only US$925 million' (Auty 1988: 275). Even with T&T's massive public sector expenditure between 1982 and

1986, total long-term debt service as a percentage of GNP was only 4.8 per cent in 1986; this figure stood at 21.4 per cent for Jamaica (World Development Report 1988). By 1987, however, T&T was in financial crisis as oil prices weakened. Debt service was projected to be US$470 million in 1988, and the Central Bank anticipated negative net foreign reserves by the end of 1988.

Upon assuming office in late 1986, the new NAR government tried unsuccessfully to secure loans from bilateral funders. Between late 1988 and 1992, T&T joined the ranks of Third World nations heavily indebted to international lending agencies, principally the IMF. The country's total debt service to exports increased from an annual average of 22 per cent between 1980 and 1987 to 50 per cent between 1988 and 1992 (World Debt Tables, Institute of Social Studies Data Base 1993), suggesting that, by the late 1980s, the cost of growth was becoming higher for T&T than for Jamaica.

Table 2.3 adds another dimension to the question of goal realization. Since the pursuit of economic growth in both countries was intended to solve chronic unemployment problems, the rate of employment can provide further evidence of goal realization. Despite the small labour force of both countries (Table 2.4) the data reveal a low employment record for the 1960s and 1980s, when economic growth was pursued (Table 2.3). It was only in the decade of change, the 1970s, that the rate of employment in T&T surpassed that of Jamaica by a full 9 per cent.

What conclusions can be drawn from the realization of economic growth goals in these two countries? Data on GDP suggest that Jamaica experienced greater economic growth in the 1960s and 1980s, the decades in which this goal was pursued. However, the cost of economic growth also seemed to be higher in Jamaica during the 1960s. On the other hand, economic growth in T&T during the 1980s was initially funded by government drawing on massive reserves and later by massive public-sector debts. Thus, by the early 1990s, T&T's public debt profile was as bad as, if not worse than, Jamaica's. The fact that employment was 2 per cent higher in T&T during the 1980s must, however, be juxtaposed against a 4 per cent increase in the rate of employment in Jamaica between the 1970s and 1980s, from 78 per cent to 82 per cent. In T&T, the rate of employment decreased by 2 per cent between the 1970s and 1980s even though the economy enjoyed the after-effects of the 1979–81 oil boom. Seen in this light, the higher employment rate in T&T during the 1980s appears inconsequential. It can therefore be concluded that during the 1960s and 1980s, when economic growth dominated the public policy agenda in Jamaica and T&T, there was greater realization of this goal in Jamaica.

Economic Change: Goals and their Realization

The question of economic change is examined in terms of:

1. diversification away from dominance by an export staple with low value-added, and
2. transfer of foreign ownership to local interests in this and other sectors, i.e., economic nationalism.

These were the issues raised by dependency economists in the early 1970s. These were also the issues around which radical social movements rallied in the late 1960s.

The place of bauxite and petroleum during the late 1960s in the economies of Jamaica and T&T, respectively, represented classic cases of staple domination. Between 1952 (when commercial mining of bauxite was first undertaken by Reynolds Metal Company) and the late 1960s, Jamaica grew to be the world's largest producer of bauxite. Quarrying and mining were the main activities taking place in Jamaica; greater value-added, in the form of alumina and aluminium production, took place in North American centres to which this commodity was exported. With 49 per cent of Jamaica's export merchandise trade dominated by bauxite in the 1960s, this sector was particularly significant in the Jamaican economy. However, multinational technical operations and vertical integration meant that only 1 per cent of total national employment accrued from this sector, and bauxite contributed only 10 per cent to GDP over the 1960s (Boyd 1988). Thus, while bauxite made a significant impact on the Jamaican economy, its returns were less than satisfactory.

While T&T's contribution to total world petroleum production stood at a seemingly inconsequential 0.5 per cent in the late 1960s, more than 50 per cent of all the country's export merchandise trade originated from this sector. Moreover, in the 1960s, this sector contributed 22 per cent to GDP, and accounted for a significant proportion of central government revenues (GOTT Annual Budget Speeches 1966 and 1967). With its 25 per cent contribution to gross capital formation in the late 1960s, petroleum was by far the most important sector of the

economy (CSO *The National Income of Trinidad and Tobago 1966–85*,
1987: 166). Although, as in Jamaica, refining dominated in the 1960s,
the presence of vertically integrated multinational corporations also
meant that value-added occurred in metropolitan centres rather than in
the country. British Petroleum, Amoco Trinidad Ltd and Texaco Trinidad Ltd were the dominant multinational corporations engaged in the
petroleum sectors in the late 1960s, with Amoco being the single largest producer.

In Jamaica, the Manley government embarked upon a process of
economic change intended to diversify the economy away from primary export of bauxite by increasing value-added in this sector. A complementary goal hinged upon a programme of resource-based industrialization, particularly in the area of agro-industry. The reduction of
foreign domination of strategic sectors in the Jamaican economy was
viewed as imperative to the success of the change programme. Manley
explains the PNP's *raison d'être* during the 1970s in this way:

> We were determined to make the process of the production and distri-
> bution of goods less dependent on external factors and local oligarchic
> control. This intention was clear and unequivocal and never wavered. It
> implied many things. The most important of these was to begin to de-
> velop what economists call 'internal linkages.' By this they mean the
> development of your own sources of raw material and other kinds of
> inputs wherever possible. It means carrying out, yourself, as many of
> the functions between production and the ultimate market-place as pos-
> sible. The first group are known as 'backward linkages' and the second
> as 'forward linkages'. (Manley 1982: 41)

Despite the inevitable conflict with international capital, this was the
course to which the Manley government was wedded in the 1970s.

In T&T, diversification into areas of resource-based industrialization downstream of the petroleum sector and economic nationalism
were also dominant goals of economic change during the 1970s. The
Third Five Year Development Plan 1969–73 spelt out the goals of economic change in terms of 'diversification of the country's structure of
production ... and making the economy more self-reliant' (GOTT
1968: 105). For the first time, diversification seemed to be addressed as
a goal of development, separate and distinct from economic growth and
full employment.

Fortunately for the PNM, the 1973 oil boom provided the necessary
revenue to make this goal attainable. It was in this period that the

PNM's most prestigious diversification projects downstream of the petroleum industry were conceived and executed (e.g., the Pt Lisas Industrial Estate, in which the production of steel was to take place). The PNM's goal of economic nationalism in the 1970s was informed by a perception of the private sector as 'innately deficient.' The 1969–73 Third Five Year Development Plan lamented the fact that, despite ample incentives, the private sector had not yet provided a high level of economic change. Thus, the plan argued for greater government and national involvement in the petroleum industry. In this regard, government proposed to create a National Petroleum Company which, among other things, was expected to protect the nation's interests in the petroleum sector.

The new policy on economic nationalism was adumbrated further in the 1970 and 1972 Budget Speeches, and in 1972 and 1975 White Papers on Public Sector Participation in Industrial and Commercial Activities. The 1972 White Paper outlined the three main reasons for increasing government participation in industrial and commercial enterprises:

(i)   to accelerate the transfer of control of foreign-owned firms to local hands;
(ii) to encourage and support new local industry; and
(iii) to save jobs in industries which, with rationalization, would be made viable. (1975 White Paper on Public Sector Participation in Industrial and Commercial Activities, GOTT 1975: 4)

By the 1980s, however, genuine commitment to economic change waned in both Jamaica and T&T. In the face of huge balance of payments deficits and increasing public sector debt, governments in Kingston and Port-of-Spain merely concerned themselves with how to contain expenditure and precipitate growth. Thus, the 1980s saw the re-emergence of growth as the primary focus of development policy-making in Jamaica and T&T.

Since the 1970s were the only period in which economic change was pursued as an end in itself, the question of goal realization is restricted to this period. Table 2.5 shows the relative dominance of the industrial sector in both economies. This is complemented by Table 2.6, which compares the export dependence of the mineral sector in the two countries. Changes in ownership patterns in the mineral sector in both countries are ascertained in the discussion following the tables.

Table 2.5   *Average annual percentage sectoral contribution to GDP in the 1970s*

Country	Agriculture	Industry	Manufacturing	Services
Jamaica	7	22	17	54
T&T	4	36	18	42

Note: All values are 1970 current prices for both countries.

Sources: Jamaica data were extracted from STATIN, *The Statistical Yearbook 1974*. T&T Data was compiled from CSO, *The National Income of Trinidad and Tobago 1966–1985*, 1986: 96–98. Some data for the 1970s for both countries were obtained from the IMF International Financial Statistics, Institute of Social Studies Database 1993.

Table 2.6   *Export dependence/percentage share of merchandise export in 1977, 1978 and 1979*

Country	Fuels, minerals & metals	Other primary commod.	Mach. & transport equipment	Other manufac-tures	Textiles & cloth-ing
Jamaica	25	28	1	45	1
T&T	91	3	1	5	0

Source: *World Development Report* (various years).

Tables 2.5 and 2.6 suggest that, while the position of bauxite in the Jamaican economy declined during the 1970s, the T&T economy remained heavily dependent on petroleum. Thus the category 'industry,' which captures the mineral economy, contributed more to GDP in T&T during the 1970s than it did in Jamaica (Table 2.5). Moreover, the dominance of the petroleum sector is shown further in Table 2.6, which indicates that 91 per cent of all merchandise exports from T&T during the 1970s were associated with this sector.

When these findings are examined against the background of the oil bonanza of the 1970s, the dominance of the petroleum sector is revealed to be even more overwhelming. This was a period in which the contribution of light manufacturing and services to GDP was driven by the demand generated by the petroleum sector. In addition to this, unlike the Jamaican manufacturing sector which was characterized by light manufacturing, petroleum refining and petrochemicals accounted for approximately one-quarter of this sector in T&T during the 1970s.

Few studies have attempted to draw out the true impact of petroleum on manufacturing and other sectors of the T&T economy (Sandoval 1983; and Auty 1988). The evidence above therefore invites the somewhat tentative conclusion that the Jamaican economy actually achieved greater diversification away from neo-colonial structures in the 1970s.

Moreover, while value-added in Jamaica's bauxite industry increased significantly between the 1960s and the 1970s, value-added in petroleum decreased during this period in T&T. Thus, Jamaica succeeded in increasing its ratio of alumina to bauxite production from 1:10 in the late 1960s to 1:1 in the mid-1970s (STATIN Statistical Yearbook of Jamaica (various years); Boyd 1988). In T&T, the ratio of the high value-added area (refining) to crude production declined from a favourable 2:1 in the 1960s to roughly 1:1 in the mid- to late 1970s (Handbook of Key Economic Statistics 1955–1985, CB 1989).

The question of how Jamaica and T&T fared in economic nationalism is addressed by looking at ownership patterns in the mineral sector—bauxite in Jamaica and petroleum in T&T. Foreign ownership in the mineral sector is particularly important because of the symbolic importance of the bauxite and oil sectors in the respective economies. Thus, critics such as the New World Group in Jamaica and the Oilfield Workers Trade Union in T&T viewed foreign ownership in this sector as proof of continuing control by external forces over the patrimony of the country. Whereas governments in both Port-of-Spain and Kingston were aware of the importance of economic nationalism for their political survival, achievements differed in the two countries by the end of the 1970s. While it must be admitted that some independent factors are important for explaining patterns of domestic/foreign ownership in this sector, the commitment of the national government to economic nationalism is an equally (if not more) important factor in explaining increased domestic ownership. This explains the readiness of the national government to tackle foreign multinationals strategically or capitulate in what has been termed a 'silent surrender.' Nonetheless, the following independent factors are recognized as being important: ownership patterns, the management style of controlling companies, the nature of technology used in this sector, the geo-politics and geo-economics of the sector, its capital intensity, and the current world market prices of the product exported, together with the extent of value-added. Consequently, while viewing economic nationalism as the outcome of national government's commitment tells only part of the story, in the context of this study it does allow for conclusions to be drawn on the subject under consideration, i.e., the articulation and realization of economic change goals.

Against this background, it should be noted that, while Jamaica was the world's largest producer of bauxite in the 1960s, this sector was still 100 per cent foreign-owned in the early 1970s (Stephens & Stephens 1986). Manley summarizes ownership in bauxite upon taking office in 1972:

> The entire investment was North American and the bulk of that US owned. The Kaiser Aluminium and Chemical Corporation, the Reynolds Metal Company, the Aluminium Company of America and the Anaconda Corporation all had major shares in this activity. The Aluminium Company of Canada owned two of the island's five alumina plants. (1982: 45)

During its two successive terms of office in the 1970s, the Manley government changed the ownership pattern in this sector from foreign to local domination. By the end of the Manley era, the government had acquired 51 per cent ownership in the Jamaican operations of the dominant Reynolds and Kaiser bauxite mining companies, and between 6 and 7 per cent of the assets of the Jamaican operations of the Alcan and Alcoa companies which were engaged in both bauxite mining and alumina processing (Stephens & Stephens 1986: 80). In addition, 10 new public subsidiary companies were created downstream of the main bauxite interests with a total investment of US$15,936,176 by 1979 (Ministry Paper No. 81, Capital Development Fund Annual Reports 1979 and 1980, MP 1980). Such companies included Jamex Bauxite Ltd., Jamaica Bauxite Institute, Bauxite and Alumina Trading Company of Jamaica, and National Gypsum & Quarries Ltd. By the end of the decade, a total of 51 per cent of the assets in the bauxite sector were locally owned.

In the case of T&T, the nationalization of British Petroleum by the PNM in 1969, coupled with the new policy of state interventionism in the petroleum industry (Third Five Year Development Plan 1969–73), implied a government commitment to economic nationalism. However, the PNM's actual record in the 1970s indicated otherwise. Throughout the early 1970s, rather than initiate any real take-overs, the PNM contented itself with imposing hefty taxes on the foreign petroleum companies dominating this sector. The PNM moved to appease the radical voices in 1974 when the holdings of Shell Trinidad Ltd. were nationalized for TT$93.6 million; the net book value of the company was assessed at TT$56.6 million. Soon thereafter, the National Petroleum Company was created as the sole domestic marketing company. However, by the early 1980s, the petroleum sector remained 73 per cent foreign-owned. Appendix Table A2.1 shows foreign ownership by sectors in the T&T economy in 1976.

There were important sectoral differences between the bauxite and petroleum industries, perhaps the most important being the share in total world output. However, commentaries on the nationalization experience of the PNP and PNM governments in the 1970s affirm the importance of focusing on government's resolution and strategies for explaining successes or failures in economic nationalism. In this regard, Stephens and Stephens (1986) observed the strategies of the Manley government for executing its policy of economic nationalism. They revealed that the nationalizing of the bauxite industry in Jamaica was part of a wider policy which aimed to reorganize the sector and increase value-added. Ultimately, Jamaica hoped to engage in aluminum smelting, and negotiations were entered into with oil-rich regional countries such as T&T, Mexico and Venezuela. Furthermore, it was noted that the Manley government institutionalized its preparatory steps to formulating and executing its bauxite strategy by establishing a Bauxite Commission. It was this Commission which established the 51 per cent nationalization target.

In contrast, commentary on the nationalization experiences of the PNM government in the late 1960s and the 1970s paints a picture of a government with no sincere commitment to nationalization, naïve about the strategies of multinational corporations, unwilling to incur the wrath of the United States, devoid of a petroleum strategy into which local ownership fitted, and unprepared in terms of the negotiating team which it sent forth. In commenting on the 1974 Shell nationalization, Farrell concluded:

> [Trinidad and Tobago] chose a target for nationalization which would have made sense only if the policy had been carefully planned and had been related to a programme for the reorganization and rationalization of the Trinidad oil industry as a whole. Secondly, the government fenced in its team from the start by foreclosing certain options for dealing with Shell through its fear of offending Shell and foreign capital. What was even worse, it telegraphed its psychological weakness to Shell who did not fail to take advantage of it. Thirdly, the failure to

conduct a proper valuation of Shell's properties and equipment and near total reliance on Shell for the information necessary for preparing the government's position led to considerable weakness and opened the door to sharp practice by Shell. (Farrell T.M.A. 1984: 45–46)

In addition, the PNM failed to make good its promise to create a National Petroleum Company (NPC) with policy formulation and holding company functions. Energy policy planning remained within the overworked and understaffed Ministry of Petroleum and to a lesser extent the Oil Audit Department of the Ministry of Finance. When the much-heralded NPC eventually materialized, it was no more than a marketing company.

In view of the above, the evidence suggests that there was greater political commitment and indeed greater economic change in Jamaica during the 1970s. It can be concluded that there was greater realization of the goal of economic change in Jamaica. In contrast, neo-colonial economic structures and production relationships seemed to dominate the T&T economy.

Women, the Goal of Social Change and its Realization

At political independence, nationalists in government in Jamaica and T&T confronted problems of social change for the underclasses created by colonialism together with the problems of take-off and growth. Together with health care and social services reform, reforms to the colonial education system became an important medium for effecting social change. Consequently, in both countries, education reforms of the 1960s aimed to expand the number of institutional places (primary, secondary and tertiary) and to ensure wider access to the system. While no specific attention was given to the problems of females in education, it was hoped that expansion and wider access would provide the necessary opportunities for all groups with restricted access, including females. In a real sense, politicians in both countries identified disadvantaged groups in terms of class and, to a lesser degree, race; gender, to the extent it was recognized, was subsumed within this perspective.

The education reforms which took place in Jamaica throughout most of the 1960s were largely spearheaded by then-Minister of Education, Edwin Allen. They were contained in the JLP's 1966 policy document, 'New Deal for Education,' whose significance is assessed by Miller:

> The New Deal reforms have had a lasting impact on Jamaican education for at least three reasons. First, they brought the largest single capital expansion of the educational system in its history since 1983. The system was expanded substantially at all levels. Secondly, they secured international assistance for Jamaican education from such multilateral agencies as UNESCO and the World Bank and from bilateral agencies as USAID and CIDA. Thirdly, they helped to galvanize public support for early childhood education through basic schools. (1989: 212).

In T&T, education reforms were informed by the PNM's anti-colonial philosophy coupled with Williams's personal and academic interest in the education system. While the Williams government did not devise special policies for women, the evidence suggests that the limited school places for girls, especially at the secondary level, were noted (Debate of the Legislative Council on the Cabinet Proposals on Education, Hansard, 25/7/1960: 2988).

It was not until the 1970s that governments in Jamaica and T&T recognized women as a distinct underclass. A goal of social change for women was articulated and programmes were devised to redress inequalities. This shift in policy has been attributed to increased awareness of women's issues, precipitated by the UN Declaration of the 1975–1985 Decade for Women. In Jamaica, the problems of women were brought to the attention of the Manley government in 1972 by activists Dr Lucille Mair and Mavis Gilmour who, in the position paper 'Women and Social Change,' argued the following:

1. Planning for national reconstruction cannot afford to overlook the special, dynamic potential of women.
2. Women can be motivated towards civic/national activism.
3. Some of the problems and grievances of women are particularly acute and carry fundamental implications for any strategy of social change.

> The official machinery required has to produce action now; it should also keep the condition of women under continuous survey. (Quoted in Blake 1984: 33)

Since this demand was compatible with the tenets of democratic socialism and the PNP's philosophy of 'equality and social justice for all,' it was warmly received by the new government, and the goal of social change for women was adopted as public policy (1972 Annual Budget Speech of the Hon. Michael Manley, GOJ 1972: 22)

The first step towards realizing the goal of social change for women was Lucille Mair's appointment as Special Adviser on Women's Affairs. In 1974, a Women's Desk was established within the Ministry of Youth and Community Development with three broad objectives: to identify the problems peculiar to women, to improve the status of women, and to formulate policy integrating women's issues into national development. Initially, the Desk had *ad hoc* status since its Director, the Special Adviser, was part-time.

Between 1975 and 1977, the Desk increased in stature and became an institutionalized arm of the Jamaican planning machinery. In 1975, the Desk became the Women's Bureau, it was relocated to the Office of the Prime Minister. A full-time Director was appointed and the Bureau's objectives were incorporated into the government's policy. In 1977, the first Minister of State for Women's Affairs was appointed.

In his book, *Jamaica: Struggle in the Periphery* (1982), Manley revealed that the PNP sought to tackle the underclass status of women on two fronts. First was through legislation on the legal status of women since 'no legislation spoke to the rights of women either in respect of their employment or generally' (1982: 49). The second front was that of education. Here, Manley pursued a strategy more anchored in class than gender analysis—to provide free education up to university level in order to increase opportunities for women as well as other underclasses (Manley 1982).

Similarly, during the 1970s, the T&T government also declared its commitment to social change for women. In T&T, this new goal had a distinctly political flavour in the sense that Williams used this opportunity to make the Women's League of the PNM the official voice of the Party on women's issues. Moreover, in 1976 a Minister for Women's Affairs was appointed for the first time in the history of T&T, and by the mid-1970s, female Ministers held important Cabinet portfolios in information, social services and community development. But the crowning glory of this decade was perhaps the 1974 *ad hoc* Commission on the Status of Women. This was established within the Ministry of Labour, Social Security and Cooperatives with terms of reference 'to review, evaluate and recommend principles and measures required to ensure the full integration of women in all aspects of national life'

(GOTT Final Report of the National Commission on the Status of Women 1978: 7). Among its many recommendations, the report of the Commission specifically focuses on the position of women and the education system, stating that:

> Education for girls as well as boys should be extended and diversified to enable them to contribute more effectively in rural and urban sectors, as well as in the management of food and other household functions. (GOTT 1978: 71)

Throughout the 1970s, the PNM's dramatic expansion of the education system was premised on the notion of equal opportunity for males and females. Against the background of Williams' struggle with conservative forces in T&T's dual education system, the reforms of the 1970s took on a decidedly class-conscious character.

As regards the 1980s it should be recognized that the problems of economic decline and structural adjustment which dominated this era consigned women's issues to a secondary position in both Jamaica and T&T. While the Seaga government in Jamaica and the Chambers and Robinson governments in T&T reaffirmed the nation's commitment to social change for women, this was a decade of intention rather than action. In addition, contraction in education expenditure due to dwindling central government revenues closed off opportunities to women as well as other disadvantaged groups in this decade. Against this background, the 1970s remain the key decade of social change for women in these two countries.

Nonetheless, a closer look at government policy on women in the 1980s is warranted. In Jamaica, the Seaga government, which assumed office in 1980, initially reaffirmed its commitment to social change for women. Henry-Wilson (1989) notes that the JLP government retained the structure of the Women's Bureau, and she credits the bureau with the landmark achievement of drafting and ratifying *The National Plan for Women*. However, Seaga soon departed from a pro-active policy on women; he chose instead to support women's occupational mobility by symbolic appointments of women to top management positions in the state enterprise sector. In the words of the JLP's Deputy Political Leader, Bruce Goulding, 'while Manley seemed to have a policy on women, the JLP did more, in practice, for women's mobility' (personal interview, May 1992).

In T&T, following the PNM's success in the 1981 general elections, the goal of social change for women was reaffirmed as official government policy by the new Chambers government. In this period, the Women's League of the Party rose to prominence. Through the 'Kitchen Cabinet,' four PNM Women's League members were allocated Ministerial portfolios in social policy areas of education, community development, social security and housing. In addition, four more National Conferences by the National Commission on the Status of Women were convened between 1981 and 1986. However, despite these initiatives, the PNM government's practical achievements in the area of social change for women were judged as inadequate (Reddock 1988). The Robinson/NAR government, which replaced the PNM in December of 1986, also reaffirmed its commitment to social change for women. Accordingly, a Minister for the Status of Women was appointed. The fact that the appointee—Margaret Hector—was a working-class women's activist signalled the government's interest in this target group. However, beyond this symbolic appointment women's issues lay largely dormant in these years of unprecedented economic decline.

To summarize, during the 1960s, the issue of social change for women was indirectly addressed through the education reforms which aimed at expansion and widened access. During the 1970s, governments in both Jamaica and T&T articulated the goal of social change for women. Expansion of the education system in both countries was expected to create increasing opportunities for women and mitigate their disadvantaged position. It must be noted, however, that in both the 1960s and 1970s, redressing class-based inequalities was the dominant motive for reforms. While the goal of social change for women was reaffirmed in Jamaica and T&T during the 1980s, economic realities coupled with contraction of the education system effectively diminished its import. The following section examines the extent to which the goal of social change for women was realized.

Women's Occupational Mobility

The question of goal realization is explored by comparing changes in the occupational mobility of women between the 1960s and the 1980s. Tables 2.7, 2.8 and 2.9 show these occupational changes.

While it would be useful to compare changes in the status of the particularly disadvantaged groups of women—i.e., African Jamaican women and rural Indian and African women in T&T—the absence of longitudinal data on African Jamaican women as a distinct group precludes this type of analysis. However, when one considers that, over the research period, more than 76 per cent of Jamaica's female population was of African ancestry, conclusions about social change for females in general can be taken as evidence of African women's advancement.

Table 2.7   Percentage change in women's occupational status, 1960–86

Occupation	Jamaica	T&T
Professional, managerial	39	10
Clerical	9	54
Crafts and technical	-14	1
Service	39	-47
Farm worker	na	-4

Note: All occupational categories are not represented due to different classifications over time and between countries. Because 'crafts and technical' was not a category in the 1960 census, 1 per cent in T&T is the change between 1975 and 1985.

Sources: STATIN Statistical Abstracts of Jamaica, various years; CSO Labour Force Report of T&T, various years.

Table 2.8   Percentage change in sectoral location of rural Indian and African female labour in T&T, 1960–80

Sector	Rural Indian females	Rural African females
Agriculture	-39	-19
Mining	2	2
Manufacturing	-10	-10
Construction	4	8
Commerce	9	15
Transport & communication	2	4
Services	7	-4

Sources: Appendix Tables A2.2 and A2.5

In the case of T&T, the absence of data cross-referencing ethnicity, sex, income, and educational attainment makes it difficult to monitor changes in rural Indian and African female populations. However, because of the concentration of Indians and Africans in certain rural administrative areas, it is possible to compare relative social changes for both groups. Thus, the occupational status of rural Indian and African women will be monitored by looking at women in the communities of Caroni and Tobago. Appendix Table A2.3 shows the ethnic concentration of Indian and African populations in Caroni and Tobago throughout the 1960s, 1970s and 1980s.

Table 2.9   *Percentage change in Indian and African women's occupational status in T&T, 1960–90*

Occupation	Indian women	African women
Professional & technical	7.8	5.8
Admin., exec. & managerial	-1.5	-0.5
Clerical	22.8	18.3
Sales	1.4	0.7
Farmers & fisherpersons	-37.0	-5.3
Production-related	-0.1	-5.7
Transport & equipment operators	-0.2	-1.0
Construction workers	-1.6	-0.9
Craftspersons	5.8	7.0
Service workers	-1.0	-22.1
Other	3.5	4.0

Sources: Complied from Reddock 1991 as captured in Appendix Table A2.6. These figures are for Indian and African women throughout T&T, and not only rural dwellers.

The data above present a rather mixed picture. Comparatively, women in Jamaica achieved greater occupational mobility than women in T&T as they moved into the topmost professional and managerial categories. This is highly significant because this category attracts better wages than the clerical occupations to which the majority of females in T&T have shifted between 1960 and 1985. Indeed, women in T&T seemed to have moved out of service work into clerical employment, presumably in the burgeoning civil service.

As regards the longitudinal question of occupational mobility for rural Indian and African women, a comparison of Appendix Tables A2.2 and A2.5 shows that Indian women in rural Caroni experienced more social change than rural African women. National-level data (Table 2.9 and Appendix Table A2.4) suggest that Indian females moved out of agricultural labour into professional occupations between 1960 and the 1980s.

Conclusions

The analysis above reveals that economic growth was the primary goal of development for the governments in Jamaica and T&T during the decades of the 1960s and the 1980s. It also revealed that the 1970s was a decade of economic change for the Manley government in Jamaica and the PNM/Williams government in T&T. The goal of social change for women was articulated by both governments during the 1970s and, to a lesser extent, in the 1980s. In the 1960s, the goal of social change for women was indirectly addressed as part of a programme to democratize the education system. In the 1970s, the governments in Port-of-Spain and Kingston sought to ensure females' access to higher education by continuing to expand the system and to ensure equality of access. In addition, women's access to social services and their legal status was considered in both countries. From a longitudinal point of view, it was seen that the status of rural Indian women improved markedly compared to rural African women in T&T.

On the question of goal realization, the evidence suggests that Jamaica had a better record in all three areas—economic growth, economic change and social change. Chapter 3 identifies the attributes of public bureaucracy that are associated with patterns of growth and change-goal realization.

From Riggs to the World Bank: Recurring Associations in the Study of Development Administration

3

The Framework of Associations

In this chapter, the explanatory framework of associations applied in this study is developed. This is constructed by searching for recurring associations over the discipline's long history, spanning from Riggs to the current hegemony of the World Bank (Walker 1996). The search for recurring associations is guided by three factors:

1. a recognition that development goals differ;
2. the selection of explanatory variables based on association rather than causality, and
3. the assumption that public bureaucracies are partially open systems.

The first factor aims to redress the tendency towards universal theories of bureaucracy's performance in areas as different as land redistribution and steel production. It is based on recognition that different types of policy goals evoke different types of political activity, especially around the unit of administration. The second guiding factor avoids the positivist trap of subjecting theory to rigorous testing based on the existence or absence of causal relations. The research question is rather modest in asking about associations and not about causality.

The third guiding factor is based on advances in organizational theory. It is no longer possible, nor useful, to try to develop a comparative framework of bureaucratic performance based solely on the environment/ecology of the organization. In this way, Riggs's 1991 ecological focus, noted in Chapter 1, is as incomplete now as it was in the 1950s.

The science of comparative development administration will not be based on 'a comprehensive ecological understanding' but on a more balanced combination of environmental and organizational factors. Thus, the promise of developing a framework of association from the literature beckons, provided that the following are recognized:

1. Development goals differ and bureaucratic requirements for realizing such goals vary accordingly.

2. Public bureaucracies are partially open systems, which means that they act upon their environment and are acted upon by environmental factors.

3. Associations between bureaucratic attributes and goal realization are a less rigorous but sufficient basis for selecting variables and explaining differences among countries.

4. Dahl's caution is heeded by checking findings from the native laboratory of development administration (the developing world) against findings from other areas (such as advanced capitalist and socialist countries).

5. Perhaps most importantly, a historical approach is taken to the literature. Such an approach must come to terms with the evolution and current state of development administration theorizing. This means that it must take cognizance of pioneering works of the Comparative Administration Group, contributions from the new development administration, along with the wider contributions of political scientists, planners, public sector neo-classical economists, along with voices from the developing world. Ultimately, this means that the term 'development administration' must be used as a broad, heuristic paradigm. It must also be in lower-case letters since Development Administration is, after all, the preserve of the Comparative Administration Group.

Against this background, theory-building around the problem of how public bureaucracy realizes development goals rests on the extent of recurrence, the persistence of the same explanatory variables, and their validation in different countries. Moreover, theory-building rests in particular on a comprehensive assessment of the organizational and environmental factors influencing the ability of public bureaucracies to realize development goals.

PART I:
Public Bureaucracy and Economic Growth: The Associations

Introduction

The literature that establishes associations between attributes of public bureaucracy and the realization of growth goals is surveyed in this section. This literature is fundamentally concerned with questions of how the size, structure and performance of public bureaucracy contribute to economic growth. This view of administration as a veritable factor of production is encompassed in the works of early development administrationists of the 1950s and 1960s, in public enterprises works, and in the development planning and neo-liberal literature of the 1970s and 1980s.

Economic growth and the organization

Organizationalists in development administration find the very existence of institutional capacity to be associated with the realization of economic production goals. Administrative capacity-building, capability building, administrative reform, administrative development, and institutional development are all terms used in this literature to describe the process whereby public sector institutions are themselves purposefully developed in order to enhance their capacity to undertake interventions designed to promote development. Such terms are often used interchangeably in the literature, with administrative capacity being the more generic concept employed.

The precise meaning of administrative capacity and its importance for development have, however, been difficult questions for development administration. Bryant and White (1982), for example, approach the question of administrative capacity by describing the symptoms of administrative incapacity. These are identified as staff shortages, poor allocation of human resources, structural inadequacy of bureaucracies, low bureaucratic responsiveness, and the inability to enforce and manage policies, the latter being a manifestation of 'state softness.' For the World Bank, which uses the term administrative capability, this is an issue of building institutions and systems for a capable public sector (World Bank 1997).

In this study, administrative capacity is a state in which administrative units are characterized by the existence and rational deployment of resources, systems and procedures towards the attainment of goals. A complementary component of administrative capacity is the ability to monitor goal realization and adjust the deployment of administrative inputs accordingly. Hence, administrative capacity-building is the strategic application of administrative development techniques to induce a state of administrative capacity. Such techniques can either be introduced from the organization's external environment, as in the case of technical assistance, or they can be brought about through purposeful organizational development strategies, such as training, structural reform or systems upgrading. Capacity-building strategies can also be either partial or comprehensive. Heady (1971) and Ilchman (1965) discuss in detail the contending philosophical bases informing different approaches to administrative capacity-building.

It must be noted, however, that the literature on public bureaucracy also points to the potential threat that a strong and capable bureaucracy constitutes to civil society, democracy, and ultimately, to political development. Indeed, this is the concern of B.C. Smith's *Bureaucracy and Political Power* (1988). Despite this fact, scholars have argued that administrative capability is indispensable to economic growth since economic production goals are invariably more tangible, technical and subject to quantification, than are change goals. Growth goals require technical inputs at all stages in the policy cycle—formulation, implementation, monitoring and evaluation. Indeed, the early development administration literature viewed increasing administrative capacity, particularly in policy formulation and planning units, to be closely associated with the realization of economic growth goals. This is not to say that capacity is not also important for change; it is, in fact, noted in the literature (Moharir 1991, Hondale 1981). The point is that while responsiveness, participation and other such variables are important for realizing change goals, administrative capacity is indispensable for addressing mundane but important questions like, e.g., how much tea or steel must be produced, what is the best way of doing so, and whether outputs should be for local consumption or export markets?

Throughout the 1960s, similar findings underscored the importance of administrative capacity for economic production and the modernization project. This could be found in such works as 'The Administration of Economic Development Planning: Principles and Fallacies' (UN

1966), Gross (1967), King (1967), Walinsky (1963), and by the International Group for Studies in National Planning's much quoted *Appraising Administrative Capability for Development* (United Nations INTERPLAN 1969). To the extent that the experience of OECD countries also suggested the indispensability of administrative capacity for economic growth (OECD 1966), an association between the two seemed to be emerging in development administration.

During the 1970s, the importance of administrative capacity for economic growth attracted less interest. This was largely a reaction to the failure of the previous decade's central-planning effort. Thus, a new development administration emerged that was more concerned with process interactions between public bureaucracies and beneficiaries than with the structures *per se*.

It was not until the 1980s that the question of administrative capacity and economic growth was again put on the agenda. The relationship was first examined in the American and British economies, which were then in crisis. Along with anti-administration measures, the monetarist response to the crisis advocated selective administrative capacity-building for the recovery of economic growth. Several important works have examined the purpose and nature of administrative capacity-building in Western economies in crisis (Fry 1986, Konig 1997, Hansen 1985, Mascarenhas 1993, McGregor 1983, Peters 1991).

Not surprisingly, aspects of the capacity-building reforms were exported from the developed countries to the developing world in the 1980s and 1990s, as part of the World Bank's larger programme on structural adjustment (Kiggundu 1990, Kitchen 1992, Smith 1993, Walker 1996). The Bank's initiative was inspired by the poor compliance record of developing countries in implementing structural adjustment programmes. Reluctantly, international lending institutions recognized that the greater the level of administrative capacity, the better the compliance record with growth-inducing adjustment policies. Administrative reforms were therefore advocated. This was reinforced by a new focus on government institutions in economics, coupled with a reawakened interest in institutional economics.

The current model of capacity building differs markedly from the technical assistance/training model of the 1950s and 1960s, which sought to build capacity by educating and training human resources. Currently, the World Bank approaches capacity building from the standpoint of systems improvement, management and effective human resource allocation to 'undertake collective actions at least cost to society' (World Bank 1997). In real terms, it is the institutional ability to support the 'macromanagement' functions of the state that the Bank defines as capability. In this framework, the institutional mechanisms of the state are required to build capacity by rule enforcement, promotion of competition, and facilitating partnerships from inside and outside the state (World Bank 1997: 77).

Sub-Saharan Africa, a region with a poor policy-enforcement record, has been the subject of intensive administrative capacity-building investment by the World Bank since the late 1980s (Adamolekun 1989, Moharir 1991). Like the programme in Jamaica, administrative capacity building in Sub-Saharan Africa includes 'strengthening and reorganization of economic planning and financial management institutions, improving formulation of economic policy, planning and management, public investment and expenditure planning, and external financial management' (Adamolekun 1989: 84). The World Bank's African Capacity-building Initiative (ACBI) aims 'at improving the process of formulation of policies on economic development issues and on the efficient implementation of policies' (Moharir 1991: 240).

The end result of the ACBI and other such initiatives is that, even under the contemporary anti-state/administration hegemony, the architects of the crime have found it necessary to empower the victim. Thus, in the discussion on economic growth and public administration in post-socialist Eastern Europe, the World Bank also argues for reforms tantamount to a far-reaching capacity-building effort (Rice 1988).

Independent findings from institutional-building organizations in the developing world further suggest the pervasiveness of capacity-building as a key strategy for overcoming economic decline. Indeed, economic revival through capacity-building initiatives such as management training has been advocated by the Caribbean Centre for Development Administration (Caricad), the Eastern and Southern African Management Institute, the African Training and Research Centre in Administration for Development, the African Association for Public Administration and Management (AAPAM), and the Special Action Program for Public Administration and Management (SAPAM) of the Economic Commission. For those taking an organizationalist perspective to the question of efficient production under uncertainty and scarcity, administrative capacity-building has emerged as an important explanatory variable. Thus, administrative capacity-building can be identified as the organizational attribute linking public bureaucracies and economic growth.

Economic growth and the policy environment

What attribute of public bureaucracy's policy environment is associated with the realization of economic growth goals? In the 1950s and 1960s, advocates of planning answered this question in terms of a policy environment characterized by a comprehensive plan (United Nations UNECAFE 1955, Waterson 1963 & 1965). In this regard, Waterson stated that 'in formulating a comprehensive national development program, planners endeavour to make realistic estimates of financial and other resources and, within the limits of these resources, to establish priorities for competing sectors and projects' (1963: 144). Mehmet (1978) observed the UN's association of planning with economic growth and attributes this to Keynesian–Harrod/Domar macro models, which linked 'aggregate output to the stock of capital by the capital-output ratio.'

By the 1970s, observers of planning in the developing world answered the question of policy environment and bureaucratic performance in opposite terms from the advocates of planning in the 1950s and 1960s (Caiden & Wildavsky 1974). For example, Caiden and Wildavsky, who were fundamentally concerned with problems of economic growth in the developing world, identified over-ambitious and comprehensive plans, unattainable in a situation of uncertainty and scarcity, as the reason for poor goal realization. Hence the title of one of their chapters, 'Planning is not the solution: it's part of the problem.' To the question of what should be done about planning, Caiden and Wildavsky (1974) posited the radical solution: 'the abolition of comprehensive multi-sectoral planning.'

> During the 1950s the developing countries sought to organize their economies on a sounder footing for growth by formulating internally consistent development plans, but the question of plan feasibility was frequently neglected. A more realistic outlook emerged with the First Development Decade, during which planners increasingly turned their attention to problems of actual plan implementation which continued to interfere with the attainment of development expectations, objectives, and specific targets. (UNECAFE 1971: 1)

In the United States, works such as *Implementation* (Pressman & Wildavsky 1973), *Planning and Politics* (Beyle & Lathrop 1970) and *The Role of the Economist in Government Policy-making* (Norton 1969) exposed the failure of comprehensive planning in American public policy. Furthermore, writing on the problems of comprehensive planning in communist countries, Charles Lindblom observed:

> What distinguishes Communist systems from others is less that they plan the methods and sequences by which they intend to achieve their great goals than that they have great goals and act boldly to reach them ... They decide upon these goals, not in any planning process different from the processes that decision-makers who do not plan employ, but in the rough and tumble of politics, emboldened no doubt by their extraordinary power over the populace and guided perhaps by a more definite ideology than those that guide leaders in the market-oriented democracies. Boldness, however, is not planning. (1975: 57)

The 1970s backlash against comprehensive economic planning typified by Caiden and Wildavsky was short-lived. As much as planning was hated, state involvement in economic interventions showed no signs of withering away, and even the new basic-needs agenda of the 1970s required planning input. As Chakravarty notes, the evidence against planning was 'by no means conclusive' (1991: 10). The relationship between the performance of public bureaucracies, the policy/planning environment and goal realization had to be reconsidered.

Scholars who were especially concerned with the failure of the economic growth policies in command and mixed economies (both in the developing world and the socialist bloc) blamed the interventionist state for the poor performance record of the 1950s and 1960s. The crisis of performance was viewed as a 'crisis in planning,' where the state either set over-ambitious goals—'fantasies' in the words of Seers (1972)—or failed to support the technical requirements of planners due to political reasons. Either way, the problem of policy failure was not just a problem of planning in scarcity and uncertainty but one of excessive interventionism by a developmental state. As Waterson puts it, 'When the time comes to implement development plans, the preference of many political leaders for maintaining investment options in their own hands and for improvisation becomes apparent' (1972: 89). Bauer's work *Dissent on Development* (1972) represents an extreme version of this argument.

In the 1970s, the solution to this problem was to be found in a double-track strategy of reducing the quantity of state interventionism in planning while simultaneously improving its quality. The belief that less government equals better and more efficient economic management was fast becoming a dominant theme in development policy studies in the 1970s. It is against this background that the following implementation strategies should be viewed: specificity in policy formulation, targeted and projectized development, process planning, and flexibility (Berman 1980, Rondinelli 1983). Paul's (1982) focus on strategic interventionism echoes these views.

However, it was the crisis of advanced capitalist economies in the early 1970s that provided the solution to the problem of state interventionism and policy failure in the developing world. This experience revealed that it was not so much the 'degree' but the 'type' of state interventionism that was associated with economic growth. The solution was to be found in a new type of facilitative implementation strategy that incorporated labour and capital, but especially capital, into policy formation and implementation. For scholars operating within a corporatist framework (Lehmbruch 1979, Panitch 1979, Pempel & Tsunekawa 1979, Schmidt 1982, Schmitter 1979), it was this crucial element—facilitation—that made the difference between economic growth and economic crisis.

The neo-liberal consensus represented by the World Bank and the Fund associates less state interventionism with economic goals in the developing world. In this regard, the World Bank and the Fund recommend a facilitative type of implementation strategy and hence a facilitative role for public bureaucracies. The new role requires public sector organizations to support interest organizations, especially the private sector, in the formulation and implementation of economic growth strategies. This position is articulated in the 1983 World Development Report, in which the Bank argues that centralized blueprint planning is inappropriate for macroeconomic management, and recommends instead 'consultation and coordination':

> To design adjustment policies and programs, consultation and coordination between policy makers and interest groups is essential. The examples of Brazil, Japan, and the Republic of Korea show that consultation and coordination among different agencies within government and between government and the private sector can provide practically sounder, if analytically less articulate, policies and programs ... Governments have found considerable merit in involving academics and businessmen in policy discussions. Their participation, usually through committees, working groups, and conferences, improves offi-

cial awareness and helps build a consensus on the means and ends of national development. (World Bank 1983: 70)

Research findings in the 1980s and 1990s seem to confirm the neo-liberal association between facilitative implementation strategies and economic growth under structural adjustment. The consensus-building quality of facilitative strategies has been identified as essential for goal realization. In this regard, Lindenberg notes that:

> Many of the more successful governments involved citizens groups in dialogue about the economic crisis and asked them to help formulate measures. In Costa Rica, President Monge mounted dialogue programs with business, labour, co-operatives, popular organizations and government officials. These groups discussed the economic crisis, the measures and possible solutions. The groups had a high sense of involvement. They were aware of and actively discussed the proposals of the IMF and the World Bank. (1989: 381)

However, another set of findings suggests an inherent logic in economic growth policies under structural adjustment, which leads to a more interventionist and, indeedan autocratic role for the state and its administrative apparatus (Nelson 1988).

The latter position questions the World Bank/IMF tendency to equate a facilitative policy content with less state interventionism. Indeed, by confusing 'degree' with 'type' of interventionism, the World Bank's entry into the discussion of public bureaucracies and the policy environment has raised more questions than it has answered. On the one hand, the Bank's focus on less state interventionism converges with that of scholars such as Caiden and Wildavsky (1974). On the other hand, its emphasis on a new type of facilitative interventionism seems to have greater philosophical continuity with the corporatist scholars writing on advanced Western economies. Because this study searches for explanatory variables based on convergence over time and applicability to other systems, the attribute—facilitative policy content—is selected as the policy environmental factor associating economic growth with public bureaucracy. Application of this attribute allows for a commentary on whether or not a facilitative policy content is, indeed, a manifestation of less state interventionism.

Economic growth and the political environment

To the question of what attribute of public bureaucracy's political environment is associated with economic growth goals, 'autonomy' from political control has emerged to be the single most sustained answer.

Indeed, the very association of the public sector with the production of goods and services in both the developed and developing world was premised on the notion that the agency of 'enterprise' should be autonomous from political interference. Thus, autonomy was taken as a prerequisite for efficiency and effectiveness. Moreover, the inculcation of a private-sector work ethic in the public sector hinged on this managerial autonomy.

Despite the ease with which the term 'autonomy' is used in the literature, its precise meaning still defies easy explanation. Dimock defined autonomy as 'concentrating managerial powers in the hands of the competent people and giving them enough free rein to achieve the desired results. It is the privilege of being left alone so long as you do not overstep the rules laid down in advance' (1949: 913). This definition implies that autonomy is not unconditional but relative. It also suggests that autonomy is in inverse proportion to control. Dimock's early definition is borne out in subsequent works on this issue. Indeed, the history of the literature on autonomy in public agencies reflects a quest for the appropriate level of autonomy/control (Islam 1993).

In Western Europe, the advent of autonomous public agencies was closely linked to the emergence of the welfare state in the post-World War II period. Autonomous agencies went by different names and were active in areas of social and economic production. In Britain, they took the form of nationalized public corporations; in France, there were *etablissement publiques (administratifs, industriels, et commerciaux)*; in Sweden, they were called central agencies *(centrala ambetsverk);* and in Germany, they were referred to as *offentliche unternehmen*. In the emerging post-World War II consensus, the autonomous public agency was called upon to undertake direct production endeavours in both the developed and developing world.

In Britain, the 'Morrisonian concept' which informed early economic public corporations sought to imbue them with the highest possible degree of autonomy—the autonomy to formulate policy. In North America, the Tennessee Valley Authority (TVA), which was established in 1933 with terms of reference to control destructive floodwaters, was granted almost unconditional policy formulation autonomy through its Board. In Latin America, the TVA constituted 'the great prototype' for autonomous agencies such as the Chilean *Fomento* (Hanson 1964). The TVA experiment was also influential in India and in Jamaica; the Damodar Valley Corporation in India and the Yallahs Valley Land Authority in Jamaica were both expected to be autonomous from the political decision-makers.

For the newly emerging nations, the idea of autonomous public agencies for the production of economic goods and services had obvious appeal. This was true both for countries pursuing socialism (e.g., India, Bangladesh, Somalia and Guyana) as well as for others that followed state capitalism (e.g., Nigeria, Peru and Barbados). However, many developing countries simply transplanted the legal form without the all-important autonomy content. Thus, so-called 'autonomous' agencies soon became a less obvious way of rewarding political cronies and winning political capital. Indeed, the misuse of the 'autonomous' public enterprise experiment in Latin America leads Wiarda and Kline (1990) to view these organizations as a fourth branch of government and an instrument for increasing centralization. Sherwood (1971) views the penchant for political interference and excessive control of autonomous productive agencies as an indicator of low political development.

By the 1970s, dissatisfaction with the poor performance of so-called 'autonomous' public agencies in both the developed and the developing world was rife. By that time, however, most scholars were more modest in their expectations of autonomy. Indeed, it was managerial autonomy over day-to-day decisions associated with policy implementation, rather than autonomy to formulate policy, that was stressed (Garner 1983, Islam 1993). Islam argues that managerial autonomy 'is expected to enhance management capacity for effective performance. Autonomy is needed for flexibility in financial decisions. It is a factor in attracting highly qualified managers as well as facilitating the process of collective bargaining. Above all autonomy would insulate the SOEs against nagging bureaucratic and political interference' (1993: 132). Writing in the 1960s, Hanson had emphasized the managerial aspects of autonomy over its more political decision-making side (Hansen 1964).

In the United Kingdom, excessive political control over 'autonomous' agencies was identified by a 1978 Government White paper on the nationalized industries as the cause of the ineffectiveness and inefficiency of British public corporations during the 1970s. Even earlier, Labour Party theoreticians such as Crossman questioned the accountability, autonomy, and efficiency of claims of public corporations. Indeed, such organizations were even seen as symptomatic of a 'New Despotism.' On the European continent, issues of control/autonomy and worker participation in the *enterprises publiques* loomed large in the 1978 French elections.

In the developing world, the African experience in particular was providing overwhelming evidence to support the view that the inefficiency of marketing boards and industrial development agencies was essentially a problem of excessive control for political ends (Ghai 1977). Similar evidence was emerging from India (Mathur 1977) and from Latin America (Boneo 1983). The UN's 1974 publication on the *Organization, Management and Supervision of Public Enterprises in Developing Countries* put the entire issue of autonomy and performance of public agencies in developing countries into comparative and theoretical perspective. Between 1974 and 1984, the International Centre for Public Enterprises in Developing Countries (ICPE) also explored this issue.

During the 1980s and 1990s, the World Bank reemphasized the importance of managerial autonomy for realizing economic growth goals. The fact that both exponents and critics of state interventionism agreed on the importance of autonomy for economic growth goals should not go without note. For opponents of state interventionism such as the World Bank, public enterprise reform in the 1980s and 1990s meant 'designing systems to hold managers accountable for enterprise performance while protecting them from undue intervention' (World Bank 1991: 293). The Bank's provocative 1995 study on *Bureaucrats in Business* further explored this theme. Antecedents to this view can be found in the World Bank's 1983 report where the success story of the Kenya Tea Development Authority (KTDA) was presented as a triumph of goal specificity and autonomy (World Bank 1983: 78).

In a real sense, this final variable—autonomy—constitutes the missing link in a chain that binds administrative capacity-building and facilitative policy content. Taken together, these attributes seem to be based on the notion of a managerial state, autonomous from the influence of interests, and collaborating with capital, in particular, in a type of corporatist model. The relationships derived from this literature are captured in the growth component of the framework of association:

> The greater the degree to which economic growth development goals are realized, the greater the likelihood of public bureaucracy having the following attributes:

(1) high administrative capacity-building;
(2) high facilitative policy content; and
(3) high autonomy from the political centre.

PART II:
Public Bureaucracy and Change:
The Associations

Introduction

Associations between attributes of public bureaucracy and change have been addressed within liberal-pluralist and radical traditions with remarkable convergence of thought. Convergence is also apparent in contributions from both Western and developing-world intellectuals. The new development administrationist writing on participation (Montgomery 1988) and decentralization (Rondinelli 1983) and foundation development administrationists writing on political development (Riggs 1971) constitute the liberal-pluralist tradition. Contributions from the neo-colonial and post-colonial state theorists represent the radical perspective on this question. Intellectuals such as Dwivedi and Nef (1982) together with what Hirschmann (1981) called the 'Underdevelopment-Dependency Movement' constitute the developing-world contribution.

Change and the organization

Decentralization and participation are twin concepts: the former addresses the issue of the internal structure of organizations, while the latter raises the issue of the policy environment in which the task of the organization is determined. Taken together, the two concepts offer an organic explanation of bureaucratic performance, linking internal and external factors. Frustrated by the inability of centrally-planned interventions to reach the poor, international development agencies such as the United Nations and the USAID searched for new delivery structures (Cheema & Rondinelli 1983, Leonard 1987, Montgomery 1988). Decentralization was a rediscovery that soon became the latest 'fashion' in development studies (Conyers 1981). Although decentralization took different forms—integrated rural development, local action in rural development and participatory development (Rondinelli 1987) —proponents of these schemes had one aim: empowerment of the dispossessed by shifting decision-making power from the centre to local levels (Griffin 1981). In this regard, 'decentralized planning' became especially popular in change perspectives (Wunsch 1991).

In the late 1970s, decentralization was imbued with magical properties. Not only was it said to be capable of contributing to economic and social change, it was also seen as a facilitator of economic growth policies since it enhanced efficiency (Cheema & Rondinelli 1983, Rondinelli 1987). However, it was in the area of integrated rural development that decentralization had its greatest appeal. Thus, think tanks on decentralization for integrated rural development mushroomed across the United States with the sponsorship of the USAID. In 1979, the USAID affirmed its commitment to decentralization for rural development in a policy paper entitled 'Managing Decentralization' (Rondinelli 1987: 103). Most notable of the USAID-sponsored think tanks were the Cornell University Rural Development Committee, established in 1970 under the aegis of the USAID Asia Bureau, and the co-operative research efforts at the University of Wisconsin at Madison and the University of California at Berkeley. In his work with the University of Wisconsin, Rondinelli attempted to refine the concept by defining it as:

> The transfer or delegation of legal and political authority to plan, make decisions and manage public functions from the central government and its agencies to field organisations of those agencies, subordinate units of government, semi-autonomous public corporations, area-wide or regional development authorities, functional authorities, autonomous local governments or nongovernmental organizations. (1987: 103)

In addition, Cheema and Rondinelli (1983) and Rondinelli (1983) characterized the four major 'degrees' or 'forms' of decentralization as deconcentration, delegation, devolution and a type of privatization.

Rondinelli's efforts notwithstanding, decentralization continued to mean different things to different people. Thus, the terms 'administrative democracy,' 'devolution,' 'deconcentration,' 'autonomy' and 'delegation' are used interchangeably with decentralization. This somewhat nebulous feature of decentralization contributed to its decline in the new development administration. Another cause for its decline was the over-optimistic expectations held for decentralization by international development organizations in the late 1970s.

Failure to clarify the meaning of decentralization became a particularly worrisome stumbling block for those wishing to engineer social and economic change in the 1970s. They faced the problem of matching the degree and form of decentralization to peculiar circumstances and of devising suitable indices of decentralization for purposes of evaluation. Moreover, many Third World governments took advantage of the ambiguity of the concept and claimed to be implementing decentralization in the form of statutory authorities, regional development corporations, federalism, local government authorities and peoples' co-operatives, while still concentrating power at the centre. Thus, the performance of decentralization interventions in Asia (Rondinelli 1983), Africa (Adamolekun & Rowlands 1979, Conyers 1981) and Latin America has been viewed as less than satisfactory (Rondinelli & Nellis 1986, Rondinelli, Nellis & Cheema 1984).

Despite the failure of decentralization experiments in the 1970s, international development institutions such as the World Bank remain convinced of the merits of this approach, especially in the area of social policy implementation. Decentralization and participation have also emerged as important building blocks in the World Bank conception of 'transparency' and 'good governance.' Currently, the World Bank uses the term loosely. Thus, decentralization has been stripped of its spatial connotations; it is used in the wider sense of endowing non-centre agencies with decision-making authority. Moreover, with the World Bank's intervention in the decentralization debate, the meaning has also shifted from the 'decentralization planning' popular in the 1970s literature, to the decentralization of implementation strategies.

In developed countries such as the United States and the United Kingdom, arguments for decentralization in the 1980s were based on the belief that autonomy from central government ensured consumer sovereignty, administrative responsiveness and, ultimately, economic and social change (Hansen 1985, Peters 1991). This view is consistent with Rondinelli's fourth level of decentralization, where privatization is a variant of decentralization rather than the anti-statist or anti-centralization conspiracy it is commonly understood to be.

That proponents of basic needs in the 1970s and World Bank economists in the 1980s seem to agree on the merits of decentralization is not surprising since they both operate within a liberal-pluralist perspective of state-civil society relations. Such a perspective assumes that power is dispersed and interest groups, both domestic and international, have equal opportunities for mobilization and action. Change is therefore a technical venture to be managed and administered through appropriate bureaucratic structures. It is this perspective that Leftwich (1993, 1994) identifies as informing the current discussions on governance in the structural adjustment dialogue of the World Bank and the IMF.

Despite criticisms and an abundance of empirical evidence against decentralization, this concept remains the most powerful and persistent organizational attribute associated with change goals. Contributions by intellectuals from the developing world (e.g., Dwivedi & Nef 1982, Indiresan 1990, Jaeger & Kanungo 1990) reaffirm the importance of decentralization for transformation and change. The persistence of decentralization therefore recommends this variable for application in this study.

Change and the policy environment

In the 1970s, participation also emerged as a reaction to the failure of the top-down central-planning model of the 1960s. Participation was perceived as the legitimate incorporation of beneficiaries and other affected groups into all stages of the policy-making process—formulation, implementation and evaluation. This new people-centred, populist model of development was spearheaded by international agencies such as the ILO. The historical antecedent of this model can be traced to three sources: American community power/pluralist debate of the 1950s and 1960s (Dahl 1961); what Midgley refers to as 'the Third World community development movement of the 1950s and 1960s' (Midgley 1986: 14); and the rise of worker participation in countries like Algeria, Chile, Peru and Yugoslavia during the 1950s.

Participation presented yet another example of the intellectual leadership given by international development agencies in the resolution of the Third World's problems. In 1971, the United Nations published 'Popular Participation in Development,' and in 1975 it published 'Popular Participation in decision-making for Development.' Midgley (1986: 21) observes that the publication of these two documents was followed by a major research programme in popular participation by the United Nations Research Institute for Social Development (UNRISD). He notes further that the declaration of the International Women's Year in 1975 gave additional impetus to participation, and that UN efforts to refine the concept reached its peak with the establishment of a UN 'meeting of experts in 1978 to consider the specific issue of community level participation' (1986: 22). However, it was left to agencies such as UNICEF and WHO to operationalize the new policy of popular participation in their various development programmes.

Prompted by the United Nations, USAID and other powerful opinion-shapers in development, Third World governments in Africa, Asia, Latin America and the Caribbean initiated participatory schemes in the 1970s. Such schemes included the 1979 Gal Oya Water management project in Sri Lanka (Uphoff 1985), the 1976 National Irrigation Administration project in the Philippines (Korten 1985) and integrated rural development projects in Bangladesh (Khan 1985). That interest in participatory schemes waned in the 1980s is not surprising as these schemes were either politicized or ignored by the politicians of developing countries.

Lessons from early participation experiments in both the developed and developing world have clarified and sharpened the concept (Bryant 1980). Thus, while early advocates of participation wavered between populist and liberal-pluralist visions of participation, in the 1980s and 1990s it is the pluralist notion of the concept that has taken root. The experience gained in the 1970s demonstrated convincingly the unmanageability of 'popular participation' in the populist tradition (Midgley 1986). The emphasis is now directed towards the participation of beneficiaries or, more specifically, representatives of beneficiary associations. In this way, non-governmental organizations (NGOs) are accorded a critical role, working with state agencies for the formulation and execution of development interventions. Models of state–NGO collaboration vary from country to country and from sector to sector (Copestake 1996).

The experiences of the 1970s have also revealed the importance of participation at the stage of policy design. But perhaps most importantly, the failures of the 1970s taught the importance of institutionalization and institution building for successful participation.

In a real sense, it is the institutionalization imperative in successful participation that dictates the three fundamental principles of participation as it is now understood—incorporation, representation, and decentralization. The current anti-state/administration revolution in development studies has also entered into the discussion of participation for change. The fundamental contention here is one of the legitimate incorporation of organized interests, constituted as NGOs, for load-shedding from the inefficient and overburdened Third World state. This is especially recommended in areas of social policy, what the World Bank calls 'people-centred development.' Thus, the 1983 World Bank Development Report advocates beneficiary participation in people-centred development interventions. The report recommends partnership with local communities by encouraging contributions of money and labour for programme success through beneficiary participation.

In a 1986 workshop sponsored by the Economic Development Institute (EDI), the World Bank reaffirmed its commitment to beneficiary participation in development interventions, people-centred and otherwise. Contributors to the workshop (Norman Uphoff, Samuel Paul and Caroline Moser) recommended the strengthening of community organizations and the incorporation of beneficiary interest representation in decision-making units (Bamberger 1991). In the developed world, community participation for improving the quality of life for underclasses, i.e., for change, has been a persistent theme in welfare states such as the Netherlands and Sweden (Hood & Schuppert 1988).

Participation and its sister concept, decentralization, have survived as important analytical and normative indicators associated with change-oriented interventions. While decentralization addresses the structure of policy-making institutions, participation speaks to the issue of the policy environment in which change-oriented policy is formulated and reformulated.

Change and the political environment

What attribute of the political environment is associated with change goals? Answers to this question come largely from political developmentalists within the Comparative Administration Group (CAG) and scholars concerned with state–society relations in neo-colonial and post-colonial societies. Political developmentalists within the CAG (La Palombara 1963, Pye 1963, Riggs 1971) explored the problematic of bureaucratic articulation with its political, social and economic environment, given different levels of development. The political environment was seen to be most influential on bureaucracy.

The highest stage of development was defined in terms of democratic political structures, an industrial economy and an associational/pluralist social structure—all characteristics of modernization/westernization. For political developmentalists, the movement of societies through stages of development constituted social change. In this way, social change as a concept was fundamentally linked with that of moderniza-tion/westernization. Underpinning this argument was a Weberian ideal-type methodology in which different stages of development were char-acterized by different ideal-types of administrative, economic, political and social structures (Verma & Sharma 1984). Riggs's ideal-types of fused, refracted and prismatic society best demonstrate this methodol-ogy.

Due to their Western lenses, political developmentalists in the CAG saw bureaucracy's articulation in traditional and transitional 'fused' and 'prismatic' societies as deviant. In such situations, bureaucracy had disproportionate power and bureaucratic neutrality was absent. Bureau-cratic politics and polity were important concepts in their analysis. On the other hand, bureaucratic articulation with political, economic and social structures was seen to be balanced in modern/Western societies. It was argued that while the threat of bureaucratic power existed in the developed world, it was checked by the dispersal of power, the capacity for mobilization and the institutionalization of checks and balances. The notion of the 'separation of powers' is fundamental to this argu-ment.

Hence the antithesis of the balanced polity was located in the devel-oping world where powers were not separate. Writing in 1963, Pye ob-served:

> The great problem today in nation-building is that of relating the administrative and authoritative structures of government to political forces within the transi-tional societies. In most ex-colonial countries there is an imbalance between recognized administrative traditional and a still inchoate political process. (1963: 31)

Fred Riggs comes to a similar conclusion:

> The colonial administration itself created a bureaucratic apparatus not subject to political control within the dependent territory, so that administrative institu-tions proliferated while political structures remained embryonic and largely extra-legal, hence unable to relate themselves effectively to control over the bu-reaucracy. (1963: 125)

The bureaucratic development argument is important for understanding how bureaucracy realizes change goals in the developing world, since bureaucrats are portrayed as having subjective interests that determine their attitude towards policies intended to change the existing status quo. Consequently, locating the politics of bureaucrats, that is to say, their subjective orientation based on class, 'clect' or ethnic bases, is a good predictor of their disposition towards the successful implementation of change-inducing policies. Furthermore, bureaucratic politics is also indicative of the relationship between public officers and the political directorate that formulates change-inducing polices.

Similarly, those concerned with state/society relations in postcolonial societies also recognize the absence of bureaucratic neutrality in the developing world. Because they see policy gains in zero-sum terms, bureaucrats' subjective disposition towards the formulators and beneficiaries of redistributive policies becomes an important predictor of policy success or failure. This argument is reflected in the works of Shivji (1973) writing on the state in Tanzania, in Meillassoux (1970) writing on Mali, Thomas (1974) writing on the Caribbean and, more recently, in the works of Hyden (1983) and Price (1975) writing on East Africa and Ghana, respectively. The more controversial of these works presents the state in the Third World as 'predatory' and bureaucrats as free agents who formulate or implement policies in accordance with subjective/non-rational factors such as 'the economy of affection' (Hyden 1983).

Recent administrative reforms in the United States and the United Kingdom sought to replace the faceless bureaucrats with a more committed functionary. Reforms were based on the assumption that a committed bureaucracy is indispensable for the execution of policies intended to alter the relationship of citizen to state and the structures of production. In this era of what Peters (1991) so appropriately calls 'conviction politics,' a politicized bureaucracy is argued to be important for change.

In the developing world, however, the handmaidens of conviction politics recommend less, not more, bureaucratic politics. A sharp distinction is made between politics and administration, i.e., between policy formulation and implementation. Bureaucracy is restricted to the area of policy implementation, while policy formulation is to be determined by the logic of the market. To undertake its role, the bureaucracy is circumscribed even further by notions of 'transparency,' 'accountability,' and:

> A legal framework for development, which means a structure of rules and laws which provide clarity, predictability and stability for the private sector, which are impartially and fairly applied to all, and which provide the basis for conflict resolution through an independent judicial system. (Leftwich 1994: 372)

Leftwich observes that such recommendations are informed by underlying Weberian notions:

> Whatever the merits and limitations of that worldview, who could possibly be against good governance, at least in its limited administrative sense, as presented by the World Bank? For is it not the case that any society—whether liberal or socialist—must be better off with a public service that is both efficient and honest, open and accountable, and with a judicial system that is independent and fair? In this sense, at least, the World Bank's conception of good governance is unexceptional: it re-identifies precisely the principles of administration that have long been argued as being of benefit to developing countries. They are impeccably Weberian in spirit, if not letter. (1994: 372)

Intellectual double standards on bureaucratic politics and its converse—bureaucratic neutrality—are rife in the literature on the question of bureaucracy and democracy in the developed and developing world. While the absence of bureaucratic neutrality and the presence of bureaucratic politics is taken as 'proof positive' of low political development in the developing world, in the developed world, similar evidence is interpreted as 'a cultural distinction.' To take the work of Heady (1979), while he finds varying degrees of bureaucratic politics amongst bureaucracies in the United States, the United Kingdom, Japan, Germany and France, these findings are presented as cultural differences, not worthy of comparative speculation about the level of political development. In contrast, his entire discussion of bureaucracy in the developing world is essentially one of the level of political development as measured by bureaucratic balance or imbalance.

In a real sense, whether or not bureaucratic politics is an indicator of political development is an academic question. The point is that the subjective disposition of bureaucrats towards policies based on shared interests with politicians and beneficiaries is fundamentally related to the nature, if not the level, of development of the bureaucracy's political environment. Thus, bureaucratic politics is a recurring theme in a wide literature that explores change and public bureaucracies. What is the socio-economic background of public bureaucrats? What schools did they attend? What is their relationship to the political ruling class? And what is their relationship to the beneficiaries of change-inducing policies? These are some of the questions explored in studies on bureaucratic alienation in developing countries (Bjorkman 1979, Srinivas 1990), and bureaucratic corruption and bureaucratic ethics (Kernaghan & Dwivedi 1983). In addition, some more general works simply treat this issue under the generic term 'bureaucratic politics.' Examples of the latter include Jain's (1989) edited volume, Puthucheary's (1978) study of the politics of administration in Malaysia, and Montgomery's (1986) study of bureaucratic politics in South Africa. It is precisely the persistence of this attribute of public bureaucracy that recommends it as the single most important political environmental variable associated with change. It can therefore be concluded that the greater the level of bureaucratic politics in support of change policies, the greater the realization of change goals.

The following association captures the relationship between change goals and public bureaucracy:

> The greater the degree to which change-oriented development goals are realized; the greater the likelihood of public bureaucracy having the following attributes:
>
> (1)   high decentralization;
> (2)   high participation; and
> (3)   high bureaucratic politics in support of goals.

The underpinnings of this association are Weberian notions of the bureaucracy in a rational-legal authority system, and pluralist notions of interest associations and state-society relations. In this view, the state is susceptible to capture by dominant interests. Table 3.1 presents the summary framework of associations between public bureaucracy and (1) economic growth and (2) change goals.

Table 3.1   *Goal realization and public bureaucracy: The framework of association*

Development goal	Location of explanatory factors		
	Policy environment	*Internal organization*	*Political environment*
Economic growth	Facilitative policy content	Administrative capacity-building	Autonomy from political control
Change (economic and social)	Participation	Decentralization	Bureaucratic politics

PART III:
Development Administration in the English-speaking Caribbean: A Special Case?

The research question of this study was partly inspired by 30 years of frustrated efforts with development interventions in Jamaica and Trinidad & Tobago. In view of the peculiar condition of the small geographical size of Jamaica and T&T, it is important to establish the relevance of the framework of association derived above. The question must now be asked: To what extent is there a special 'development administration' for small countries?

A second distinguishing factor, more nebulous but equally interesting, which characterizes these two islands, is their location in a region known for its successful transplantation of Westminster parliamentary government. Moreover, the Westminster model of government is supported by a transplanted 'Britishness' that is particularly associated with the former West Indian colonies. This invites the question of whether there is a peculiar development administration for the Commonwealth Caribbean? Answering these two questions requires close scrutiny of the development administration literature on small size, and on public bureaucracy in the Commonwealth Caribbean region.

To address the first question, it is important to note that attempts to theorize the administrative implications of small size were first made in 1968 with the publication of a United Nations Public Administration Division of the Economic and Social Affairs Department (UNPAD) study entitled, 'Comparative Analysis of the Distinctive Public Administration Problems of Small States and Territories.' The findings of the UNPAD study were incorporated into two successive publications of the United Nations Institute for Training and Research (UNITAR): 'Status and Problems of Very Small States and Territories' (1969) and 'Small States and Territories, Status and Problems' (1971). Murray (1977) notes that, prior to these publications, UN public administration reports, such as the 1951 'Handbook of Public Administration' and the 1969 study 'Appraising Administrative Capability for Development' simply ignored the question of size. Murray writes that the UN was guided by the basic assumption 'that analyses and prescriptions are not affected by the scale on which a state operates—or not affected to a degree that makes the prescriptions inapplicable' (1977: 567).

Since the publication of the early UN studies, several scholars have taken up the challenge of trying to build a theory of development administration and small size. They include: Murray (1981, 1985), Thynne (1981), Tisdel and Fairbairn (1983) and Ghai (1990), writing on the Pacific; Jones (1976), Mills (1971), Kersell (1985, 1987), Kemp-Hope (1983) and Khan (1982) writing the English-speaking Caribbean; and Bray (1992), who compared Ministries of Education in 15 small British Commonwealth countries. The journal, *Public Administration and Development*, has been the organ of expression for most of these articles. Interest in this area of research has also been supported by the International Association of Schools and Institutes of Administration (IASIA). Within the IASIA, Working Group V was established in 1983 with terms of reference to explore the special case of public administration in small developing countries. A recent publication entitled *Public Administration in Small and Island States* (1992) featuring articles from a wide cross-section of such states, represents the culmination of this nine-year research effort.

A review of the myriad works on the special case of public administration in small developing countries reveals a lack of consensus on the meaning of size, and a failure to reach conclusions on the relevance of small size for administration. Several different definitions of size are offered. They include population size (e.g., the early UN studies referred to above), physical size, size of the economy, and vulnerability, the last being a new dimension introduced by the Commonwealth Secretariat in 1985. While acknowledging the obvious difficulty of finding an objective definition of size, most applied studies in this area use population size as an arbitrary but convenient yardstick. A minority of studies, however, employ the concept without defining it (Wijeweera 1992: 392).

Further complicating the discussion is the distinction between size and 'scale.' Raadschelders (1992) and Jones (1976) have discussed the question of scale as presented in the 1967 publication by Benedict entitled *Problems of Small Territories*. In addition, the distinction between microstate, island state and small state has not been clarified. To compound the definitional problem, agreement is also lacking on the administrative significance of small size (whatever the definition of size). To be sure, several scholars identify human resource limitations, the absence of a critical mass, the existence of a large interventionist state, over-politicization of the bureaucracy, experimentation with non-

Weberian structures and practices (for example, team management and multifunctionality), and the absence of a strict separation of powers as characteristics of the administrative system of small developing countries. However, the same scholars are also quick to point out that these characteristics are not peculiar to small countries, nor are they necessarily a consequence of smallness (Wijeweera 1992: 398).

Consequently, while it is true to say that public administration in small developing countries seems to share certain general characteristics, it cannot be concluded that this is due to small size; neither can it be concluded that these characteristics are not apparent in large developing countries. Based on their review of the literature on this debate, Schahczenski (1992) and Wijeweera (1992) come to a similar conclusion. Contributions in a 1994 special edition of the *Asian Journal of Public Administration* devoted to 'Governance of Small and Island States' have come no closer to constructing a special development administration for small countries.

As regards the second question on a Caribbean development administration, it should be noted that, prior to political independence, the Colonial Office treated the question of administrative performance for development as a problem of training and institution building for governance.

With the transition from internal self-government to full independence in the 1960s, indigenous scholarly works in development administration emerged. Gladstone Mills emerged as the foremost development administrationist during this period (Mills 1966). Clearly influenced by the Riggs's ecology paradigm, Mill's early works concentrated on the ecology of Caribbean bureaucracies. He identified small size, a colonial past and the transplanted nature of institutions as important features of the bureaucracy's ecology. He explored the relationship between such ecological factors and the internal organizational structures and functions of public bureaucracies in the Commonwealth Caribbean. Other significant works by indigenous scholars during this period included Hamilton (1964), the MSc thesis of Jones (1968), the PhD thesis of Ryan (1965), and Collin's study of the civil service strike in Guyana (1964).

Similar to Mills, the works of early Caribbean scholars betrayed a preoccupation with the legacies of colonialism and its impact on the ecology/environment of public administration. The attitudinal, social, cultural and political legacies were viewed as a hindrance to bureaucracy's role as a change agent. Overcentralization, politicization, low professionalism, low representativeness and a law and order mentality were the chief organizational factors retarding the bureaucracy's development role. Creeping into the definition of development in these studies was the concept of change—change from the old colonial economic, social and political structures. Not only was the developmental impact of bureaucracy judged in terms of its contribution to employment generation, its contribution to creating a new and more democratic economic, political and social order was also viewed as vital.

The 1960s were also characterized by what can be loosely called 'efficiency studies' by the World Bank and USAID in particular, and by local commissions appointed by national governments to consider the question of how to make the bureaucracy more efficient in the implementation of economic growth policies. Several solutions were posited, including training, administrative reform, reclassification and salary upgrading, and technical assistance.

In keeping with the expansion of public services and the commensurate growth of the bureaucracy, the 1970s saw an outpouring of development administration literature. While most contributors to this literature expressed disappointment with the development impact of public bureaucracies, they took different views on the meaning of development, the unit of analysis and the explanation of performance. Those who took statutory authorities and planning agencies as the unit of analysis viewed efficiency as the key indicator of performance. They also saw development in terms of increased production of goods and services. For others, whose unit of analysis remained 'the bureaucracy,' development was seen as change, and their methodology borrowed generously from political economy. Edwin Jones's PhD thesis (1970) and subsequent work (1975) represent this new preoccupation with change. At the level of *realpolitik*, the calls for change either resulted in the election to office of political parties on the left or in the radicalization of incumbent political parties throughout the English-speaking Caribbean. Hence the advent of democratic socialism under Manley in Jamaica in 1972, the emergence of the New Jewel Movement in Grenada in 1979, and the emergence of corporate socialism in Burnham's Guyana of 1974. So intense was the new wind of change sweeping through the English-speaking Caribbean that the doctrine of ideological pluralism became an article of faith in the Caribbean Economic Community (Caricom).

Against this background, Caribbean development administrationists, particularly those writing on the Jamaican experiment of democratic socialism, tried to prescribe an optimal role, structure and function of public bureaucracies for the management of change. It is in this light that the works of Nunes (1976) and Jones (1976) should be viewed. These works criticized the Weberian model of bureaucracy and called for a more politicized and innovative public administration. Administrative innovations included aspects of the current thinking on participation, decentralization and team management. Small size was seen as a facilitative factor in this process.

The publication of two readers, *Notes on Organization and Change* by Nunes and Draper (1974) and *Issues and Problems in Caribbean Public Administration* edited by Ryan (1977) demonstrated the intellectual crossroads at which Caribbean development administration found itself in this period. A review of the contributions to the readers reveals a continuing preoccupation with explaining how the environment of the bureaucracy retards its propensity to contribute both to economic growth and change. While some contributions continued the tradition of tracing the problems of the environment to the legacies of colonial rule (e.g., Nunes & Draper 1974), others avoided the historical approach. Instead, the environment was taken as a given, though problematic, variable and scholars sought only to explore its impact on administrative performance. Yet other contributions reflected a concern for internal issues of management, structure, systems and procedures, factors they linked with the efficient production of development outputs (e.g., sections VI & VII of Ryan 1977). A related organizational issue also linked to the efficient production of development outputs was the legal framework within which development administration operated. Interestingly, during this period external observers of development administration in the region maintained their interest in ecological factors, particularly size, when analysing the developmental performance of Caribbean public bureaucracies. This is the context in which Garcia-Zamor's 1970 and 1977 works should be located. Garcia-Zamor's 1977 work is particularly important since it remains the only extensive macro-level comparative study of administration and development in the region.

In the 1980s, the balance-of-payments problems affecting the Caribbean countries resulted in development administration issues being addressed largely in terms of efficiency. It is in this light that the various publications of the Caribbean Public Enterprise Project should be viewed. In addition, the 1980s also witnessed the publication of studies on the Office of the Ombudsman in Jamaica, Trinidad and Tobago and Guyana (e.g., Barrett 1985).

In the 1990s, Caribbean development administration has found itself torn between a high-road constructed on old theories and themes and a normative orientation guided by the realities of efficiency management under structural adjustment. Examples of the former include *Issues and problems in Caribbean Public Administration* (Ryan & Brown 1992) and *Public Policy and Administration* (Mills 1990a). Both works are disappointing since they are largely reprints of old essays and theories from the 1960s and 1970s. They also lack a common theme and theoretical focus. Examples of the normative orientation can be found in the numerous reports and studies by public-sector management networks such as the Caribbean Management Development Association (CMDA) and the Caribbean Centre for Development Administration (CARICAD). The efforts of CMDA and CARICAD have been supported by the Commonwealth Association for Public Administration and Management (CAPAM). The recent work edited by Garrity and Picard (1996), entitled *Policy Reform for Sustainable Development in the Caribbean*, demonstrates the theoretical inadequacy of the contemporary management focus. Key words such as policy reform, sustainablity, administrative reform, and governance are employed without substantial theoretical grounding. Moreover, the relationship between these points of reference is often assumed in the various contributions. The absence of a comparative framework through which theoretical insights can be derived from the two main country studies which dominate the work, Jamaica and Trinidad &Tobago, is also a major deficiency.

This is the juncture at which development administration in the Commonwealth Caribbean now finds itself. The argument for a special case of development administration in the Caribbean has not been sustained, especially in recent times when the realities of structural adjustment have emerged as a common denominator in developing countries as different as Jamaica and Nigeria (Walker 1997). While it is true that peculiar factors will shape the course of the adjustment programme the absence of a theory of development administration that is region-specific means that the framework of association derived above can be used to explore the research question of this study.

Summary, Conclusions and Fulcrums of the Empirical Inquiry

This chapter set out to explore the question: What attributes of public bureaucracy are associated with the realization of economic growth and change goals in situations where the state has a central role in the development process? The relationship between public bureaucracy and development was found to be fundamentally bound up with the status and integrity of Public Administration as a discipline. Early scholars in the Comparative Administration Group used development administration as the testing ground for developing a science of public administration. Because they failed, and because scholars from other disciplines have subsequently shaped discussions, it became necessary to consider a wide cross-section of literature in order to come up with an answer to this research question.

An eclectic approach was taken in order to construct an explanatory framework. This approach addressed specific questions of growth and change to the literature, it focused on associations rather than causality, it viewed public bureaucracies as partially open systems, and it selected explanations based on recurring and converging themes. A framework of association was constructed with two aspects, the first relating public bureaucracy to economic growth goals, and the second relating public bureaucracy to change goals. Differences in the realization of development goals discerned in the previous chapter will be explored through the Most Similar Systems Research Design in the chapters that follow.

Public Bureaucracy and Economic Growth: The Associations

Introduction

This chapter examines whether Jamaica's relative success at realizing economic-growth goals in the 1960s and 1980s was associated with a greater administrative capacity-building effort, more autonomous implementing agencies and a more facilitative policy environment. Evidence of such relationships is seen as supporting the economic growth component of the framework of association.

Part I explores associations at the macro level of public sector agencies. In Part II, the same associations are explored at the micro- or case-study level of the Industrial Development Corporation.

PART I

Public Bureaucracy and Economic Growth: Macro-level Associations

Economic growth and capacity building

It is important to situate the discussion on administrative capacity-building in Jamaica and T&T in the 1960s against the background of the following factors: political independence in 1962, the state-sponsored economic growth model being implemented at the time, and an inherited colonial civil service whose main activities revolved around revenue collection and the maintenance of law and order. In the 1960s, the new governments in Jamaica and T&T encountered the problem of how to reorient and restructure the colonial civil service to support the new goal of economic growth. What reforms were initiated and what institutions were created to enhance the public service's capacity to support the economic growth programme?

The PNP's establishment of a Central Planning Unit in the Office of the Premier, Norman Manley, in 1955 marked the first step along the road to capacity building for an independent Jamaica. Although the Unit's staff was small and inadequately trained in the techniques of planning, it succeeded in producing the 1957–67 National Plan and the 1963–68 Independence Plan for Jamaica.

The in-service training programme was based on a human resource assessment of the Central Planning Unit's Manpower Research Unit. The assessment concluded that 'Vacancies exist at the moment as far as can be ascertained for 1,191 persons in the Government service in which there are degrees of difficulty in finding the right persons for recruitment' (Annual Budget Speech, GOJ 1967: 12). Similarly, in a 1964 address to the Civil Service Association, the Deputy Prime Minister and Minister of Finance, Donald Sangster, identified the greatest problem facing his government as 'the need to create a sufficiency of capable persons to fill the posts existing in the service, which will make for increased efficiency' (Barnett 1977: 176). The JLP government proposed to tackle the problem by increasing the 1967 training vote by 3 million pounds sterling over the previous year, whereas the vote for 1966 was 11.3 million pounds sterling (GOJ Annual Budget Speech 1967). Stricter conditions on bonded overseas training were also proposed and senior officials were prevented from taking vacation leave in excess of three months. Furthermore, the option to retire at 50 with permission was restricted to cases of 'ill-health or inefficiency' (Barnett 1977: 177).

Secondly, in the 1960s the JLP government also made deliberate efforts to woo foreign expertise to supplement existing capacity. In the first instance, the services of planners were obtained through technical assistance arrangements from agencies such as UK/ODM, USAID, Canada External Aid, West German Aid, VSO/UK, Canadian Volunteers and German Volunteers (CPU Technical Assistance Newsletter 1960–1969). In addition, efforts were made to recruit professional Jamaicans residing in the UK and the USA.

Thirdly, in the period immediately following political independence, deliberate attempts were made to upgrade the capacity of the Central Planning Unit. The Manpower Research Unit was relocated to the Central Planning Unit; co-ordination of technical assistance was added to the Unit's functions; staff training, upgrading and reorganization was initiated; and a Ford Foundation manpower planning team was assigned to the Unit to build capacity in manpower planning.

Fourth, arguably the most important capacity-building effort of this period was the comprehensive public-service reform programme to take place between 1966 and 1968. The reform programme was based on the recommendations of the 1965 United Nations study on public administration in Jamaica. The impetus for the UN study stemmed from a 1961 resolution of the Jamaica Civil Service Association. The occasion of the resolution was the Association's 42nd annual conference.

By June of 1964, the adviser to the UN team had arrived in Jamaica to pave the way for the 1965 study. Based on the recommendations of the UN report, the JLP government undertook a massive public-service reclassification and salary upgrading exercise intended to bring a modern public service into existence. In his 1967 Budget Speech, then-Minister of Finance Edward Seaga affirmed his government's commitment to the UN's recommendations and to a modern public service. Aspects of the UN report which called for budgeting and financial management reforms were also implemented in the late 1960s.

During the 1960s, the PNM government in T&T also faced the problem of how to implement a state-directed economic growth programme with a law and order civil service. In 1959, a Commission of Enquiry headed by former permanent secretary to the Chief Minister, Ulric Lee, was set up to review and make recommendations to implement an earlier 1958 report (i.e., the King Report) on civil service reform. Although the Lee report contained several far-reaching recommendations, it was placed on hold as yet another civil service inquiry, the 1964 O'Neil Lewis Committee, was convened with terms of reference to consider 'The role and status of the civil service in the age of independence.' Winston Mahabir, then Minister of Health, gives some personal insights into why the Lee Report was shelved:

> For reasons upon which we all speculated unproductively, Williams made the prodigious error of assigning Lee to re-organise the Civil Service. I refused to co-operate with Lee, having little regard for any quality he had demonstrated thus far. In any case his assignment was never approved by Cabinet. The end result was called Lee-organisation. It created waves of verbal rebellion in Cabinet and in the Civil Service

itself. The press talked sarcastically about the drift to Lee-wards. (Mahabir 1975: 50)

The O'Neil Lewis Committee identified the problems of overcentralization, slow decision-making and poor co-ordination in government as obstacles to civil service performance.

Recommendations centred on the issue of training (extensive short- and long-term training and the establishment of one centralized training body), closer politician-civil servant relations and a comprehensive upgrading of salaries. In 1966, the PNM implemented the salary-upgrading proposal, but reorganization and decentralization recommendations made in this and previous reports were sadly neglected. Consequently, up to 1966, capacity building in T&T was largely interpreted as salary increases. Given that the Civil Service Association disagreed with the amount and categories of increases, the PNM was investigating the Association for 'subversive activities,' and that 1966 was also an election year, the capacity-building potential of salary increases became lost in the quagmire of politics.

It was not until the closing years of the 1960s that yet another committee—the Dolly Committee—was assembled to 'recommend on the re-organization and streamlining of Public Service practices and procedures' (GOTT Dolly Report, 1969: 16). But even here, results were disappointing, and the same findings of overcentralization, slow decision-making and poor co-ordination were again raised.

By the late 1960s, a succession of administrative reform reports (Dolly 1969, King 1958, Lee 1959, Lewis 1964) contained a full range of recommendations to improve the administrative capacity of the T&T public service. The PNM's reluctance to implement these recommendations reflected its implicit mistrust and fear of a public service then under investigation for 'subversive activities.' Towards the end of the 1960s, however, the PNM appeared to be yielding to the notion of a professional civil service as two new capacity-building institutions were created—the Organization and Management Division and the Central Training Unit. However, these were not without their problems.

In 1967, the Organization and Methods Department (O&M), first established in 1959 as a unit of the Colonial Secretariat, was reorganized and renamed the Organization and Management Division of the Ministry of Finance. Cabinet Minute No. 1394 of 1969 expanded the new O&M's functions accordingly: 'The consultation function of the O&M Division of the Ministry of Finance and Planning should be widened to include the main and supporting services of Ministries and Agencies of the Government of Trinidad and Tobago, and in particular those relating to personnel, supply, financial and office management' (GOTT *Major Achievements of the O&M Division 1956–86*, 1986: 1). However, in the late 1960s the new O&M promised far more than it delivered. Firstly, appointment to the elite O&M staff became a highly political issue, and secondly, the division was patently understaffed, (with a staff of only 24) even though the O&M was expected to support a civil service numbering 28,250 by 1969 (Dolly Report, republished in Ryan 1972: 104). Thirdly, legacies of the O&M's past organization and methods meant that the organization was soon relegated to forecasting the clerks and cleaners requirement of the civil service rather than serving as a proactive institution for public service human resource development.

In 1966, a Central Training Unit (CTU) was established to co-ordinate the training needs of the T&T civil service. During the 1960s, the CTU suffered from acute staff shortages, operating as it did with only five training officers, as well as a general lack of political confidence in the organization, and poor co-ordination with government Ministries on training capacities and needs. Consequently, by 1974 the Unit had to be completely reorganized and upgraded.

Thus, the end of the 1960s found civil servants in Jamaica reasonably satisfied with salary increases, content that the JLP would heed the Association's call for administrative reform, confident that the government was committed to administrative improvement, and optimistic about the much talked about and heralded Ministry of the Public Service. The prospect that the PNP could be returned to office in the upcoming 1972 elections made them even more optimistic.

In contrast, in T&T a battle of attrition was taking place between the Civil Service Association and the PNM, as the PNM viewed civil servants as a veritable opposition cell. The following chapter, which deals with economic change, reveals how this drama was played out in the 1970s. Suffice it to say, however, that, in the 1960s, civil servants took to the streets on the eve of political independence. They bore grievances over the government's failure to implement civil service reform recommendations, the politicized nature of the awarding of scholarships, the deficiencies in the Civil Service Regulations, and the structure and classification of the Civil Service. Under the leadership of

James Manswell, the Civil Service Association resisted co-optation and participation in constructing solutions to the problems it identified.

As regards the 1980s, the second decade when economic growth was pursued, this period was marked by a structural adjustment programme supported by an administrative reform initiative in Jamaica, both of which were formulated, implemented and monitored by the World Bank. Indeed, the reform programme emerged out of a World Bank observation on the adverse impact of low administrative capacity on 'some aspects of the 1980–82 IMF agreements and the first World Bank supported structural adjustment programme' (Glaessner 1992: 335). The programme aimed at:

a. narrowing the gap between remuneration of the Civil Service's PMT [Professionals, managers and technicians] group and that of comparable staff of statutory bodies and public corporations;
b. reforming the budget, expenditure control and cash management systems as part of restoring the effectiveness of the Finance Ministry; and
c. improving the policies and operating methods of the Ministry of the Public Service and the Public Service Commission which, together with the narrowing of the compensation gap, would restore the government's capacity to fill key civil service positions. Progress in improving the functioning of the core agencies would set the stage for an improvement of line Ministry effectiveness. (Ibid.: 336)

The World Bank evaluated the Administrative Reform Programme in favourable terms as it accorded the new Seaga/JLP government the flexibility to redeploy and attract staff in pursuance of its economic recovery programme. The Seaga government relied heavily on foreign technical expertise in implementing the reform programme, particularly in the area of education administration reform and the strengthening of the Ministry of the Public Service. Thus, for the year 1981 alone, the value of managerial and technological know-how transferred to Jamaica was estimated at US$10.5 million. In 1982, it was US$10.8 million, and in 1983, it was US$10.9 million (World Bank/ GOJ 1984).

In 1983, the Jamaican government and the World Bank entered into a technical assistance loan agreement. The Planning Institute of Jamaica, the successor to the Central Planning Unit and the National Planning Agency, had responsibility for co-ordinating these activities. A World Bank review of technical assistance in Jamaica during the 1980s concluded that it was 'more than moderately successful in con-

tributing to achievements of Structural Adjustment Programme goals'
(World Bank/GOJ 1984: 8).

In contrast, in T&T the early 1980s found the PNM government un-
sure about the administrative capacity-building strategy needed to support its new growth model. The PNM resorted to its standard solution
by appointing yet another administrative reform commission in 1984.
The myriad submissions to this commission were neither compiled,
published nor implemented. The exercise was widely viewed as a waste
of resources. Indeed, the voice of conservatism—the Sunday Guardian
Special Correspondent—ridiculed the appointment of the Commission
in a newspaper column:

> Yet another committee has been appointed to review the Public Service
> ... The Public Service, however, has always been singled out for more
> than its fair share of attention. What is particularly exasperating is that
> after much fanfare at the start of each investigation, followed by ladles
> of publicity when the great and always 'startling' discoveries and rec-
> ommendations are finally released, precisely NOTHING happens. Once
> the impressively bulky documents are handed over by their relieved
> authors, the whole scene goes into quite anti-climax. In this way, the
> unspoken motto of 'look busy but do nothing' is served with distinc-
> tion. (*Guardian* 19/2/84)

In August of 1987, yet another commission was appointed by the
Cabinet with terms of reference 'to review all existing administrative
reform proposals.' Although Cabinet accepted the commission's recommendations, it was not until September of 1988 that the new NAR
government introduced an Administrative Reform Programme (ARP)
with terms of reference to support the economic growth strategy outlined in the Macro Medium Planning Framework of 1988–95. Between
1988 and 1990, the NAR's efforts at implementing administrative reform were hampered by the Public Service Association (PSA), which
interpreted the 'R' in 'reform' as 'retrenchment,' and by a lack of clear
perspective on how the country's large public service should be re-
formed. There was talk about a shortened working week, job-sharing
and termination of long-term 'temporary' public sector employees. In a
real sense, the PSA's perspective on reform was not far from the truth,
since the Voluntary Termination Employment Scheme (Act No. 19 of
1989, GOTT) was the new government's main achievement in the area
of administrative reform. The PNM government, which took office in

1991, established a Ministry of the Public Service and affirmed its commitment to capacity building through reform.

The discussion above seems to support an association between greater administrative capacity-building in Jamaica during the 1960s and 1980s and greater achievement of economic growth goals. In contrast, the government of T&T seemed more committed to the idea than the practice of administrative capacity-building. This situation can be explained, in part, by the adversarial relationship between the government and public servants in T&T. This relationship made the PNM government wary of the idea of a developed public service.

Economic growth and the autonomy of public-sector agencies

Was the realization of economic goals in Jamaica in the 1960s and 1980s associated with the greater autonomy of public-sector agencies? This question is explored by comparing the formal/legal status of key public-sector agencies in the industrial sector of both countries. The industrial sector is defined as including mining, construction and manufacturing. In Jamaica and T&T, industry was expected to play a critical role in economic growth by increasing production and creating employment. This inquiry seeks to determine whether the legal status of agencies constituting the industrial sector in the 1960s and 1980s was one of the following:

1. controlled government department,
2. semi-autonomous public corporations subject to supervision by the responsible Minister, or
3. autonomous public companies subject to the control of shareholders.

To pave the way for the subsequent discussion on the facilitative policy content these agencies are further classified according to their degree of interventionism, i.e., whether they engaged in direct production or merely facilitated private-sector initiatives. Facilitative agencies can either be regulatory or engage in the provision of infrastructure for private sector consumption. Findings are presented in Tables 4.1a & b and 4.2a & b.

Table 4.1a   Legal status of industrial public bureaucracies by degree
of interventionism in the 1960s, Jamaica

Legal status	Direct production	Facilitative/ infrastructural	Facilitative/ regulatory
Department		Central Planning Unit	
Public corporation	Jamaica Railways Corp.	Jamaica IDC, Land Develop. & Utilization Comm., Urban Develop. Corp., Scientific Research Council, Jamaica National Exports Corp., Port Authority, Water Comm., Small Business Loan Board	Bureau of Standards, Public Utilities Comm.
Public company	Jamaica Ice Co., Zero Processing & Storage Ltd, Jamaica Woolens Air Jamaica	Jamaica Develop. Bank, Things Jamaica Ltd, Jamaica Frozen Food Ltd., Caribbean Preserving Co., Guild Prod. Ltd., Victoria Crafts Markets	

Sources: GOJ Annual Budget Speeches, Estimates of Expenditure, Ministry Papers to the House of Representatives, and The Laws of Jamaica.

Table 4.1b   Legal status of industrial public bureaucracies by degree
of interventionism in the 1960s, Trinidad & Tobago

Legal status	Direct production	Facilitative/ infrastructural	Facilitative/ regulatory
Department		Central Statistical Office, Economic Planning Division	Central Tenders Board
Public corporation	T&T IDC, Public Transport Service Corp., T&T Electricity Comm., Port Authority, Water & Sewage Authority, Development Finance Corp., British West Indian Airways Corp.		Bureau of Standards, Public Utilities Comm.
Public company	Trinidad Tesoro Oil Co.	Telephone Co.	

Sources: GOTT Annual Budget Speeches, Estimates of Expenditure, and The Laws of T&T.

Table 4.2a Legal status of industrial public bureaucracies by degree of interventionism in the 1980s, Jamaica

Legal status	Direct production	Facilitative/ infrastructural	Facilitative/ regulatory
Depart-ment		Trade Commissioners Service, Marketing Service Centre	Collector General, Comm. of Public Ac-countability, Divestment Committee
Public corpora-tion	Petroleum Corporation of Jamaica	Jamaica IDC, Jamaica National Export Corporation, Urban Development Corporation	Bureau of Standards, Pub. Utilities Comm., Pub. Utilities Ombudsman
Public company	Petrojam, Jam. Cement, Esso Refinery Co., JAMALCO bauxite/alu-mina, South-ern Processors Ltd, Cotton Polyester Ltd, Rural Ice and Cold Storage Ltd	Factories Corp. of Jam., Nat. In-dustrial Develop. Co., Jam. Pro-motions Ltd, Jam. Nat. Invest, Promotions Ltd, Jam. Nat. Invest. Bank Ltd, Nat. Commer. Bank, Statistical Inst. of Jam., Jam. Pub. Service, Free Zones Com-panies, Planning Inst. of Jam., Industrial Build. & Properties Ltd, Food Tech. Inst., Toolmakers Inst., Jam. Mortgage Bank, Nat. Invest. Bank of Jam., Jam. Mar-ket. Co., Jam. Export Trad. Co.	Project Analysis & Monitoring Company

Sources: GOJ Annual Budget Speeches Estimates of Expenditure, Ministry Pa-pers to the House of Representatives, and the Laws of Jamaica.

Tables 4.1a & b suggest an association in the 1960s between higher economic growth in Jamaica and a preponderance of autonomous agen-cies. Thus there were four times as many public companies in industry in Jamaica than there were in T&T, where the semi-autonomous public corporation was the dominant legal form of public bureaucracies.

Table 4.2b　Legal status of industrial public bureaucracies by degree of interventionism in the 1980s, Trinidad & Tobago

Legal status	Direct production	Facilitative/ infrastructural	Facilitative/ regulatory
Depart-ment		Central Statistical Office, Project Analysis Unit, Ministry of Planning	
Public corpora-tion		T&T IDC, Management Development Centre, Development Finance Corp., Port Authority, National Energy Corp.	Central Tenders Board, Bureau of Standards, Pub. Utilities Commission
Public company	Iron and Steel Co., Point Lisas Ind. Co., Trinidad Nitrogen Co., Fertilizers of T&T Co. Ltd, Trincity Garment Man., CUTTAGE Bulk Buying Fabric Co., Lake Asphalt of T&T Co. Ltd, Nat. Agro Chem. Co., Nat. Gas, T&T Oil Co. Ltd, T&T Methanol Co., Trinidad Marine Petroleum Co., TRINTOMAR	National Secondary Roads Management Co., National Petroleum Marketing Co., National Property Development Co.	

Sources: GOTT Annual Budget Speeches, Estimates of Expenditure, and The Laws of Trinidad & Tobago.

Tables 4.2a & b suggest that, in the 1980s, no clear association existed between goal realization and the autonomy of public-sector agencies. In both cases, the 'autonomous' public company seems to be the dominant legal form for public agencies. In Jamaica, important industrial public bureaucracies such as the National Industrial Development Company, the Jamaica National Investment Promotions Company and the Jamaica Free Zones Companies enjoyed the highest degree of autonomy. Similarly, in T&T, flagship public agencies such as the Iron and Steel Company, TRINTOMAR, and the Pt Lisas Industrial Company also enjoyed the highest degree of autonomy.

The fact that the majority of autonomous companies in Jamaica had facilitative roles while those in T&T engaged in direct production suggests that, in the decade of the 1980s, the legal status of the company was less closely associated with goal realization than the role of the organization. This will be explored in the case study inquiry presented in Part II.

Economic growth and the facilitative policy environment

This section explores whether higher growth in Jamaica during the 1960s and 1980s was associated with an economic policy environment that facilitated private-sector involvement. The findings of Tables 4.1a & b and 4.2a & b suggest an answer to this question in the affirmative. However, it is important to go behind formal/legal structures and unravel the actual intent and the impact of decisions taken by governments in pursuit of the goal of economic growth.

Chapter 1 noted the centrality of the state in development in Jamaica and T&T; this was balanced by a nascent private sector. The fact that the Jamaica Labour Party, which governed Jamaica for most of the 1960s, had its base in the local private sector and subscribed to capitalist development ideals suggested a favourable disposition towards facilitating private capital in Jamaica.

Consequently, while in T&T the PNM quietly took over the utilities in the 1960s (water, electricity, telephones and transportation), in Jamaica the JLP government appeared reluctant to intervene in areas of economic production. Thus in the 1960s, the Jamaican Telephone Company remained a subsidiary of the London Telephone and General Trust, the Jamaica Omnibus Service Ltd. was owned and controlled by the UK conglomerate British Electric Traction Ltd., and the electric company, the Jamaica Public Service, was owned by the Montreal Trust. During the 1960s, the JLP government's only sojourns into direct production were the Jamaica Ice Company, Zero Processing and Storage Company, Jamaica Woolens, and Air Jamaica (Table 4.1a).

In addition to its limited intervention in the economy during the 1960s, the JLP further endeared itself to the private sector by putting in place a legislative framework of incentives and concessions to encourage investment, especially in the manufacturing sector. Not only were these incentives generous, they also discriminated in favour of the local private sector (Ayub 1981, Jefferson 1972). Widdicombe notes:

> Ownership of those firms receiving benefits under the incentive laws
> after independence in 1962 became an important issue in industrial
> policy development in Jamaica. Some 82 out of the 185 companies op-
> erating under the incentive laws as of December 31, 1969, were 100%
> Jamaican owned. In addition there were 28 joint venture firms in which
> local Jamaican participation was 50% or more. This means that 44.3%
> all incentive firms were at least 50% owned by Jamaicans. As for for-
> eign ownership, 21.1% of the incentive firms were wholly owned by
> US interests, 4.4% by UK interests, and 2.7% by Canadian interests.
> (Widdicombe 1972: 249)

Moreover, the fact that the JLP government neglected issues of redistribution and social justice, focusing instead on capital expenditure for
economic growth, further endeared it to the private sector in this period. In his 1967 Budget Speech, then-Minister of Finance Edward
Seaga, justified the government's policy choices in this way:

> [We] were not interested in our social problems, but whether there was
> security involved for an economical investment. (GOJ Annual Budget
> Speech, 1967: 1)

Despite an obviously pro-capital stance, by 1968, Seaga's efforts to
nationalize/Jamaicanize private industry and amend the Income Tax
Law (Ministry paper No.15 as appended to the 1969 Budget Speech)
were interpreted as profoundly anti-business by the overprotected and
over-pampered Jamaican private sector (Senior 1972). In a real sense,
these reforms were not inconsistent with the JLP's pro-business stance,
since the proposed amendment promised to reallocate mobilized resources to infrastructural development, and nationalization promised to
incorporate the domestic private sector. That the policies put the government on a collision course with capital and contributed to the JLP
losing the 1972 general election had more to do with the autocratic
style of the man spearheading these initiatives—Edward Seaga—than
the content of the policies *per se*.

What the Jamaican private sector construed as a threat in the late
1960s was the norm throughout the 1960s in T&T. In T&T, the private
sector had long since felt threatened by the personalization of power
around Prime Minister Eric Williams, the nationalism and anti-colonial
rhetoric of the PNM, the regime's involvement in the public utilities
(Table 4.1b), and the government's courtship of labour.

Although the 1964–1968 Development Plan presented the PNM as committed to a private sector-led development strategy, the first half of the 1960s witnessed punitive taxation policies against capital, both local and foreign. The tax reforms proposed in Jamaica in the late 1960s were already initiated in T&T in 1963. Moreover, with the fall in petroleum prices in 1963, the PNM government embarked upon a programme of tariff and fiscal reforms aimed to restrict non-essential consumption and raise revenue through increased corporate taxes.

However, the final blow to the private sector came in 1966, with the passage of the Finance Act. The man widely thought to be the author of the bill, then Minister of Finance under the PNM, A.N.R. Robinson, describes the Act's objectives:

1. To improve the administration and efficiency of tax collection and provide better means of satisfying taxpayers' complaints.
2. To minimize tax evasion.
3. To collect taxes in money then being unjustifiably diverted to foreign countries.
4. To lower the taxes of skilled and professional employees.
5. To achieve a system of taxing profits appropriate to the country's needs.
6. To remove the inducements to distribution and consumption and replace them with incentives to reinvestment.
7. To offer incentives for the expansion of productive employment and exports.
8. To introduce a tax on capital gains formerly untaxed or evaded.
9. To provide for relief from double taxation. (Robinson 1987: 90)

Robinson chronicled the negative reaction of the private sector to the proposed bill, and recalled the memorandum to the Minister of Finance from the Southern Chamber of Commerce where the negative implications of the proposed legislation were spelled out (ibid.: 94).

In addition, foreign multinationals involved in the oil sector in T&T were especially targeted by the progressive taxation structure of the Petroleum Act of 1969.

Although the PNM tried to restore private-sector confidence in the economy by amendments to the Finance Act and introduction of the anti-labour Industrial Stabilization Act of March 1965, both local and foreign capitalists remained unconvinced of the government's commitment to facilitating private sector-led economic growth. This view runs counter to Parris's conclusion that the PNM took capital's side against labour in this period (Parris, C.D. 1976). Indeed, at this time the PNM's dilemma was not a simple one of capital or labour.

By the late 1960s, the domestic private sector in T&T became even more disturbed by what was perceived as the increasing autocracy of the PNM, coupled with its increasing interventionism into the economy. Evidence of the latter could be found in the government's 1969 nationalization of British Petroleum and its subsequent joint venture with Tesoro of Texas. The Third Five-Year Development plan published in 1968 also laid out the policy framework for a more interventionist role for the state in development.

Turning now to the 1980s, how facilitative were the economic policies of the governments in Kingston and Port-of-Spain in this period? Tables 4.2a & b suggest that more facilitative public agencies existed in Jamaica than in T&T during the 1980s. With the exception of the acquisition of the Esso refinery and the take-over of the Alcoa Company in 1984, all new public-sector agencies were created during the 1980s to support a private sector-led recovery strategy. Bureaucracy's new facilitative role was based on Seaga's industrial policy. The policy identified seven priority sub-sectors as the basis for take-off and growth.

Under the Caribbean Basin Initiative of the Reagan administration, Jamaican exports secured preferential access to US markets. The Seaga government hoped to persuade the foreign and domestic private sector to invest in priority sub-sectors in order to create employment and boost Jamaica's export production (Pantin 1990). Moreover, the government especially targeted Jamaica's thriving business communities in Miami, New York and Toronto (i.e., Ja-mericans as they are called in Jamaican patois) to invest in Jamaica's recovery.

Under the new industrial plan, institutional support was to come from these public-sector promotional agencies: National Industrial Development Company Ltd. (NIDCO), the Jamaica Industrial Development Corporation (JIDC), the Jamaica National Investment and Promotional Limited (JNIP), the Jamaica National Export Corporation, the Trade Commissioner Service, the Free Zone Company, the Marketing Service Centre, Jamaica Marketing Company, and Jamaica Export Trading Company. The policy instruments implemented by these agencies aimed to grant concessionary terms and provide soft loans, information and physical infrastructure for investment. Accomplishments included the establishment of an export development fund, the operation of a re-discount window at the Bank of Jamaica, and the provision of factories in the Kingston and Montego Bay Export Free Zones.

During this period, private-sector agencies, both local and foreign, worked in close collaboration with the Seaga government and its development agencies. In a 1985 private sector/JIDC 'consultation' appropriately entitled 'Side by Side,' both groups searched for solutions to promote growth and recovery. Following this consultation, JIDC's Chairman of the board, businessman Lascelles Chin, is reported to have said:

> Jamaica ... is in quite a predicament and the only thing that we can't afford is that the private sector and the government keep apart because the only way we are going to solve this problem is for both sectors to combine together—it will not be easy—but we have to, because it is the only way it can be done. (*Gleaner*, 7/7/1985)

Indeed, the success of the 1986 Expo was in fact due to private sector/government collaboration, in particular the efforts of the Jamaica Exporters Association and the Jamaica Manufacturers Association (*Gleaner Expo 1986 Supplement*, 3/19/86). The Manley government, which took office in 1989, distanced itself from its former Democratic Socialist ideology, under which public agencies were used as productive enterprises. The new Manley government sought to win the confidence of both the foreign and domestic private sectors and to continue the facilitative policies of the Seaga government. In this way, policy continuity was consistent with the new realities characterized by the denationalization of policy formulation, the exigencies of economic management, and the end of ideology in national governments struggling to pass IMF tests.

Two important caveats must be made to the general thrust of this discussion so far. The first has to do with Seaga's autocratic style of leadership, which is said to have alienated powerful elements of the private sector (personal interview with representative of the Private Sector Organization of Jamaica, April 1992). The second caveat is that in pursuing its facilitative policy, the Seaga government was assuming an increasing interventionist role. Indeed, between 1981 and 1988, the public sector contributed 58 per cent to gross fixed-capital formation in Jamaica, while the private sector's share was only 41 per cent (Charlton 1991). In T&T, for the same period, government's contribution to gross fixed-capital formation stood at 36 per cent, while that of the private sector was 64 per cent (CSO *National Income of Trinidad and Tobago*

1981–1991, 1993). Thus facilitation and interventionism appeared to be compatible in Jamaica. In addition, the take-over of the Alcoa aluminum plant and the Esso refinery increased the size of the public sector under Seaga.

Chapter 2 revealed that, in T&T, the PNM's primary development goal of the 1980s aimed to precipitate growth through a heavy export-led diversification programme downstream of the petroleum industry, and revive export-led light manufacturing. Since the IDC case study that follows focuses on the second aspect of the goal, only the first aspect—the export-led heavy diversification thrust—is discussed in this section. Under the resource-based diversification programme, products such as steel, natural gas and fertilizer were intended for the export market. Against this background, a facilitative implementation strategy implies that government institutions and legislation should support private-sector enterprises actually undertaking production.

However, in their efforts to reorient the role of public agencies to support private-sector initiatives, both the PNM and NAR governments confronted similar obstacles:

1. The fact that, unlike Jamaica, the government in Port-of-Spain had no 'special relations' with the government in Washington;

2. The huge capital investment requirements of the government's diversification programmes;

3. The pressure for economic nationalism exerted by one of the country's most radical unions, the Oilfield Workers Trade Union (OWTU); and

4. The spectre of political and administrative corruption associated with multinational involvement in the oil industry. T&T's largest political corruption scandal had been over payments made to then-Minister of Industry and Commerce, John O' Halloran, by Tesoro Oil Company of Texas.

Consequently, while the 1981 amendment to the 1974 Petroleum Taxes Act demonstrated the PNM's commitment to facilitate private-sector investment, the reality of economic nationalism forced the government to simultaneously introduce a new Supplementary Tax on the 'realized income' of petroleum companies. Not surprisingly, multinationals viewed this measure as a disincentive. Texaco and Tesoro, the second and third largest multinationals in petroleum, left Trinidad and Tobago in the 1980s. The PNM government acquired the assets of Texaco in

March 1985 for TT$189 million, and those of Tesoro soon after for 3.2 million barrels of residual fuel oil.

With the exception of joint ventures with Amoco (Fertrin) and Grace (Tringen), the PNM's years in office during the 1980s were marked by government's increasing involvement in both the oil and non-oil industrial sectors (GOTT *Natural Gas. An Investor's Guide*, 1985). Thus the government's major diversification projects—the natural gas pipeline, the Pt Lisas Port and harbour facilities, an electricity plant and water supply system, two ammonia plants (Fertrin and Tringen), a methanol plant and a steel plant (ISCOTT) valued at TT$6 billion—were funded from the public coffers. The lumpiness of these investments, Washington's disaffection with the PNM for failing to support the 1983 American-led invasion of Grenada, coupled with sustained pressure for economic nationalism from the OWTU, explains the PNM's go-it-alone attitude.

During the NAR's tenure, a more concerted effort was made to facilitate foreign investment in the heavy diversification programme. In this regard, one of the government's first measures was a 35 per cent reduction of the dreaded Supplemental Petroleum Tax. The government also initiated steps to repeal the Aliens Landholding Ordinance and update the 1929 Company Law. Additional measures were 'the revision of the tax regime to encourage increased production and exploration activity and a system of lease-operatorships and farms-outs on land' (GOTT Annual Budget Speech, 1989: 19). Amoco and CONOCO, a subsidiary of Du Pont, were to be the major private investors.

Such initiatives were questioned by angry observers (i.e., the trade unions, the opposition PNM, and former Permanent Secretary in the Ministry of Petroleum Hamel Legall), who accused the NAR of profligacy with the national patrimony. Moreover, when it was discovered that two NAR-appointed chairmen (Anthony Beaubrun, Chairman of the National Gas Company and Reuben; and Charles Dash, Managing Director of Trintoc and Chairman of Trintomar) were major shareholders of private companies with interests in the public companies that fell under their responsibility, the spectre of corruption in this sector made the NAR government less enthusiastic about private ownership. To compound this situation, the fact that the NAR inherited diversification projects (e.g., ISCOTT and TRINGEN) with long gestation periods and lumpy expenditure commitments dictated an increasingly proactive role in the economy. For 1987 alone, debt service on government and state enterprise external debt stood at US$397 million. It is against this background that the new NAR government negotiated two yen-loans totalling US$107 million specifically to finance the TRINGEN II project (Farrell, T.W. 1989: 8).

Consequently, by 1990, the NAR's public-sector investment pro-gramme envisioned a major public investment in the energy sector. Indeed, 54 per cent of project public-sector investment for 1990 was to be spent on the energy sector. To conclude, because of factors peculiar to the energy sector in T&T, both the PNM and NAR governments were less able to employ facilitative strategies in pursuit of economic growth during the 1980s. Thus, the evidence above seems to support an association between greater goal realization in Jamaica during the 1960s and 1980s, and a policy environment more facilitative of the pri-vate sector.

PART II:
Public Bureaucracy and Economic Growth: Micro-level Associations

Industrial development corporations (IDCs) and economic growth

The labour riots of the late 1930s and the chronic unemployment prob-lems that precipitated them were the two most significant factors to influence British West Indian public policy in the period immediately following World War II. The emergence of the industrial development corporations (IDCs) must be seen in this context. In the 1950s, the IDCs of Jamaica and T&T were the most important development insti-tutions of the soon-to-be-independent Jamaica and T&T. The Jamaica IDC was established in 1952 and the T&TIDC in 1958. In both coun-tries, the IDCs were expected to be the catalyst for economic growth through employment creation and increased industrial production.

To be sure, the fact that an IDC was established as early as 1952 in Jamaica was no small achievement. The Jamaica Industrial Develop-ment Corporation (JIDC) was established after ten long years of battle with Colonial Office officials and 'independent' British scholars such as Galletti, all of whom were convinced that Jamaica's future lay in primary-export production.

It was Arthur Lewis who provided the intellectual justification for industrial development. The Bustamante/JLP government gave political support and policy direction to Lewis' strategy, and Jamaican industrialist and engineer, Robert Lightbourne, provided the leadership and know-how to bring industrial development to fruition. Robert Lightbourne was a Jamaican who established himself as an industrialist in wartime Britain. He returned to Jamaica in 1955 and was persuaded by Norman Manley to help bring to life the dream of industrial development in Jamaica (personal interview with Robert Lightbourne, Jamaica, June 1992).

> In January 1952 a bill to establish the Jamaica Industrial Development Corporation was introduced in the House by Sir Harold E. Allan, Minister for Finance and General Purposes. In presenting the bill, Sir Harold belaboured the point that the JIDC was expected to be an autonomous, professional, industrial promotion organization giving assistance 'to undertakings of a nature that is not easily obtained on a strictly commercial basis'. (Quoted in Widdicombe 1972: 92)

The bill was approved on 7 February 1952, and the JIDC was established under Acts No. 13 and 45 of 1952 with terms of reference to 'stimulate, facilitate and undertake the development of industry in this Island' (GOJ Act No. 13 of 1952).

As Jamaica's oldest industrial promotions agency, the JIDC's role and functions have changed according to the policy goals emphasised by the government at the time. In the 1960s and 1980s, the JLP governments in Kingston emphasized economic growth. What role was the JIDC expected to play during these periods? This question is best answered by looking at both the policy utterances and actual policy preferences of the governments. The 1957–67 Ten Year National Plan identified 'increased industrialization' as a major plank in the government's growth strategy. In this regard, the JIDC's goals were spelled out as such:

> This organization [the JIDC] would assemble market information, technical information on power, water, wage rates, availability of site, etc. It would know and pass on to the potential investor information on relevant laws likely to affect his trade. It would make all the preliminary contacts with the several government departments usually involved and render technical assistance whenever possible. (GOJ 1958: 28)

Although agricultural development and redistribution were the stated goals of the second plan (1963–68), economic growth through industrialization was the actual policy emphasis of the JLP government (see Chapter 2). In this regard, JLP Budget Speeches of the 1960s specified and delimited the JIDC's role purely in terms of promotion and support to big business. Thus, the Corporation's loan administration portfolio was taken away and reassigned to the newly created Development Finance Corporation in 1963, and the JIDC was merely felt to provide the physical infrastructure to prospective investors, administer incentive legislation, and provide information on export markets (GOJ Annual Budget Speeches 1961 to 1969).

In the 1980s, the JIDC's role in economic growth became the subject of politics. Immediately following Seaga's 1981 election victory, the very future of the JIDC came under question. The fact that the JIDC's management supported Manley in his bid to change the neo-colonial structure of the Jamaican economy during the 1970s did not escape Seaga. Not surprisingly, the Seaga government was reluctant to do business with the JIDC, which it saw as partisan and staffed by 'very few people of calibre, vision, drive, and motivation' (Cabinet submission of the Minister of Industry (MOI), MIC 34/5/109, 1984: 6).

Therefore, in September of 1982, the new Seaga government established a parallel 'JIDC' called the National Industrial Development Company Ltd (NIDCO) as a subsidiary of the JIDC to support the country's diversification programme. Between 1982 and 1983, the 'rump JIDC' was only expected to provide and maintain the physical infrastructure and undertake productivity training, while the new NIDCO took the lead in promoting industry. NIDCO's role and function was to support industry operating under the government's new industrial policy. As noted above, the new policy identified seven priority sub-sectors to spearhead government's diversification thrust.

Following a 1983 World Bank study recommending the merger of Jamaica's four premier industrial-promotion agencies—the National Industrial Development Company (NIDCO), the Jamaica Industrial Development Corporation (JIDC), the Jamaica National Export Corporation (JNEC), and the Jamaica National Investment Promotions Company (JNIP)—the NIDCO was merged into the JIDC in early 1984. Between 1984 and 1988, the new JIDC, which then included NIDCO, was expected to render critical support to the priority sub-sectors programme. Specifically, the Corporation was expected to: provide physical infrastructure through its factory construction programme, provide training in the new technologies of the sub-sectors, provide information and advice on Jamaica's incentive legislation, support a factory retooling and refurbishing programme, and attract foreign investment (*Gleaner Expo 1986 Supplement* 19/3/1986).

Throughout its lifetime, the JIDC existed within a network of incentive legislation designed to 'woo and fawn' investors. The most significant of these were:

- The Pioneer industries [Encouragement] Law No. 46 of 1954
- The Industrial Incentives Act No. 45 of 1958
- The Export Industry Encouragement Law No. 49 of 1956
- The Factory Construction Act No. 9 of 1961
- Industrial Incentives Act No. 45 of 1965
- The International Finance Companies Income Tax Relief, Act No. 1 of 1971
- Kingston Free Zone Act No. 3 of 1980

Although the official title of the JIDC's governing Ministry changed from time to time, the Ministry designated with responsibility for Industry and Commerce was generally responsible for the Corporation. Between 1952 and 1990, when the JIDC was finally dissolved as a legal entity, two years after its merger with the JNEC and the JNIP, the organization went through several transformations but remained Jamaica's premier industrial development agency.

In contrast to Jamaica, the emergence of the Trinidad & Tobago Industrial Development Corporation in 1958 took place in an environment of consensus and support from the colonial status quo. This was partly due to the fact that the battle against the Colonial Office had already been fought and won in Jamaica during the early 1950s. More importantly, though, the British government's representative in T&T, Governor Sir John Shaw, had supported industrialization in T&T from as early as 1947, and recommended the formation of an Industrial Board.

In response to this recommendation, an Economic Advisory Board was established in 1948 with the following terms of reference:

> To explore the possibilities of establishing new industries ... to examine applications from private enterprise wishing to expand or establish new industries. (Hansard, 22/3/1957: 1306)

On 26 February 1959, the T&TIDC was created to replace the Economic Advisory Board and assume the responsibilities of the Hotel Development Corporation. The latter had been established under Ordinance No. 23 of 1956.

The impetus for creating the T&TIDC was a 1957 Motion passed in the Legislative Council. The mover of the motion, then-Chief Minister and Minister of Finance, Planning and Development, Dr Eric Williams, justified the proposed industrial development programme and the creation of the IDC on the basis of its job-creation potential.

The T&TIDC was established as a quasi-autonomous public corporation under Act No. 11 of 1958, with terms of reference to 'stimulate, facilitate and undertake the development of industry and hotels in Trinidad & Tobago.' In furtherance of this end, the act gave the IDC wide-ranging powers.

The inclusion of hotel development in the Corporation's portfolio stemmed from its inheritance of the staff and the functions of the Hotel Development Corporation. In the research period (1960–90), the T&TIDC's industrial policy was largely determined by the Ministry of Industry and Commerce, and between 1966–88, the T&TIDC's personnel policy was controlled by the Statutory Authorities Services Commission. In 1988, the T&TIDC attained an 'autonomous' legal status.

Similar to Jamaica, the T&TIDC's role in economic growth in the 1960s was established in medium-term development plans. The First Five Year Plan (1958–62), which was predicated on private sector-led development, prescribed that the T&TIDC should provide industrial loans, technical support and physical infrastructure to private entrepreneurs. The Second Five Year Plan (1964–68) shifted its emphasis to human resource development, and in this regard, new goals were prescribed for the T&TIDC. In addition, the second plan also specified functional categories of IDC expenditure, namely (a) development of industrial sites, (b) assistance to industry, (c) industrial financing, i.e., direct loans to industry, and (d) development of the hotel industry.

The 1980s were a period of uncertainty for the T&TIDC. Dissatisfaction with the organization's performance resulted in the 1985 Scotland Commission being appointed, and in December of 1986 the government changed for the first time in 30 years. These events created a policy environment in which narrow and somewhat conflicting policy guidelines were given to the Corporation.

During the PNM years in the 1980s, the IDC was expected to contribute to economic recovery by supporting the export-led light manufacturing thrust of the Chambers' government. This meant a reorientation of the Corporation's 1970s functions. In the 1970s, the Corporation supported the government's economic change policies. In addition to its support to export-led light manufacturing in the PNM years of the 1980s, the T&TIDC was also expected to support the government's small-business lending programme. While stimulating the small-business sector was the official reason given for this function, in reality the Corporation's small business programme was a form of transfer payments to the party faithful and the ambitious but underprivileged.

At first, the NAR government, which took office towards the end of 1986, supported the IDC's goals under the PNM, with the addition of promoting agro-industry. By 1988, however, the NAR lost confidence in the IDC's ability to manage the small-business programme. A Small Business Corporation was created in 1988 and the IDC was restricted to supporting light export promotions. This was to be facilitated by the 1986 devaluation of the T&T dollar. In the NAR's years, the IDC's functions were spelled out in Annual Budget documents and *ad hoc* policy statements of the National Advisory Council.

Throughout its lifetime, the T&TIDC also existed within a web of incentive legislation. These included:

- The Aid to Pioneer Industries Ordinance Ch. 33 No. 3 1950
- The Income Tax (In Aid of Industry) Ordinance Ch. 33, No. 2, 1950
- Customs (Amendment) Ordinance 1959
- Hotel Development (Encouragement) Act, 1962
- Cement Industry (Development) Ordinance No. 41 of 1951
- Nitrogenous Fertilizer Industry (Development) Ordinance No. 3 of 1958
- Petrochemicals Industry (Development) Act, NO. 4 of 1962
- The Tyre Manufacturing Industry (Development) Act, No. 39 of 1967
- The Fiscal Incentives Act 1979
- The Free Zones Act of 1988

The purpose of this legislation was to support an industrialization programme intended to create jobs and increase manufacturing output. Throughout its life, the creation of jobs remained the most important goal of the T&TIDC.

In conclusion, although the Jamaica and the Trinidad & Tobago IDCs were established in different contexts, were guided by different laws, developed different structures and functions, and experienced different fortunes, both organizations were conceived of as important implementing agencies in the struggle for economic growth through employment creation and increased manufacturing outputs.

How well did the two IDCs undertake these tasks? Furthermore, to what extent was their performance associated with the following attributes:

1. administrative capacity-building,
2. autonomy, and
3. a policy environment which facilitated private sector involvement?

As regards the first question, the IDCs' contribution to economic growth can be assessed in terms of:

1. the number of jobs directly created by firms operating under IDC-administered incentive and concession legislation;
2. the number of firms operating under IDC-administered concession legislation;
3. the average investment of firms operating under IDC-administered concession legislation.

Table 4.3 compares the performance of the two IDCs using the indicators stated above. An additional column on actual IDC expenditure (recurrent and capital) gives some indication of their relative efficiency in undertaking their roles.

Despite obvious data gaps in Table 4.3, the JIDC seems to have made a greater contribution to economic growth in both periods. In the 1960s, the JIDC created more jobs, promoted more firms and generated substantial investments, and in the 1980s it could be credited with creating more than three times the number of jobs created by the T&TIDC for approximately one-third less than the T&TIDC's expenditure. Indeed, the JIDC's performance in the both periods must be seen against the background of the relative strength of the manufacturing sector in Jamaica and of manufacturing's contribution to employment creation. In the 1960s, the annual average contribution of manufacturing to GDP stood at 15 per cent in Jamaica compared to 10 per cent in T&T. In the 1980s, the manufacturing sector in Jamaica contributed 20 per cent to GDP, and 14 per cent of the employed work force was in this sector. In contrast, for the same period, the manufacturing sector in T&T contributed only 7 per cent of GDP, and only 11 per cent of the employed work force was in this sector.

Table 4.3   *IDCs' contribution to economic growth in the 1960s and 1980s*

	Ave. annual expenditure (capital & recurrent) in current US$ millions	Firms operating under IDC-administered incentive legislation (annual averages)		
		No. of jobs	No. of firms	Investment in current US$ millions
JIDC				
1960-69	2.7	4,821[a]	70	71[b]
1980-88	2.4	5,325	n.a.[c]	n.a.[c]
T&TIDC[d]				
1960-69	2.7	951	36	n.a.
1980-90	3.3	1,420	56	71

Notes:
a   This figure represents the years 1959–64.
b   This figure is for investments as of March 1969.
c   In the 1980s, Jamaica National Investments Promotions Ltd. took credit for all new companies established in Jamaica and all related investments. Thus, the 1988 JNIP annual report estimated that 890 investment projects were established in Jamaica between 1981–88 with a total investment of J$2.4 billion. The JIDC Annual Reports only claimed responsibility for job creation, an average of 5,325 for the 1981–88 period.
d   Figures for T&TIDC in the 1960s exclude firms granted concession under the 1962 Hotel Development Act, and the 1980s exclude the small businesses. The 1980–90 figures for T&TIDC only include data for the years 1987 and 1989. Data for other years were unavailable.

Sources:
JIDC: Annual Reports and Annual Financial Statements of the Jamaica IDC, 1960–70 and 1980–88; Widdicombe 1972; *A Review of the JIDC 1956–64*; *Developments in Industry*, Ministry paper No. 38, 1967; and Ayub 1981.

T&TIDC: Annual Reports and Annual Financial Statements of the T&TIDC 1960–70 and 1980–89; *Record of Major Achievements of T&TIDC 1959–81*; and *IDC Report on Second Five-Year Development Programme*, 1968.

The following analysis explores whether the JIDC's successes at realizing economic growth goals were associated with a greater administrative capacity-building effort, greater autonomy, and a more facilitative policy environment.

IDCs, economic growth and administrative capacity-building

Because data on several aspects of administrative capacity-building (e.g., training, personnel policy and technical assistance) are largely unavailable for the two IDCs in both the 1960s and 1980s, this question is explored in terms of administrative reform to the *structure* of the IDCs of Jamaica and T&T. To begin with the Jamaica IDC, during the 1960s, reform to the structure was initiated twice—in 1961 and 1965. In 1961, a reform programme was undertaken following the findings of a foreign management consultant on the JIDC. The consultant was asked by the outgoing PNP government to recommend reforms to enable the JIDC to better discharge its promotion function. The resulting recommendations were geared towards supporting the Corporation's industrial promotion goals. Widdicombe describes the structural reforms that took place:

> As a result of a study by a management consultant firm, JIDC's 98 staff members were organized along the following departmental lines: (1) industrial development, which included promotion, development of new industry, development of hotels and resort, publicity, and public relations; (2) planning and research, which included economic research, incentive and taxation investigation, long-range planning, international trade, and JIDC's industrial development library; (3) industrial services, which included fostering the expansion of existing industry, industrial relations, and industrial information; (4) engineering, which included civil engineering and consulting engineering; (5) finance, which included investments, accounts, and office management; (6) legal counsel; and (7) overseas offices. (Widdicombe 1972: 209–10)

In late 1965, far-reaching structural reforms took place in the JIDC as a result of the resignation of the Corporation's long-serving General Manager, Harold A. Braham. Consequently,

> the Industrial Development Department was renamed as the Promotion Department and assigned a number of the functions of the old Planning and Research Department. Also, the economics staff of the Planning and Research Department was made into a single Economic Department as it had been before the 1961 reorganization. (Widdicombe 1972: 210)

During the 1960s, six IDC administrative reform commissions were appointed by the T&T government, with terms of reference that encompassed structural reform. They were: the Julien report (1966), the Neilson report (1967), the Wyeth report (1967), the General Manager's report (1968), the IDC Board's Conclusions on the Reorganisation, and the Tripartite Commission's Committee on Industrialisation report. Because of its coverage of structure, function, systems and procedures, the 1967 Wyeth report was, arguably, the most comprehensive study of this period. Not surprisingly, given the PNM's record of failure to implement administrative reform recommendations and its hostility to foreign expertise, by the end of the 1960s, they had failed to implement the recommendations.

A short digression on the Wyeth study is necessary here. As a result of the PNM's general dissatisfaction with the Corporation's performance in the 1960s, a reluctant approach was made to the United Nations in 1966 for 'expertise' to reform and restructure the IDC. The UN-dispatched British industrial 'expert' Ralph Wyeth made a series of recommendations intended to decentralize the structures of decision-making within the IDC and widen the participation of interest groups on the Corporation's Board. Not surprisingly, Wyeth's recommendations were wholly rejected. The reason given was that 'they were not in the national interest' (*Express* 6/4/1968 & 3/4/1968). Thus, for most of the 1960s, the structure of the T&TIDC remained virtually unchanged.

Towards the end of 1960s, however, the PNM's efforts to broaden the scope of the IDC's functions put the issue of structural reform on the agenda once again. This time, the government came up with its own homegrown comprehensive menu of reforms. The Third Five-Year Development Plan published in 1968, together with the 1969 annual budget, spelled out the PNM's reform proposals for the IDC. In addition, the 1969 budget spoke of the creation of 45 new posts and five new divisions in the IDC. The divisions were to be: Economic Studies and Planning, Secretariat, Financing, Industrial Promotions, and Industrial Liaison. Top Jamaican economist Steve de Castro was specially contracted from the Economics Department of the University of the West Indies, Jamaica, to head what was to be the nerve centre of the restructured T&TIDC—the Economic Studies and Planning Division.

Once more, the PNM was reluctant to implement the structural changes proposed. Consequently, by October 1969, the Director of the Economic Studies and Planning Division, Steve de Castro, resigned from his post and openly criticized the government for its failure to implement reforms. With the exception of the renaming of some departments, the structure of the T&TIDC had remained effectively un-changed.

As regards the decade of the 1980s, structural reform in the JIDC was wholly attributable to the priority sub-sector emphasis of the government's new industrial policy. Thus, following the merger of JIDC with the National Industrial Development Company (NIDCO) in 1984, the new 'JIDC' had four new divisions, each corresponding to a functional area under the current industrial policy: Research and Statistics, the Priority Sector Programme Division, the Management Services Division, and the Industrial Estates Division (*JIDC News* 1 (1) August 1984: 1). Furthermore, for the fist time, a legal department was created in the JIDC. Despite several recommendations urging the establishment a legal department in the T&TIDC, this never materialized. In the T&TIDC, all legal opinions are obtained from private law firms. In 1988, the JIDC underwent its final structural reform. Along with two other public industrial development agencies—the JNEC and the JNIP—the JIDC was merged into the new, Jamaica Promotions Ltd (Jampro). Although the 1988 merger effectively brought about the end of the JIDC, it was consistent with the government's administrative capacity-building effort for the entire industrial sector.

During the 1970s and for most of the 1980s, the structure of the T&TIDC remained unchanged. However, this situation was to be altered in 1987, when the new NAR government took steps to implement the recommendations of a 1985 study into the Corporation's performance, the Scotland Committee Report. Thus, in 1987, under the new NAR government, two new Divisions were created in the IDC: Evaluations and Information Services; two posts of Manager were created, one for each new Division, and one post of Assistant to the General Manager was also created effective 1 July 1987. Furthermore, some minor restructuring took place in the organization in order to accommodate its new function as Secretariat to the Investment Co-ordinating Committee—a 13-member Cabinet-appointed committee made up of representation from selected government ministries (*Sunday Express IDC 30th Anniversary Supplement*, 26/2/1989).

Beyond these initiatives, however, reforms consisted simply of changing the names of existing Divisions; their basic functions remained the same. For example, Financial Administration became the Finance and Accounts, the Economic Studies and Planning Division became the Industrial Planning and Business Development Division, and the Public Relations and Promotion Division became Industrial Counselling.

The discussion above reveals a greater and more sustained commitment to capacity building in the JIDC compared to its T&T counterpart. Indeed, it was this commitment that eventually led to the merger of the JIDC in 1988. In contrast, the structure of the Corporation in T&T remained relatively unchanged throughout the 1960s, 1970s, and most of the 1980s. While many recommendations were made for structural reform, the PNM government appeared to lack the political will to carry them out. The implied association between greater capacity-building effort and economic growth seems to be apparent from the discussion above.

IDCs, economic growth and autonomy

The question of the autonomy of the two IDCs will be explored in terms of managerial autonomy—i.e., the freedom and scope of the IDC's management, including its board, to take final decisions in furtherance of the organization's stated goal of 'promoting and facilitating industrial development.' In view of the designated role and functions of the IDCs in the 1960s and 1980s, four important decisional areas can be identified:

1. Personnel policy (recruitment, promotions, discipline),
2. Industrial estate development and property management policy (location, construction leasing, and maintenance of estates),
3. Marketing policy (market identification), and
4. Incentive administration (granting concessionary terms under relevant laws).

Table 4.4 below tries to capture actual autonomy rather than the formal/legal autonomy stated in the governing legislation. It suggests that there was greater managerial autonomy in the JIDC during the 1960s. This finding is consistent with the association between greater goal realization and autonomy. Three important factors explain the differences in the level of autonomy in the Jamaica and T&T IDCs during this period. First, the governing legislation that brought the JIDC into existence conferred executive management status on the board of directors; this was not the case in T&T. In addition, under the Act, the General Manager was also a member of the Board of Directors and was integrated into executive decision-making.

Table 4.4   Managerial autonomy of the Jamaica and T&T IDCs in promoting industry, 1960s and 1980s

	IDCs	Personnel policy	FINAL DECISION IN POLICY AREAS		
			Industrial estate development & management policy	Marketing policy	Incentive administration policy
1960s	JIDC	IDC management	Generally with IDC management; for location of estates and setting of rents final decisions lies with MOI	IDC	IDC advisory role, final decision lies with MOI
	T&TIDC	Civil Service Commission prior to 1965; Statutory Authority Services Commission post-1965	IDC advisory role; final decision lies with MOI	IDC advisory role, final decision lies with MOI	IDC advisory role, final decision lies with MOI
1980s	JIDC	MOT&I and PM	MOT&I and PM	World Bank, MOT&I and PM	World Bank, MOT&I and PM
	T&TIDC	1988, appointment of GM was especially subject to political interference upon resignation of GM Eldon Warner	T&TIDC	MOI, since IDC overseas offices closed in 1983/84	MOI

Key: MOT&I—Ministry of Trade and Industry; PM—Prime Minister; GM—General Manager; and MOI—Ministry of Industry.

Sources: Annual Reports of the Jamaica and T&T IDCs 1959–69 and 1979–89.

The board's executive management status was especially effective in matters related to personnel policy, where the board, including the General Manager, exercised its power without recourse to higher political authority. In the T&TIDC, the field was left open for political interference in personnel policy during the 1960s. Prior to 1965, the Civil Service Commission had responsibility for IDC personnel policy, but with the creation of the Statutory Authority Services Commission in 1965, this body took over such responsibility. To the extent that both Commissions were the object of political interference in the 1960s and thereafter meant that political intervention was exerted in IDC personnel policy. Thus the hiring, promotion and firing of T&TIDC staff became contentious political issues on which the fortunes of the PNM government of the day often hinged. It is against this background that the dismissal in 1961 of four IDC officers, two of whom (Max Ifill and Ben Primus) were top managers should be viewed. This event occasioned a question to the Minister of Industry and Commerce, John O'Halloran, in the House of Representatives. In his reply, the Minister took responsibility for the dismissals but justified them on the grounds of the officers' 'incompatibility with the government's intent for the IDC'. Letters to the editor on this issue in the daily newspaper lamented the IDC's loss of autonomy (*Guardian*, 9/6/1961).

Second, while appointment to the board of the JIDC was a political issue, the fact that the JIDC's topmost management of the 1960s (Executive Director Carrol G. da Costa, Manager of Training Mr Bertie Morris, and Mr Beresford Bennett) were founding members from the 1950s and had a proven management track-record made the JLP government less inclined to exert political influence over management. Moreover, the fact that the JLP Minister of Industry in the 1960s, Robert Lightbourne, was the *de facto* founder of the JIDC meant that he had worked with these officers in the 1950s. He had also acquired respect for their professional competence (personal interview with Robert Lightbourne, June 1992). Therefore, decisions, especially those requiring technical expertise such as property management, were left exclusively to the management team.

In T&T, there was no such continuity of management, nor did the politicians accept that the T&TIDC managers had any professional competence. In fact, for most of the 1960s, the Minister of Industry, John O'Halloran, was especially unhappy with the IDC's non-executive board and its executive management for its poor performance and inefficiency. Thus, in the 1965 budget debate, the Minister indicted the IDC's board for the organization's poor performance and the failure of government's industrial policy. The board's defence was that 'the minister was never prepared to delegate authority to the board to take decisions' (*Daily Mirror*, 22/1/1965). In 1966, the PNM government sought to remedy this problem once and for all by handpicking a 'competent, dynamic and new' General Manager. In doing so, however, the government flouted the recruitment procedures of the Statutory Authority Services Commission. Without advertising a vacancy, and bypassing T&TIDC's Assistant Manager, P.J. Burke, the new incumbent—Eldon Warner—was seconded to the IDC in the post of Deputy General Manager. One year later he was appointed General Manager.

The third factor pertains to the JIDC's greater autonomy in marketing policy. This point stems from the fact that the JIDC had built up competence in this area due to the fact that its overseas offices were established since the mid-1950s. Indeed, the JIDC's external strengths were so well developed that, when Jamaica achieved political independence in 1962, it was JIDC offices that temporarily took on the job of representing Jamaica oversees. Moreover, the fact that it was the Executive Director, Carroll C. da Costa, who had established the Corporation's overseas offices in New York, London and Toronto meant that politicians dared not question the JIDC's competence in international marketing. In contrast, the first T&TIDC overseas office was only opened on 1 June 1964 and largely revolved around the initiative of a single itinerant officer, Clyde Namsoo.

An interesting conclusion to this discussion of the Corporations' autonomy in the 1960s is to juxtapose the biggest IDC scandals of the era in the two countries. In Jamaica, the Jamaica Woolens affair dominated the late 1950s and most of the 1960s (Widdicombe 1972). It was a sad story of JIDC management being autonomous enough to make its own investment decisions, but unlucky enough to suffer losses equivalent to 619,207 pounds sterling (Ministry Paper No.57 1964, Memorandum by JIDC General Manager on Jamaica Woolens Ltd. 1962). The PNP government of the day was held accountable for this scandal, and for this and other reasons lost the 1962 general election.

While there were many IDC scandals in T&T in the 1960s, they generally revolved around the same theme—resignations over political interference and lack of autonomy. The resignation statement of board member George Dhanny best captures this scenario:

Within the past few months particularly, I have witnessed duplicity, favouritism, discrimination, nepotism, intrigue and political interference in the running of the IDC and on a scale that has filled me with disgust … The ordinance that created the IDC intended that it should operate largely along recognised commercial lines and enjoy a considerable measure of autonomy, without red tape and without directives on details … What in fact it has become is a Civil Service bureaucracy staffed with seasoned civil servants and reflecting all the shortcomings of the Civil service department of delays, indecision and lack of purpose and direction. (*Guardian* 22/9/1966)

As regards the 1980s, findings in Table 4.4 do not confirm an association between greater goal realization and autonomy in the 1980s. Although the T&TIDC became more autonomous in the 1980s, it did not contribute more to economic growth. Indeed, it was the more controlled JIDC that seemed to make a greater contribution to economic growth. What explains these differences, and do they in fact challenge the association under consideration? To answer this question, it must be recalled that the JIDC's role in the 1980s was determined by the JLP's new industrial policy and by recommendations in the World Bank's industrial sector report. The net effect of these two factors, combined with the fact that Seaga took personal responsibility for Jamaica's economic recovery, resulted in increased control over the JIDC. Between 1981 and 1984, the 'rump JIDC' was designated the task of training and managing 19 new subsidiaries created in the Manley era; NIDCO, the JIDC's newest subsidiary, effectively took over the JIDC's role under the new industrial policy. However, the involvement of the Prime Minister, the World Bank, and the Ministry of Foreign Affairs, Trade and Industry severely circumscribed the decisional space of both the JIDC and the new NIDCO. Important marketing decisions on the garment sector were determined by the Ministry's 807 trade agreements with the United States. Promotional decisions were determined by the designated priority sub-sector. Decisions related to industrial estates and property management were taken over, first by the Ministry of Foreign Affairs, Trade and Industry, and later by a new holding company, Factories Corporation of Jamaica Ltd. Finally, personnel decisions fell under the purview of the Prime Minister, a development that must be viewed against the background of the government's public-sector reduction programme.

Between 1984 and 1988 (when the NIDCO was merged into the JIDC), managerial autonomy continued to be almost non-existent. Managerial decision-making continued to be determined by the same factors listed above. Indeed, a memo from the Financial Secretary to the Permanent Secretary of the Ministry of Industry spells out the World Bank and IMF impingement on the JIDC during this period. The memo reads as follows:

> It should be recognised that JIDC as a major public enterprise falls under the scrutiny of both the World Bank and the IMF and that it is essential that a detailed 3-year programme be identified to the Ministry of Finance & Planning showing the projects and programmes to be undertaken, the related cash flow implications of the activities of the corporation and a projected profit and loss and balance-sheet position covering the 3-year period. (MIC Memo from the Financial Secretary to the Permanent Secretary, Ministry of Industry and Commerce, 13 January 1984)

Then Minister of Industry, Douglas Vaz, also took personal responsibility for JIDC matters as they pertained to the USAID, World Bank, and UNIDO industrial-sector strengthening programmes. It is in this context that the letter from Mr Martin V. Dagata, Acting Director of the USAID to Minister Vaz should be viewed. The letter states:

> In our meeting of April 2, 1985, you requested that *we deal directly with you* on matters relating to our proposed assistance to the garment sector. Accordingly, I am enclosing an outline of the proposal we have worked out with the Jamaica Industrial Development Corporation. This is an internal document, but I believe it accurately reflects the understanding that was reached between USAID, Warren Woodham [General Manager of the JIDC] and other JIDC staff ... We appreciate the personal interest you have shown in this matter and look forward to the implementation of a successful program in this important sector (MOI, 26 April 1985)

Moreover, decisions related to JIDC's properties and industrial estates were taken over by the Ministry and the Prime Minister. Thus, against JIDC's advice, its management was directed on which of its properties to divest, to whom it had to be divested, and at what cost. Indeed, the following comment from the Permanent Secretary of the Ministry of Industry must be viewed in the light of the Prime Minister's insistence on divestment despite the advice to the contrary from JIDC's management:

> I fully understand the *raison d'être* for such sales in light of JIDC's needs. However, I am a little concerned about the general principle of sale of JIDC's holdings, which in principle are owned on behalf of the Government of Jamaica. Should these sales be made without specific Cabinet Authority? Should the Divestment Committee be involved? What of the approval of the Accountant General, where he is involved? (MOI, Memo to the Minister of State from Permanent Secretary, 26 May 1987)

With the JIDC's merger with the Jamaica National Export Corporation (JNEC) and the Jamaica National Investment Promotions Ltd. (JNIP) to form the new Jamaica Promotions Ltd. (Jampro) in 1988, managerial autonomy continued to be circumscribed by political interference. On this occasion, however, the macroeconomic management implications of structural adjustment were the reasons advanced for political encroachment into JIDC decision-making. The two most important management decisions affecting the future of Jampro in the late 1980s—redundancies of over 100 Jampro staff, and the decision to close Jampro's Washington and Hong Kong offices—emanated from a political source, PNP Senator Barclay Ewart, who was also Chairman of Jampro. Senator Ewart defended these decisions on the grounds of cost savings to the Jamaican economy (*Gleaner* 2/12/1989).

On the other hand, the T&TIDC's increased autonomy during the 1980s can be attributed to two factors. Firstly, in the PNM years (1980–86) it was due to the government's confidence in the Corporation's management and board. This stemmed from the fact that both the Chairman of the Board, Jack de Lima, and the General Manager, Eldon Warner, had served in the Corporation's management since the 1960s and had good working relations with the PNM government. It was largely due to this confidence that the Manager of the IDC's Small Business Division and the General Manager of the Corporation were granted permission to authorize loans up to TT$20,000 and TT$50,000, respectively. The management of the Corporation had been struggling for this right since the mid-1970s.

Secondly, in the period before the new NAR government approached the IMF, the Corporation enjoyed increased autonomy because of the personal efforts of then-Minister of Industry Ken Gordon. Gordon encouraged the Corporation's management to formulate its own investment policy, an issue that was bitterly resented by the Ministry's staff. He also succeeded in removing the Corporation from the control of the Statutory Authority Services Commission.

With T&T's approach to the Fund in late 1988, however, the Corporation's new-found autonomy was at risk. A Jamaican type of scenario evolved where the involvement of external actors encouraged government to exert greater control for reasons of financial accountability. Thus, during interviews in 1992, top management expressed concern about rumours of retrenchment and merger, and the increasing involvement of external agencies, such as the Inter-American Development Bank, in formulating T&T's industrial policy. Not surprisingly, by April 1995, the T&TIDC had been dissolved, and a new organization—the Trinidad and Tobago Tourism and Industrial Development Company (TIDCO)—was brought into existence by Act No. 4 of 1995. Most of the IDC's staff were dispersed with the creation of TIDCO.

In conclusion, while there was an association between economic growth and IDC autonomy in the 1960s, in the 1980s, greater control in the JIDC was found to be associated with economic growth.

IDCs, economic growth and the facilitative policy environment

Given that the JIDC had a better record of realizing economic growth goals in the 1960s and the 1980s, its policy environment might have also permitted a more facilitative role for the Corporation. This association is explored by looking at the actual functions of the organizations and the pattern of expenditure allocation. Such a focus should reveal whether the IDC was a direct producer or facilitator of industrial-led growth.

In the 1960s, this association must be located against the background of the Arthur Lewis import-substitution industrialization model of economic growth then being implemented. Facilitating private sector investment was the linchpin of this model of development. However, that was the ideal; the reality of a nascent private sector and a state-directed growth model dictated direct state involvement in productive enterprises. Did governments approximate the ideal or did they succumb to more centrifugal forces?

Following the ill-fated Jamaica Woolens venture, the JIDC seemed wary of undertaking similar ventures. It therefore restricted its activities to supporting private-sector investment through its factory building and incentive administration programme. Thus, throughout the first half of 1960s, the Victoria Crafts Market constituted the only substantial business venture of the JIDC. The Victoria Crafts Market was established as a subsidiary of the JIDC in 1956. By 1964 total investments in the Crafts Market were the equivalent of 12,950 pounds sterling and total profits amounted to the equivalent of 15,000 pounds sterling (JIDC Annual Reports, 1961 & 1964). Three other JIDC subsidiaries—Jamaica Wood Products, Glass Blowing Project, and Alabaster House of Jamaica Ltd.—were either moth-balled or sold to private investors by 1963 for an estimated total cost price of only J$125,000 (Widdicombe 1972). Against this background, the JIDC annual reports of the 1960s copiously documented and emphasized the organization's facilitative functions and activities.

As regards JIDC expenditure, Widdicombe's 1972 study shows that expenditure in the 1960s went overwhelmingly to supporting private enterprise through factory construction and land development. This study estimates that, by 1970, a total of 376 firms operated in Jamaica under incentive legislation administered by the JIDC. Of this number, 82 per cent were owned by interests from Jamaica. The bulk of JIDC expenditure in promoting these enterprises went into factory construction and land development (Widdicombe 1972: 209).

In 1967, however, this situation was somewhat altered when a new wholly-owned subsidiary of the JIDC—Jamaica Frozen Foods Ltd.—was established by Ministry Paper No. 6. The new enterprise aimed 'to assist in developing the full potential of agriculture by minimizing the losses of the Agricultural Marketing Corporation, thereby enabling the Corporation to improve the marketing facilities it is increasingly providing to farmers' (Ministry Paper No. 6, 1967: 1). Since data on JIDC expenditure on this venture in the 1960s are not available, the impact on the Corporation's overall expenditure pattern during this period cannot be ascertained.

During the 1960s, the T&TIDC was also mandated to support private-sector investment in industry. Unlike the JIDC, however, the PNM interpreted support to mean direct investment in private enterprises through purchasing debentures in companies and by direct loans to industry. The fact that the Corporation had an interest in the so-called 'private companies' in which it bought shares begged the question of a facilitative role.

This feature of the T&TIDC can be traced to the Corporation's responsibilities under the Act, and to the fact that it inherited an active loans portfolio from the Hotel Development Corporation. Thus, the construction of the 261-room Hilton Hotel at a total cost of TT$13.3m was listed as the first major achievement of the Corporation for the 1960s (*Record of Major Achievement*, T&TIDC 1981). Not surprisingly, the Corporation's hotel-development portfolio dominated its activities. Feasibility studies, project identification and development, all activities associated with direct production, also dominated the Corporation's functions in the 1960s.

In the 1980s, the JIDC was expected to contribute to economic growth by supporting the government's seven priority sub-sectors industrialization programme. As shown above, the JIDC also lost its autonomy during this period. Thus the Corporation was directed to divest directly-owned subsidiaries brought over from the Manley days and to redirect its activities and expenditure in support of the private sector. As a consequence, a new business advisory services function was included in the Corporation's portfolio in 1986, a sewing academy (Garmex) was established in 1987 to support the Montego Bay and Kingston Free Zones, a technical assistance programme was established in 1985 to support the electronics and footwear priority sectors, and a series of diagnostic studies on the export market were undertaken for the furniture sector between 1983 and 1986 (JIDC *Annual Reports* 1983–88).

On the question of expenditure, the Corporation's consolidated income and expenditure account for the 1980s shows the shift in expenditure from subsidiaries deficit financing inherited from the Manley era to the priority sub-sectors and industrial estate development. Consequently, while one-third of total expenses for the year 1978 was spent on loss-making JIDC subsidiaries, 50 per cent of total JIDC expenditure in 1987 went toward the priority sub-sectors project; expenditure on subsidiaries was less than 1 per cent of total expenditure (*Financial Statements*, JIDC 1978 & 1987).

The 1980s saw the T&TIDC charged with the responsibility of supporting the government's light export manufacturing programme. In the 1970s, the Corporation's activities were dominated by small business loan administration. Of the 3,146 small business loans granted between 1970 and 1984, only 1,004 went towards manufacturing ventures, while the remaining 2,142 went toward personal and other services (T&TIDC

Scotland Committee Report 1985). Against this background, manufacturers, both large and small, were especially unhappy with the Corporation's performance in the early 1980s (*Express* 13/3/1986). Moreover, since the Corporation closed its Toronto and New York offices between 1983 and 1984, export manufacturers felt particularly abandoned. The PNM took cognizance of these views, and the 1985 Scotland Committee was mandated to outline a new and more facilitative implementation strategy for the Corporation. The Committee also indicted the Corporation for its past role as an entrepreneur, stating that 'it is neither desirable nor appropriate for the Corporation to operate enterprises on a continuing basis' (1985: 38). Furthermore, the Committee recommended that the 'wasteful' small business loans programme be discontinued.

The report concluded with a number of reforms intended to make the Corporation more facilitative, i.e., the introduction of a one-stop shop, emphasis of the Corporation's investment-attracting and promotional functions, relocation of the financial assistance role to the Development Finance Corporation, termination of the small business loan scheme, and emphasis on incentive legislation administration.

Between 1985 and 1986, none of these recommendations was implemented. With the change of government in December 1986, however, several new developments took place: the One-Stop-Shop was introduced; an industrial promotions division was created; the IDC became the Secretariat for the intra-departmental Investment Co-ordinating Committee; industrial counselling, exhibitions, and trade fairs were mounted for potential foreign investors; and the Corporation hosted two missions from the US-based Private Investment Corporation (OPIC) in 1988 (*Express* 21/5/1988). The 1986 devaluation of the TT dollar made export manufacturers particularly receptive to these initiatives from the IDC.

However, the effects of these facilitative efforts were muted by the fact that the Corporation continued to pursue the same old non-facilitative activities for which it was reprimanded in the Scotland report. Thus, the IDC initiated three major investments in the late 1980s: the Aloe Vera Plant project, the French Thyme and Persian Lilac project, and the Fabric Bulk Buying Company known as CUTTAGE Fabrics Ltd Resuscitation of the garment industry was the rationale given for establishing CUTTAGE (T&TIDC Annual Report 1989). Moreover, the Corporation continued its small business lending scheme. In fact, the Corporation designated 1988 as 'small business year' and approved 99 applications, to which TT$1.1 million was loaned (T&TIDC Annual Report 1989). Small-business lending only came to an end in November 1989 with the creation of the Small Business Development Company Ltd. While financial statements for the late 1980s are not available the Corporation's balance sheet at 31 December 1987 that accompanied the 1987 Annual Report does show that only 9.2 per cent or TT$3.1 million of total expenditure was spent on assistance to industry; 42 per cent or TT$14.3 million of total expenditure was spent on loans to industry. In many of the latter cases, the Corporation was a majority shareholder.

The discussion above suggests that the JIDC had a more facilitative role during the 1960s and 1980s, thus confirming the association made in the development administration literature between goal realization and a facilitative policy environment.

Conclusions

What conclusions can be drawn from the macro- and micro-level applications of the framework of association above? Firstly, both macro and micro applications confirm a strong association between the organizational attribute—administrative capacity building—and goal realization. Thus there was a stronger political commitment to implementing capacity-building initiatives in Jamaica through techniques such as institutionalizing the use of foreign technical assistance. In T&T, there was considerable initiative but little political will to implement capacity-building recommendations. This was manifested by a general weariness of foreign expertise and a reluctance to empower public servants through administrative development. Consequently, while at the micro level the JIDC underwent continuous reform and restructuring in both the 1960s and 1980s, the in T&TIDC was characterized by structural constancy due to a lack of political will to implement reforms.

Secondly, as regards the political environmental variable—autonomy—the explanatory powers of this factor seemed to be restricted to the 1960s. This was so at both macro and micro levels. At the macro level, greater goal realization in Jamaica was associated with a greater incidence of autonomous productive enterprises in the 1960s, and at the micro level the JIDC was also characterized by managerial autonomy. In the 1980s, however, no such association could be confirmed at the macro level. The macro application suggested that the nature of the policy environment was more strongly associated with goal realization than autonomy in the 1980s. More light was shed on this finding in the micro case study application. Here, the more-controlled JIDC was associated with greater goal realization, and the less-controlled T&TIDC was associated with less goal realization. This suggests that the structural adjustment and stabilization imperatives which dominated the 1980s require more control over parastatals for success. Another important finding was the association between autonomy and management continuity. The experience of the JIDC during the 1960s and the T&TIDC during the PNM years of the 1980s brought this finding to light, suggesting that managerial autonomy from politicians has to be earned and that there is a time dimension to this factor.

Thirdly, both the macro- and micro-level applications confirmed an association between more facilitative implementation strategies and a greater realization of economic growth goals in Jamaica. In both the 1960s and the 1980s, the JLP's *raison d'être* was to facilitate private sector-led growth. The functions and expenditure patterns of agencies such as JIDC provided evidence of this point. In contrast, a largely entrepreneurial state developed in T&T that directly owned and controlled productive enterprises. This could be attributed to the politics of foreign ownership associated with oil, the lumpiness of heavy industrial investments, and the anti-colonialism of the PNM. However, the finding of a facilitative policy environment coexisting with an interventionist state in Jamaica during the 1980s suggests that facilitation is a type of interventionism rather than a matter of degree.

At the end of this inquiry, it can be argued that the findings are generally consistent with the relationships suggested in the framework of association.

Public Bureaucracy and Economic Change: The Associations

Introduction

Chapter 2 revealed that economic change was a dominant goal pursued in the 1970s, and that Jamaica was better able to achieve this goal than T&T. In view of such findings, the development administration question arises: Was the realization of economic change goals in Jamaica associated with greater decentralization of economic decision-making structures, greater beneficiary participation in economic decision-making, and greater bureaucratic politics? This question is addressed in the macro-level exploration that follows in Part I. Part II addresses the role and function of the Jamaica and T&T Industrial Development Corporations in the decade of change. The relative contribution of the two IDCs to change is first outlined, then their differences are explored in terms of the three development administration variables: decentralization, participation and bureaucratic politics.

PART I:
Public Bureaucracy and Economic Change: Macro-level Associations

Economic change and decentralization

Centralization is a recurring theme in Caribbean development administration (Mills 1990b, 1971). Despite the small size of these islands, what passes for 'decentralized' decision-making is very often no more than deconcentration; real decisions are taken at the level of the Office of the Prime Minister and the Cabinet.

Against this background of centralization, the inquiry below focuses on the structures of economic policy formulation in Jamaica and T&T during the 1970s. The object is to determine whether greater goal realization in Jamaica was associated with greater decentralization in economic policy formulation. Tables 5.1 and 5.2 capture the key structures involved in policy formulation in both countries during the 1970s, their functions, the actual degree of authority vested in these bodies, and their composition. Information on composition provides the background to the discussion on participation that follows.

The fact that economic policy formulation largely took place in structures staffed by functionaries from the centre in both Jamaica and T&T is the first important finding to note from Tables 5.1 and 5.2. The principal planning structures—the Economic Planning Council of Jamaica, and the National Planning Commission of T&T—were headed by the respective Prime Ministers and had no regional offices. Hence the persistence of the centralization factor in policy formulation.

Beyond these similarities, further comparison of the two tables reveals that there were more policy formulation structures in Jamaica overall, and more structures in which decision-making authority was vested. While there were only seven structures for policy formulation in T&T, there were 11 in Jamaica. Of the 11, only one, the Bank of Jamaica, was purely advisory; all others were vested with some authority to formulate aspects of economic policy. Of the seven structures engaged in economic policy formulating in T&T, real decision-making authority was only vested in two structures: ministries and parastatals. Ministries were vested with authority under the PNM government's sectoral planning strategy, and parastatals were vested with decision-making authority based on profitability, age of the enterprise, or confidence in the board and management. In the case of the Co-ordinating Task Force, in a real sense decision-making power was devolved to its chairman, Professor Ken Julien, and not to the structure *per se*. The three remaining structures—the National Economic Advisory Council, the Central Bank, and the National Advisory Council—only functioned in an advisory capacity.

Table 5.1   Decentralization and economic policy formulation structures in the 1970s, Jamaica

Structure	Functions	Actual decision-making authority	Composition
Central Planning Unit (1955-72), National Planning Agency (1972-89)	Planning and co-ordination of economic development policy	Delegated authority	Headed and staffed by public officers, Gladstone Bonnick/Director
Bank of Jamaica	Monitoring and implementation of fiscal and monetary policy	No decision-making authority but had some influence over policy	Headed and staffed by public officers, G. Arthur Brown/Governor of the Bank
Economic Planning Council	The premier planning body. It formulates, implements and evaluates economic and social policy	Devolution from Cabinet but still centralized due to ministerial composition	Prime Minister as Chairman, Minister of Finance and Deputy Prime Minister as Deputy Chairman, Ministers of Industry, Mining, Agriculture, Labour, and Public Utilities
Technical Advisory Committee	To advise the Economic Planning Council and the National Planning Agency on draft plans	Limited delegation	Chief Technical Directory of the NPA as Co-ordinator, Governor, Central Bank of Jamaica, Finance Secretary, one economist and one sociologist
Consultative Committee	To permit, encourage and make provisions as far as practicable for the regular participation of the private sector in planning the development of the country	Limited delegation of authority, function mostly advisory	Each committee composed of leading private-sector representatives, officials from the relevant Ministries, & a technical secretary from the National Planning Agency. Chairman of each committee was the Minister under whose portfolio the sector falls. The Parliamentary Secretary for Economic Planning was an ex-oficio member of all sector committees

(Continued)

Table 5.1   *(continued)*

Structure	Functions	Actual decision-making authority	Composition
Ministries	To formulate and implement government's economic policy	Delegation of limited authority	Public officials
Ministry of Mobilization & Human Resources (1977–90)	To supervise and co-ordinate people's programmes. To formulate an alternative to the IMF path for Jamaica	Devolved authority to formulate plan	Headed by the PNP's left, close formal and informal liason with farmers, unemployed, small business persons
Economic Stabilization Commission (1976–1980)	To achieve understanding and consensus in advising government on anti-inflationary policies	No decision-making power; purely advisory; reports directly to the Economic Council	Headed by Exec. Chairman Dr Headley Brown, with representatives from trade unions, employers federation, manufacturers associations, Chamber of Commerce, Consumers League, farmers' organizations, co-operative movements, credit unions and financial sector
Capital Development Fund	To identify public investment for the use of revenue from bauxite levy	Developed authority	Big businessmen
Parastatals (JIDC, Bauxite Commission)	To formulate and implement government's economic policy	Delegated authority to formulate economic policy	Headed by private sector representatives, e.g., Bauxite Commission headed by Meyer Matalon
Community Councils & Community Enterprise Councils	To enable communities to formulate and implement economic development projects	Devolution of authority to identify economic projects	Labour, party supporters, small business persons and the unemployed

Sources: Constructed from GOJ Annual Budget Speeches, 1969–80; Stephens & Stephens 1986; Economic & Social Planning in Jamaica, May 1972, Ministry Paper No. 10; The National Development Planning Function, memorandum to all permanent Secretaries, Office of the Prime Minister, August 1972; Henry-Wilson 1985, and personal interviews with Professor Norman Girvan, May 1992.

Table 5.2　Decentralization and economic policy formulation structures in the 1970s, Trinidad & Tobago

Structure	Functions	Actual decision-making authority	Composition
National Planning Commission (1963-74)	To formulate annual, medium- and long-term plans	Little real authority since final decisions lay with the Prime Minister who held portfolios of Chairman of the Commission, Minister of Finance, and Minister of Planning and Development	Prime Minister as Chairman; Ministers of Finance, Agriculture, Industry, Petroleum, Labour; Director of Statistics; representative of the Central Bank; PS to the Prime Minister, and CEO of the IDC
National Economic Advisory Council (1963-74)	To assist in the formulation of development plans and goals	No decision-making authority but did have some influence over policy formulation	5 members selected by the Labour Advisory Council, 5 members selected by the Business Advisory Council, 2 persons selected by government from small farmers associations, friendly societies and similar bodies of voluntary sector
Coordinating Task Force	To co-ordinate and implementT&T industrial development projects	Devolution of authority to the chairman and not to the structure	University Prof. K.S. Julien as Chairman, CEO of the IDC, and public servants—G. Rampersad, B. Ali, S. Martin and C. Hee Hong
National Advisory Council (1978-80)	To advise government on formulation of economic and social policy	None, only influenced policy	University Prof. K.S. Julien as Chairman, representative from private sector, labour and the University—Prof. J. Spence and Dr St Cyr

(Continued)

Table 5.2 *(continued)*

Structure	Functions	Actual decision-making authority	Composition
Central Bank	To formulate and supervise fiscal and monetary policy	Advisory function but delegation of limited decision-making authority	Public servants
Infrastructural Advisory Group (1975-1979)	To co-ordinate the public sector infrastructural development projects	Limited advisory function	All public servants: representatives of the Ministries of Planning, Works, the Electricity Commission and the Water & Sewage Authority
Parastatals	To formulate and implement policy	Limited delegation to some parastatals based on profitability, e.g., Trinidad Tesoro; age of parastatal, e.g., the electricity co. established in 1952; or confidence in board & management, e.g., the telephone co. TELCO	Headed by public servants and professionals; little representation from labour and business on boards
Ministries in the oil-boom period (1974-80)	To formulate and implement sectoral policy	Limited authority delegated based on confidence in Minister and sectoral planning	Headed by public servants

Sources: Constructed from: GOTT Annual Budget Speeches 1969-1979; Barclay 1991; Francis 1979; and personal interviews with Lennox Seales, of the Organization and Management Division, Office of the Prime Minister, Jan 1992 and with ex-government Ministers of the 1976 Cabinet, July 1992.

Taken together, a complex picture emerges of limited decentralization to Ministries, parastatals and to the Task Force in T&T. The latter was subjectively determined since authority was entrusted to the person who headed the agency and not to the agency itself. This picture must be complemented by the extreme centralization of power in the hands of the Prime Minister at the time, and the fact that even decisions to decentralize or not to decentralize were based on his personal likes and dislikes (personal interviews with ex-Ministers, May 1992). This is not to say that decision-making under Manley was not personalized. On the contrary, Henry's unpublished study of decision-making under Manley cited in Stephens and Stephens (1986) demonstrates that it was personalized. However, in Jamaica the dominance of interest organizations (labour and capital), Jamaica's balance of payments problem, and Manley's philosophy of participatory development led the PNP into more meaningful decentralization. Therefore this finding of greater realization of economic change in Jamaica and more decentralized structures of economic policy formulation is consistent with the association in the framework. But did greater decentralization facilitate greater participation? This question is explored below.

Economic change and beneficiary participation

The interests

Because the demand for economic change emanated from radical social movements in the two case countries, it is important that the question of participation be widened beyond 'direct beneficiaries' to include the participation of these groups. In Jamaica, the Unemployed Workers Council, the Independent Trade Union Advisory Council, the Young Socialist League, and the New World Group, an association of university lecturers and professionals writing in 'Abeng' demanded economic change. In T&T, the National Joint Action Committee, the New Beginning Movement, the Oilfield Workers Trade Union, the Transport and Industrial Workers Trade Union, and the Tapia House Movement led the battle for economic change.

Regarding the question of beneficiaries, research in the Commonwealth Caribbean shows that indigenous entrepreneurs operating in what has been termed 'the residentiary sector' are the chief beneficiaries of economic change. This theme is addressed in the works of V. James (1994), Davies (1984), Reddock (1980), LeFranc (1989), Fisseha and Davies (1981), Witter and Kirton (1990), Nunes (1974) and Thomas 1974. Research on this sector reveals that, unlike established compradorial enterprises operating as agents of international capital, indigenous entrepreneurs are characterized by local ownership, high value-added and imaginative outputs contributing to diversified production (Davies 1984). Furthermore, it is also shown that they almost always were black—in contrast to the white ex-plantocracy dominating screwdriver industry in most of the Caribbean—and they operate in small business enterprises, usually in the informal sector. A further characteristic is their low level of organization in interest associations (Reddock 1980). In contrast, compradorial elements of domestic capital have constituted themselves into associations from the early 1950s.

In view of this scenario, it is important to identify the associations representing big and small business interests in Jamaica and T&T in the 1970s. In that decade, big-business interests in Jamaica were represented by: the Jamaica Manufacturers Association, established in 1947 with terms of reference to 'promote and encourage industry, science, commerce in Jamaica'; the Jamaica Exporters Association; the Jamaica Chamber of Commerce, incorporated in 1950 to 'promote and protect trade, business, commerce, agriculture and industries in Jamaica'; the Employers Federation and the Construction Federation; and the Private Sector Organization of Jamaica (PSOJ), established in 1976 as an umbrella organization for business organizations of all sectors. The Small Business Association of Jamaica, credit unions and cooperatives represented the interests of indigenous entrepreneurs in Jamaica.

In the 1970s, associations of big business in T&T included, among others: the Chamber of Industry and Commerce, established with terms of reference to 'enhance the investment climate of Trinidad and Tobago'; the South Chamber of Industry and Commerce, a splinter association of the Chamber of Commerce, formed in 1956 to advance the idea of industrial development downstream of petroleum for the south of Trinidad; the T&T Manufacturers Association; the Kiwanis; the T&T Businessmen Association; the Employers Consultative Association; the Hardware Owners Association; and the Junior Chamber of Commerce, established in 1949 to promote business and commerce among young entrepreneurs. An important point to note at this juncture is that private-sector associations in T&T were characteristically fragmented. Divisions existed on the basis of race, region and sectoral interests. For example, while the Northern Chamber of Commerce represented the interests of the white ex-plantocracy engaged in import re-tailing and import-substituting businesses, the membership of the Southern Chamber of Commerce was largely Indian or mixed, and the major focus was on the petroleum industry. Moreover, the interests of Indian businessmen in Northern Trinidad were generally represented by the T&T Manufacturing Association. In addition, associations established in the 1970s, such as the Hardware Owners Association, were mainly Indian-dominated and somewhat hostile to traditional white capital. It is against this background that Williams' incisive comment on the T&T private sector in 1961 should be noted:

> What we have today is a large segment of the community-union of this, that or the other, Chamber of Commerce North and South, Manufacturers' Association, Businessmen's Association, Agricultural Society of the island or of parts, each pulling this way or that way, each seeking to establish itself and promote its own interests, even at the expense of others, not caring about the others, each seeing an individual tree in the whole forest. This gets us nowhere, and the community, subjected to a barrage of propaganda from all sides, itself cannot see the wood for the trees. (Quoted in Ryan 1972: 260)

Against this background an important umbrella effort with unifying potential—the Employers Consultative Association—failed to attract support from the Syrian/Lebanese, Indian and Tobagonian business community. This was due to its close association with the white Northern Chamber of Commerce. Indeed, it was not until 1991 that Joe Pries, Jr spearheaded a broad-based drive—the Nova Committee—to unify private-sector interests and incorporate them with those of labour and the state. Joe Pries, Jr is the son of Joe Pries, Sr, Chamber of Commerce President (1987–89) and the T&T Businessmen Association President (1981–83). From all indications this effort did not meet with success because it was viewed as an initiative of the Northern Chamber of Commerce.

In the 1970s, credit unions and co-operative societies represented the interests of some indigenous entrepreneurs; in the 1970s, T&T had no small-business associations. To be sure, the necessity of an association to represent the interests of small black business came out of the state-sponsored 1978 Small Business Consultation. The T&T Small Business Association, which was established in 1979, has had a history of fragmentation and conflict revolving around personality differences, politics and regionalism. This conflict culminated in 1982, when the

Association fractured into two, with the Eastern interests of the Association breaking away from the Central, Western and Southern interests. Thus, the 1970s were characterized by an essentially fragmented small- and big-business private sector in T&T.

In contrast, in the same period, big business in Jamaica was coming together in the umbrella Private Sector Organization of Jamaica to ensure that their interests were taken into consideration. To what extent were advocates and beneficiaries of change (radicals and indigenous entrepreneurs) incorporated into the structures of economic policy formulation during the decade of change in Jamaica and T&T?

Radicals and participation in economic change

That the PNM survived the 1971 'no vote campaign' while the JLP lost the 1972 general election to the PNP is not surprising, since the former had the political acumen to reinvent itself in the language and colour of change. Throughout the 1970s, the PNM demonstrated its expertise in the politics of survival by promoting younger and more politically acceptable cadres from within its ranks, thereby conveying a somewhat false impression of change.

Consequently, in 1976, the PNM's inner circle of cabinet ministers and parliamentary secretaries evolved from being almost completely dominated by whites and browns in the late 1960s, to dominance by black 'progressives' such as Patrick Manning, Hugh Francis, Selwyn Richardson, Desmond Cartey, and Marilyn Gordon. Of the 18 members of the inner circle, 15 were black, 2 were Indian (Errol Mahabir and Kamuluddin Mohammed) and one was mixed-race (Mervyn de Souza); there were no whites. This contrasts with Winston Mahabir's incisive comments on the complexion of the inner circle of PNM decision-makers in 1956:

> From the perspective of proportional representation, the whites were vastly over-represented. If PNM really stood for Pure Negro Movement then Pure Negroes were grossly under-represented. 'Pure' Indians were reasonably well represented. (Mahibir 1975: 94)

Having reinvented itself as pro-change, the PNM proceeded to clamp down on radical social movements during the 1970s. In this light, attempts were made to introduce two draconian pieces of legislation: the Public Order Bill and the Firearms Bill of 1970. Although these bills failed to pass into law, aspects of their content were later incorporated into the Sedition Act and Summary Offences Acts, both of 1971. Moreover, a new Minimum Wage Act of 1973 extended 'the restrictions on speech by providing that the place of employment may be searched for "any class of workers" in any industry and reviews settlement of labour disputes' (C. Parris 1976: 231). In addition, a state of emergency was declared in the sugar sector, the Industrial Relations Act was passed in 1972, and the government moved to crush the most radical social movement of all, the National Union of Freedom Fighters (NUFF) with a search-and-destroy campaign. In the face of this evidence it can be concluded that the PNM did not incorporate radicals into economic policy-making structures, since the party itself was ostensibly 'radicalized'.

The new Manley government taking office in Jamaica also moved against the more radical social groups by passing punitive legislation such as the Industrial Relations and Public Service Relations Bills.

> However, the Manley government also incorporated radical intellectuals from the New World Group (for instance, George Beckford, Louis Lindsay, Trevor Munroe, D.K. Duncan and Norman Girvan) in strategic decision-making and advisory capacities in economic policy formulation. (Heaver 1986)

In addition, George Beckford and Louis Lindsay served as advisers and were part of the team that constructed the socialist alternative to the IMF—the Emergency Production Plan of 1977. In summary, while both the PNM and the PNP exercised state power against radical social movements during the 1970s, Manley balanced these moves by appointing University radicals to advisory and decision-making positions.

Beneficiary participation in economic policy formulation

To what extent were beneficiaries of economic change incorporated into economic policy formulation in Jamaica and T&T during the 1970s? As Table 5.1 shows, business secured representation in four sites of economic policy formulation in Jamaica: the Consultative Committee, the Economic Stabilization Commission, parastatals, and the Capital Development Fund, which functioned as a *de facto* parastatal. However, in all cases, members from established capital 'represented' the interests of business in Jamaica. Thus Henry-Wilson notes:

> Pat Rousseau, a lawyer in one of the leading legal firms and founder of the island's first fully-owned insurance companies, was appointed Chairman of [the Bauxite Commission] with Mayer Matalon—perhaps Jamaica's wealthiest business magnate—its Vice Chairman. (1985: 75)

She notes further that Karl Hendrickson, a Director of National Continental Corporation, was made Chairman of the Jamaica Public Service; Larry Sharpe, a businessman, was put in charge of the Agricultural Marketing Corporation; and Mayer Matalon was appointed Chairman of Jamaica Telephone Company. Henry-Wilson seemed especially troubled by the implications of appointing big-business representatives to the Capital Development Fund.

In addition to these appointments, the interest aggregation and demand-making role of the umbrella Private Sector Organization of Jamaica (PSOJ) constituted an informal forum for big-business participation in policy formulation. Not only was the PSOJ unrelenting in its attack on the Manley government, it also put forward alternative policies and suggestions (*Gleaner* 28/1/1970), thus sometimes acting as the *de facto* opposition to the government. By its actions, the PSOJ helped to institutionalize private-sector interests in policy formulation fora, such as the Economic Stabilization Commission of 1977.

However, two important qualifications must be added to the impression of big-business dominance. Firstly, some parastatals such as the Jamaica Industrial Development Corporation and the Agricultural Development Corporation encouraged small-business participation through co-operatives. This point will be discussed in Part II, which deals exclusively with the industrial development corporations (IDCs). Secondly, as Jamaica's balance of payment situation worsened in 1976, the PNP incorporated more representation from associations of indigenous entrepreneurs (small business associations, credit unions and co-operative movements) in its search for alternatives to the IMF. Thus the 1975/76 Annual Budget announced the creation of a Commission for Economic Stabilization comprised of 'Trade Unions, Employers Federation, Manufacturers Associations, Chambers of Commerce, Consumers League, Farmers' Organisations, Co-operative Movements, Credit Unions and Financial Sectors' (GOTT Annual Budget Speech 1976: 18). In addition, the Ministry of Mobilization and Human Resources created in early 1977 undertook close consultation with representatives from small business, the credit unions, and the co-operative sector in preparing the 1977 Emergency Production Plan. Similarly, the *raison d'être* of the Community Enterprise Councils centred on project identification from grassroots organizations. It must be said, however, that the impact of indigenous entrepreneur's participation in the Emergency Production Plan, the Commission for Economic Stabilization and the

Community Enterprise Councils was nullified with the government's approach to the Fund in 1977.

As regards T&T, Table 5.2 shows that representatives from indigenous entrepreneurs were only present in one policy formulation structure in the 1970s—the IDC. Indeed, the premier policy formulation structures to which decision-making power was devolved, i.e., the National Planning Commission and the Co-ordinating Task Force, consisted of politicians and technocrats, in particular one 'super-technocrat', Professor Ken Julien. Other than the IDC experiment, which will be discussed in Part II, no attempt was made to incorporate the voice of indigenous entrepreneurs into economic policy formulation. In the previous decade, participation by this group was facilitated by the consultative machinery around the medium-term plans. In the 1970s, the end of medium-term planning was associated with greater centralization of decision-making power into the hands of politicians, supported by technocrats and a select group of public servants. Unlike the incorporation of the New World Group into policy formulation in Jamaica, however, representatives from the University of the West Indies in T&T (Professor Ken Julien and Dr E.B.A. St Cyr) were not included for their radical ideas on economic change. Rather, William's fascination with academic achievement recommended anyone who had distinguished himself academically to occupy a chosen place in the structures of policy formulation. Precisely because of its dearth of scholastic credentials, the T&T private sector was de-selected. With the exception of a few personal favourites from the private sector (e.g., Jack de Lima, Gerald Montano and the Southern Chamber of Commerce), the private sector was largely excluded from the sites of economic policy formulation in the 1970s. This was facilitated by the fact that, unlike Jamaica, there was no united private-sector voice.

Consequently, while Manley sought to incorporate radicals and elements of the private sector into economic policy formulation, Williams alienated himself and the PNM from this interest in the 1970s. Ryan (1989: 212–22) gives a captivating account of the heated debate between the PNM government and the private sector conducted in the *Guardian* and the House of Representatives at that time.

In concluding this discussion it must be said that, in both countries, the real power to formulate economy policy lay at the centre. To the extent that decision-making authority was decentralized, however, there seems to have been a greater effort to incorporate radical advocates of change and potential beneficiaries in Jamaica. In T&T, a po-litico-technocratic alliance developed in the 1970s which effectively excluded all other interests including large and small businesses.

Bureaucratic politics and economic change

Introduction

Was the realization of economic change in Jamaica associated with bu-reaucratic support for the goals of change? This question is explored in two stages. The first stage entails identifying shared interests between top bureaucrats and those with an interest in change, i.e., beneficiaries, advocates of change, and the political directorate. Shared interests include socioeconomic background as indicated by schools attended, shared ethnic grouping, and economic class as determined by income. Consistent with the bureaucratic politics literature in development administration, evidence of shared interests is treated as sufficient condition for support. The second stage of the inquiry requires close scrutiny of the actions of bureaucrats either in support of or against economic change.

Top bureaucrats, radicals, indigenous entrepreneurs and politicians: An exploration into shared interests

In the 1970s, the profile of the top Jamaican public servants changed significantly. First, the emergence of new parastatals introduced a breed of 'public officers' who had as much impact on economic development policies as Permanent Secretaries, thus robbing the latter of their status. Nunes's work on 'The Declining Status of the Jamaican Civil Service' (1990) provides an important point of entry into this discussion. In this work, Nunes shows that the character of the civil service and indeed of civil servants reflected the changing social structure of Jamaican society in the 1970s. Nunes shows that, whereas the civil servants of colonial times were an elite group, in the 1970s their status fell as the group became more heterogenous and representative of the new black middle class.

In Jamaica, a new breed of bureaucrats occupied the top positions in both the civil service and the parastatals during the 1970s. They were mostly black, male, young and educated at the University of the West Indies rather than abroad (personal interview, Permanent Secretary, Ministry of the Public Service, May 1992).

Table 5.3   Ethnic group of top civil servants of T&T, 1975

Name of officer	Designation	Ethnic group
Mr George Patrick	PS Min of Labour	Afro-Trinidadian
Mr Euan Nunez	PS Min of Public Utilities	Mixed
Mr Mottley De Pieza	PS Min of Industry & Commerce	Mixed
Mr Teasely Taitt	PS Min of Health	Afro-Trinidadian
Mr George H. Legall	PS Min of Petroleum	Afro-Trinidadian
Mr Lennard Farfan	PS Min of Works	Mixed
Mr Joseph Herrera	PS Min of Agriculture	Mixed
Mr George A. Phillip	PS Min of Education & Culture	Afro-Trinidadian
Mr Edward Braithwaite	PS Min of West Indian Affairs	Afro-Trinidadian
Mr Ulmot Pierre	PS Min of Local Government	Afro-Trinidadian
Mr Frank Barsotti	PS Min of Planning & Development	Mixed
Mr Eugenio Moore	Economic Advisor to the Prime Minister	Afro-Tobagonian
Mr Isidore C. Rampersad	Advisor in the Prime Minister's Office on Community Development	Indo-Trinidadian
Mr Wilfred Mc Kell	Director of Personnel Administration	Afro-Tobagonian
Mr Ovid O. Fernandes	Special Advisor to the Minister of Petroleum	Afro-Trinidadian

Sources: Personal interviews with ex-Ministers and civil servants, field notes, 1992.

Complementing this group were some older civil servants fitting the 1960s prototype who continued to hold critical positions in the 1970s. Notable examples are: G.A. Brown, Governor of the Bank of Jamaica; Sir Egerton Rudolph Richardson, Permanent Secretary of the Ministry of the Public Service and head of the Permanent Secretaries Association; Oscar Gordon Wells, Permanent Secretary in the Office of the Prime Minister (1975–79); Gladstone Bonnick, the Director of the National Planning Agency; and Horace Barber, Financial Secretary. With the exception of Richardson, these men were central to economic policy formulation in Jamaica during the 1970s. A closer look at their profile reveals a strong link with the colonial past 'in the service of the Crown,' to borrow a phrase from Gladstone Mills.

The distinction between the new entrants and the old colonial civil servants is important for exploring the shared socioeconomic and ethnic factors of top bureaucrats and those with an interest in change in the 1970s. While the older career civil servants shared with Jamaica's compradorial business class a common alma mater (Jamaica College and Calabar High School), membership in Lodges, and a British tertiary education, the new entrants, especially those in the parastatals, shared the UWI experience with radicals from the New World Group. They also shared an assertive black identity with indigenous entrepreneurs (The Gleaner Publishing Company 1990; Levy 1973, 1979; Nunes 1990; and personal interview with the Permanent Secretary of the Ministry of the Public Service, May 1992).

In the case of T&T, the biographical profile of top bureaucrats that follows is based largely on personal interviews due to an absence of published data on such officers. The uppermost echelon of public officials within the civil service of T&T were almost all male and, with a few exceptions (notably the two Rampersad bothers and Mr Frank Barsotti), were largely comprised of Trinidadians and Tobagonians of African descent. Table 5.3 lists the top civil servants for the year 1975 and their ethnic origin.

Unlike the top bureaucrats of the 1960s, who had made a quick exit to the private sector by the mid-1970s, this group had fewer years of experience in the civil service and was also younger. In the main, they came from urban working-class families and had not attended prestigious schools such as St Mary's College. In contrast, schools such as Queens Royal, College Osmans' High, and Modern Academy were their alma mater. Many of them had also obtained first and second degrees while in the civil service as part of an in-service training programme.

The experience of the Permanent Secretary of the Ministry of Petroleum and Mines at the time is somewhat typical of this group. He joined the civil service (Treasury Dept) in 1946 after 'doing well' at Modern Academy. He came from an urban, black working-class family (his father was a tailor in the Police Service) and by 1975 rose to the level of Permanent Secretary of the country's most prestigious Ministry (personal interviews, January 1992).

That this group was almost all black Afro-Trinidadian and Afro-Tobagonian (Victor Bruce, Governor of the Central Bank, and Eugenio Moore and Dodridge Alleyne, both Permanent Secretaries) was indicative of the fact that civil service employment was the highest aspiration of blacks in the 1940s and 1950s. With the exodus of the white and Chinese bureaucrats of the 1950s, the lower-ranking black civil servants were poised to fill vacancies at the top. This group of senior black civil servants of the 1970s was also sympathetic to the nationalist philosophy of the Peoples' National Movement. Because black civil servants in the pre-independence era could aspire to no higher rank than Chief Clerk, the new group was also fundamentally anti-colonial in its orientation.

Although a new breed of public servants assumed leadership of parastatals in the 1970s, the old civil servants continued to play an important role. The new breed of public servants consisted largely of returnees from North America. They had migrated in the not-so-good-days of the 1950s and 1960s in search of a better life. They qualified in technical disciplines such as planning and engineering, mainly at Howard University and University of Toronto (personal interviews with managers at the Public Transport Service Corporation, Trinidad and Tobago Telephone Company, the Water and Sewerage Authority, and the Agricultural Development Bank, July 1992). In the 1970s, they were relatively young (approximately 36 years old), black, male and took their political point of reference from the black power ideology of North American blacks. Thus, in T&T, both returnees and career civil servants in the 1970s seemed to share a common nationalist ideology with the PNM. To the extent that returnees in the parastatals, civil servants, politicians and indigenous entrepreneurs were all predominantly black suggests that bureaucrats would be favourably disposed to economic nationalism that sought to create a class of local black business men and women.

In summary, the 1970s saw changes in the bureaucracy in both Jamaica and T&T. There was an infusion of new blood in both countries; nationals returning from abroad in the case of T&T, and in Jamaica, new recruits from the University of the West Indies. In T&T, bureaucrats seemed to share greater socio-economic and ethnic factors with those interested in change, while in Jamaica the persistence of career civil servants from the pre-independence era introduced an element of reservation to change. Now onto the examination of whether the actions of these bureaucrats supported or opposed economic change.

Bureaucratic actions: Support or opposition to change?

Studies on democratic socialist experiments in Jamaica in the 1970s have noted the conflict that ensued between senior bureaucrats on the one hand, and on the other hand, the Manley government, its cadre of radical economists from the University of the West Indies, and grass-roots beneficiaries of change programmes (Bartilow 1986, Crichlow 1988, Henry-Wilson 1985, Kaufman 1985, Lee 1988, Stephens & Stephens 1986). These studies present an intricate picture of conflict arising more as a reaction to Manley's attempt to politicize the bureaucracy than as a result of the content of the change policies *per se*. In turn, Manley's attempt to politicize the bureaucracy is also explained as a reaction to the slow pace of change in the first years of the government.

In order to modernize the civil service, a new Ministry of the Public Service was established in 1973 and an Administrative Staff College was established in 1976. Furthermore, in the early years of his administration, Manley also tried to reform the structures and functions of key agencies in the economic policy-making network. These agencies included the National Planning Agency, the Office of the Prime Minister, the Office of the Finance Secretary, the Ministry of Finance, and the Central Bank.

Because these experiments failed to yield the desired results, and because change continued at a snail's pace, in the mid-1970s Manley introduced a new parallel structure of special advisors into the Jamaican bureaucracy. These were handpicked cadres of politically committed and competent functionaries from the business community and the University of the West Indies, who were installed in strategic decision-making centres.

Concurrently, Manley also elaborated a new and more political role for bureaucrats of all levels, consistent with the principles of democratic socialism. In his various addresses to the Civil Service Association in the 1970s, the new role was revealed. For example, in his 1976 address to the Civil Service Association, he crystallized his new thinking thus:

> The very word 'neutral' connotes the idea of the car whose gear is in neutral, that is 'cautious to commit.' It is a negative concept and Third World countries cannot survive the neutrality of their citizens. If a Third World country is to have a hope of survival, the first challenge is not that of this loftiness of neutrality, but the earthly ground-based reality of commitment. ... But, the problem is, how to be committed

without ever crossing the line of your professional integrity as a civil servant. (Manley's address to the Civil Service Association, quoted in Mills 1977: 227)

An unintended consequence of Manley's attempts to reform and politicize the bureaucracy in the interest of change was the reassertion of professionalism, and a closer adherence to systems and procedures. It is against this background that the Association of Permanent Secretaries was formed and the actions of top civil servants were now construed as foot-dragging and deliberate sabotage. Moreover, the public service became polarized between a minority who accepted the new philosophy of commitment and a large majority who asserted professional standards. An example of the former position is the commitment of the Jamaica Industrial Development Corporation's management to economic nationalism and diversification (personal interview, senior JIDC manager, May 1992). The latter point will be discussed further in the case study that follows.

For the majority of bureaucrats who were cautious about the new changes, the final straw came in 1977 with the creation of a Ministry of Mobilization and Human Resources, and with Manley's attempt in January of 1977 to install sympathizers on the Civil Service Commission.

The new Ministry of Mobilization encroached on the planning functions of established structures such as the National Planning Agency, the Ministry of Finance, the Ministry of Labour, and the Central Bank. Unlike these agencies, however, its *raison d'être* was planning through mass mobilization and mass participation. The new Ministry also institutionalized the role of University of the West Indies radicals in economic policy formulation. The resignations of Arthur Brown as the Governor of Jamaica's Central Bank and Gladstone Bonnick as Director of Planning were attributed to the activities of this Ministry.

Thus, by the end of the Manley era the bureaucracy was polarized between those who supported the government's economic change programme (usually younger career bureaucrats and new political appointees in strategic decision-making agencies) and those who opposed it because of the PNP's modus operandi of politicizing the bureaucracy. The latter were invariably the older career civil servants.

The experience of bureaucrats in T&T during the 1970s differs from the Jamaican case. In T&T, Williams' relationship with the top bureaucrats worsened in the early 1970s. Despite the fact that Williams and top bureaucrats belonged to an elite group of educated black professionals, he remained suspicious of their role in the transformation process upon which T&T had embarked. Moreover, the Prime Minister's 1977 budget speech summed up the frustration and impatience of the PNM government encumbered by a bureaucracy unable to keep pace with the government's radical diversification and economic nationalism policies.

Unlike Manley in Jamaica, however, Williams did not attempt to win commitment for the new change policies by politicizing the public service. Rather, Williams effectively excluded bureaucrats from the transformation process of the 1970s by centralizing decision-making power in the hands of an elite team over which he presided. The team included, among others, University of the West Indies Professor Ken Gordon; Eldon Warner, General Manager of the Industrial Development Corporation; George Legall, Permanent Secretary in the Ministry of Petroleum; and Frank Barsotti, Permanent Secretary in the Ministry of Planning and Development. The elaborate system of multiple and interlocking directorships in which these officers were involved reinforced centralization in T&T.

Thus, George Legall, Permanent Secretary of the Ministry of Petroleum, was also a member of the following boards in the 1970s: the Trinidad & Tobago National Petroleum Marketing Company, the Trinidad-Tesoro Petroleum Company, and the Fertilisers of Trinidad and Tobago Ltd. Frank Barsotti, Permanent Secretary of the Ministry of Planning and Development, was Chairman of the Board of four parastatals: T&T Export Credit Insurance Company, T&T Development Finance Company, Caroni Ltd, and Forres Park Ltd; he was also a board member of the Orange Grove National Company. Eldon Warner, General Manager of the Industrial Development Corporation, was also a board member of five parastatals, vice-chairman of the Trinidad Bagasse Products Ltd and Chairman of the Management Development Centre. Appendix A5 provides a selected list of public servants on parastatal boards as at 1978.

However, it was University Professor and 'super technocrat' Ken Julien who epitomized the interlocking directorships and centralization of decision-making. Julien was Chairman of the Trinidad and Tobago Electricity Commission, the National Advisory Council, the National Energy Corporation, the Industrial Development Corporation, the Iron and Steel Corporation of T&T, Fertrin, Trinidad and Tobago Electronics, and the Co-ordinating Task Force. In response to a question on Julien's directorship in the House of Representatives from the Member of Parliament Hector McClean, the Minister of Petroleum and Mines at the time justified Julien's multiple roles with the comment that 'the challenges of our economic development required the multiple use of our best brains' (*Express* 6/5/1978, *Guardian* 7/5/1978).

To complete his centralization effort, Williams moved to exclude other senior bureaucrats through his well-known tactic of 'exile.' This was a Machiavellian strategy which those close to him saw as characteristic of his 'make or break' leadership style (Mahabir 1975). What exile effectively meant was exclusion by demotion, banishment, reassignment, being kicked upstairs, retirement, or worst of all, retention with no responsibility, duties, or communication from the Prime Minister—in short, being put in the corridor of the Ministry with a desk, a writing-pad and a pen.

In the historic civil service 'shake-up' of November 1975, Mr Frank Rampersad, former Permanent Secretary in the Ministry of Finance, was relieved of his job, sent on 18 months leave, and later kicked upstairs to the Commonwealth Secretariat. Other civil servants who suffered a worse fate included Dodderidge Alleyne, former Permanent Secretary to the Prime Minister, the officer around whom the drama of the 'small ambitious minority' revolved, and Eugenio Moore, former Permanent Secretary in the Ministry of Planning and Development. They were both demoted and assigned lesser portfolios without any real responsibility. Mr Harold Leacock and Mr Leo Nanton, former Permanent Secretaries in the Ministry of Education and Culture and Ministry of West Indian Affairs, respectively, were retired. Isidore C. Rampersad, brother of Permanent Secretary Frank Rampersand and former Permanent Secretary in the Ministry of Local Government, was assigned to the Prime Minister's Office in an unspecified capacity dealing with the administration of Community Development. Finally, Ovid O. Fernandes, former acting Permanent Secretary in the Ministry of Petroleum and Mines, was replaced by Mr George Legall and demoted to the post of special adviser to the new Minister (*Express* 2/12/1975).

By the end of the 1970s, the question of bureaucratic politics in support of the PNM's economic change programme was a redundant one. While Jamaica's economic change programme was characterized by politicization to foster commitment, in T&T centralization and alienation were the hallmark of the diversification programme of the

1970s. These findings both challenge and qualify the bureaucratic politics explanation. The challenge comes from the finding that shared interests with politicians and beneficiaries is not necessarily a sufficient condition for favourable disposition to change. In other words, bureaucratic support for change policies does not rest on commonalities with beneficiaries of change—rather, support has to be engineered through politicization. The more broad-based and inclusionary the politicization strategy, the greater the association with change. The more centralized and elitist the bureaucratic change team, the lesser the association with change.

PART II:
Economic Change and the Industrial Development Corporation: Micro-level Associations

IDCs, *the goals of economic change and their realization*

What were the goals of the Jamaica and T&T IDCs in the decade of economic change, and to what extent were they realized? In the 1970s, the JIDC occupied a central position in Manley's economic change policy. The JIDC was expected to contribute to diversification by developing and supporting labour-intensive resource-based industrialization, particularly in the agricultural sector. In this regard, a small business division of the JIDC was established in 1972. Disbursements to the JIDC also increased from an average of US$3 million in the 1960s to US$8 million in Manley's first year in office. Of this sum, a substantial proportion was to be spent on research and development for displacement of imported processed food items (Financial Statement and Annual Report for 1973, JIDC). Although the foreign exchange crisis which engulfed Jamaica in the later years of the Manley government resulted in falling revenues to the JIDC, the Corporation was still charged with the responsibility of developing replacements for products which the country could no long afford to import. Even the Emergency Production Plan of 1977 envisioned a key role for the JIDC in a new resource-based industrialization strategy. On this occasion, however, the emphasis was to be put on export promotion. Throughout the 1970s, the JIDC's role in economic nationalism was also underscored by the Manley government (JIDC Annual Reports 1973, 1974).

Similarly, the Trinidad and Tobago IDC was expected to contribute to economic change by supporting resource-based light manufacturing. However, outputs were intended for the export market rather than for import displacement. The year 1970 was designated Small Business Year, which the IDC was responsible for organizing. Following the success of the Small Business Year, and based on the recommendations of a 1969 Cabinet-appointed Small Business Development Committee, the PNM government entrusted the IDC with the permanent responsibility for resource-based industrialization through small business. Thus the new resource-based thrust of the IDC in the 1970s was to be implemented through a small-business development scheme in which priority would be given to the domestic sector. This was in keeping with the government's new foreign investment policy which discouraged foreign ownership of productive enterprises in T&T (MacDonald 1986). The 1969–73 Development Plan (GOTT Third Five Year Plan 1969–73, 1968) therefore charged the IDC with the responsibility to 'formulate and implement a programme for small local industry development.' The Plan went further to prescribe that the programme include 'a package of technical, management and marketing assistance and the provision of finance.'

The Chairman of the IDC Board, Mr Bernard Primus, summed up the IDC's policy thrust for the 1970s in this way:

> We have put the emphasis on the Trinidad investor. Our promotional effort is directed to nationals at home and abroad. We go out of our way to help nationals abroad who have certain types of experiences to come back. ... We also have, as you know, the small business section. (*Guardian* 7/9/1975)

The Small Business Loans Division of the IDC was created in 1970. It would subsequently dominate the T&TIDC's activities throughout the decade.

In addition, the T&TIDC was also expected to play a pivotal role in formulating the government's heavy resource-based industrialization policy. In this regard, IDC's General Manager was incorporated into the nerve centres of industrial policy-making. Accordingly, the new Economic Studies and Planning Division was called upon to undertake wide-ranging feasibility studies to promote the use of local materials in heavy industrialization.

The question of the relative performance of the Jamaica and T&T IDCs in realizing the goals of the 1970s can be best explored in terms of the efficacy of the respective small-business programmes in contributing to resource-based diversification. This, however, requires close scrutiny of the outputs of IDC-supported small businesses to determine whether or not they were contributing to diversification. Poor and sporadic reporting of JIDC in the 1970s makes this task extremely difficult. To the extent that Annual Reports and Financial Statements exist for this period, no separate data were presented on the outputs of small businesses supported by the JIDC. For example, under the heading 'Small Business Division,' the 1976/77 Annual Report merely stated that 'a total of 644 projects were identified, of these 218 were completed, with a total capital investment of [J]$3,682,432 and generating direct employment of 1,308' (JIDC Annual Report 1977: 31). This situation existed despite the fact that the IDC was obliged to report on categories of loan disbursements following a US$7 million World Bank Loan for Small Scale Enterprise Development in 1977.

Because of such difficulties, the question of IDC realization of economic change goals will be assessed in the area in which there has been greatest reporting in the two Corporations—majority-owned IDC subsidiaries. Table 5.4 lists IDC subsidiaries according to whether their contribution to resource-based industrialization has been 'high,' 'moderate,' 'low' or 'not at all.' However, a further problem exists since the Governing Act of the T&TIDC did not specifically recognize a holding company function for the Corporation despite the fact that it had performed such a function since its inception. Indeed, it was not until 1978 that the T&TIDC was assigned special 'supervisory responsibility' on behalf of the Corporation Sole (the Minister of Finance) for majority public-owned industries funded or directly created by the Corporation by Cabinet decision (*Record of Major Achievements of the IDC 1959 to 1981*, T&TIDC 1981: 19). Thus Table 5.4 captures both subsidiaries officially recognized in the 1978 Cabinet decision and *de facto* subsidiaries funded, managed and/or supervised by the T&TIDC throughout the 1970s.

Table 5.4 suggests that subsidiaries of the Jamaica Industrial Development Corporation made a greater contribution to resource-based industrialization than the subsidiaries of the T&TIDC. While the majority of T&TIDC subsidiaries in the 1970s were in hotel development, in Jamaica subsidiaries supported agro-industrial undertakings. Moreover, when these findings are read in conjunction with available data on the small business loan scheme in the T&TIDC, the position of the JIDC appears even more favourable. The Scotland Committee Report (T&TIDC 1985: 22) revealed that of the 3,146 small business loans issued between 1970 and 1984, less than one-third (1,004) went towards manufacturing enterprises. The majority of loans went towards services (1,469), while 673 were loans categorized as 'other,' the latter largely consisting of loans for hotels and guesthouses.

Table 5.4   *IDC subsidiaries in the 1970s and contribution to resource-based industrialization*

Contribution	JIDC Subsidiary	T&TIDC Subsidiary
High	Jamaica Frozen Foods Hanover Spices Ltd Southern Processors Ltd Jamaica Jute Industries Ltd Agriunabo Textiles Ltd Food Technology Institute Toolmakers Institute National Cassava National Tool and Die Ltd Darliston Community Foods Cornwall Dairy	Metal Industries Company Ltd Trinidad Bagasse Products Ltd Universal Metal Company Ltd
Low	Kingston Dry Dock	
None	Hague Apparels Ltd Cotton Polyester Ltd Fashion Knits Jamaica Ltd Industrial Building and Properties Ltd	Cowboy Jack Hideaway Farrell House 1979 Hotel Ltd Allied Innkeepers of T&T (Hilton Hotel) Caribbean Hotel Development Company Ltd (Crown Reef Hotel) Sea Island Development Company Ltd (Chagacabana Hotel) Inter Caribbean Hotels Ltd Trincity Garment Manufacturing Company Ltd T&T Electronics Ltd

Sources: Annual Reports and Financial Statements of the Jamaica and T&T Industrial Development Corporations 1969–79.

On the basis of such evidence, it can be concluded that the JIDC had a better experience at realizing the goal of resource-based industrialization. Was goal realization also associated with decentralization of structure, greater participation of beneficiaries, and greater bureaucratic politics in support of change policies? These questions are explored below.

IDCs, economic change and decentralization

The inquiry which follows compares the extent to which decision-making authority was vested in divisions of the two IDCs by the political centre, i.e., the responsible Ministry and other supervisory bodies. In this regard, the boards of directors are also defined as a division of the Corporation and not as part of the political centre. Table 5.5 suggests greater decentralization of decision-making authority by the political centre to divisions of the Jamaica IDC. This was aided by the existence of a JIDC executive management board with a long-standing tradition of autonomy from central government based on a proven track record (see Chapter 4). The fact that JIDC divisions also had the authority to make decisions within their sphere of control is indicative of two things—the autonomy of the JIDC management from the political centre, and the internal management style that predominated in the 1970s. In this period, when the JIDC was an instrument of the PNP's economic change policies, the Corporation's management climate was shaped by the new philosophy of democratic socialism and bureaucratic commitment.

The JIDC's management was also very much involved in the search for alternatives to the IMF (personal interview with JIDC executive manager, May 1992). Against this background, divisions were given the latitude to experiment, create and manage the industrial aspects of socialist transformation effectively. Thus the JIDC's Planning Division contributed significantly to the manufacturing section of the 1977 Emergency Production Plan. Because the JIDC's commitment was not questioned by central government, divisional heads in JIDC Institutes, subsidiaries, and the Productivity and Industrial Services Division were vested with the necessary authority to identify, develop and implement new resource-based manufacturing projects (personal interviews with former head of the Productivity and Industrial Services Division, May 1992). This was the case despite the fact that private-sector representatives dominated the JIDC board in the 1970s.

Table 5.5   Decentralization of decision-making authority in the Jamaica and T&T IDCs, 1970s

JIDC		T&TIDC	
Division	Decision-making authority	Division	Decision-making authority
Board of directors	Delegation of authority in specific areas of policy formulation, devolution in implementation	Board of directors	Non-executive board, limited delegation, Ministry has final say on policy and implementation decisions
Office of the General Manager	Delegation of decision-making authority		
Planning & Research	Devolution of authority, e.g., formulate industrial policy in Emergency Production Plan	Economic Studies & Planning Division	Limited delegation in the area of project identification, however vetted by Ministry
Productivity & Industrial Services	Devolution of authority to formulate and implement policies & programmes	Industrial Liaison & Extension	Devolution in ares of implementation, policy formulated by Ministry
		Industrial Promotions Division	Delegation of decision-making authority

(Continued)

Table 5.5   *(continued)*

JIDC		T&TIDC	
Division	Decision-making authority	Division	Decision-making authority
Property & Engineering	Devolution in areas of implementation	Industrial Estates Division	Devolution in site identification, building and maintenance
Finance	Functions closely supervised by GM and board	Financing	No decentralization, close supervision by Ministry, board and GM
Public Relations	Functions closely supervised by GM and board	Secretariat	No decentralization, even decisions related to legal opinions made by GM and vetted by Ministry
Small Business Division	Limited deconcentration	Small Business Division	No decentralization, Ministry reserves right to approve loans
Personnel	Functions closely supervised by GM and board	Personnel	No decentralization, Ministry and SASC has final decisions
Subsidiaries	Devolution of decision making in production targets and mode of production	Subsidiaries	Deconcentration, with close monitoring by Ministry
		Productivity Centre	Delegation of authority in formulation and implementation

Sources: Personal interviews; the Annual Reports of the JIDC and the T&TIDC for the years 1970 to 1979; JIDC 30th Anniversary Gleaner Supplement 24/11/1980.

Private-sector board members were selected because of loyalty to the PNP, their belief in Manley and sympathy for the aims of democratic socialism. This peculiarly Jamaican phenomenon perhaps explains the anomaly of William Albert Easton, then-Director of the Jamaica Manufacturers Association, simultaneously serving as Executive Director and Deputy Chairman of the JIDC's board throughout the height of democratic socialism (1976–79).

In contrast, during the 1970s, decision making in the T&TIDC fell under the exclusive control of the political centre. This was largely due to the political nature of the Small Business Loans portfolio which then dominated the Corporation's activities. While the T&TIDC could recommend approval or rejection of loan applications, the final decision lay with the Ministry of Industry and Commerce or, perhaps better said, with the Minister of Industry and Commerce. It was not until the mid-1980s that the Corporation's management finally won the right to approve small business loans (T&TIDC Scotland Committee Report 1985). Thus, by the late 1970s, the deployment of staff at the Ministry greatly matched staff distribution at the IDC. Within the Ministry, economists, clerks, and administrative officers were hired to monitor and supervise the work of the IDC's various departments. Not surprisingly, IDC staff members were incensed by such a high degree of political control. Personal interviews with IDC functionaries from the 1970s reveals that officers were especially disappointed that the General Manager at the time, who was thought to be on good terms with the PNM, failed to use his office to win greater internal decision-making powers for the Corporation.

The evidence above paints a picture of different internal management styles within the two IDCs, different organizational/ central government relations, and different climates of economic change. The fact that JIDC divisions had greater authority to make decisions was due to its long-standing autonomy from the Ministry of Industry, the mood of democratic socialism with which the JIDC staff was infected, and the internal management style of JIDC executive management. In this case, greater goal realization was associated with greater decentralization.

IDCs, economic change and beneficiary participation

To what extent were representatives of indigenous entrepreneur associations (small business, credit unions, and co-operatives) incorporated into decision-making divisions of the two IDCs? With regard to the

JIDC, it is important to recall that this organization subscribed to the new participatory management ethos of democratic socialism. The JIDC therefore actively encouraged representation of indigenous entrepreneurs in its subsidiaries and institutes. Thus the President of the Small Business Association of Jamaica at the time, Adolph Brown, was appointed as Chairman of Industrial Building Properties Ltd, a JIDC subsidiary. This was a strategic appointment since this was a subsidiary that owned, leased and managed factory spaces and industrial estates. Brown's presence was expected to facilitate small businesses gaining access to such accommodation.

In addition, craftsmen's guilds were incorporated in the formulation of the training programme in the JIDC's Toolmakers Institute, and in the late-1970s the Technology Institute worked together with farmers associations in Community Enterprise Organizations to develop cassava-processing projects. Most significant, however, was the role of farmer community organizations in these JIDC agro-industry subsidiaries: Cornwall Dairy Development Company, Southern Processors Ltd, Hanover Spices Ltd, National Cassava Products, and Darliston Community Foods Ltd. In some cases, farmers associations were incorporated into the boards of these subsidiaries. Moreover, through the many growing pains that dogged these projects, farmers were involved in decision making related to production targets, processing techniques and marketing of the final product (JIDC Annual Reports, and personal interview with a JIDC board member of 1976–77, June 1992).

In contrast, the evidence from T&T reveals only one short-lived and somewhat cosmetic experiment of incorporating representation of indigenous entrepreneurs in the 1970s. In 1970, a Small Business Council was established within the IDC as a parallel body to the Corporation's non-executive board. The Council had an advisory function in matters related to small business; the Ministry still retained the final decision-making authority. Throughout its lifetime, the Council was headed by IDC board member and trade unionist Mr Gaston Benjamin. It also included three representatives from small business, a representative of the Trinidad Co-operative Bank, a representative from the Credit Union Bank, the secretary of the Trade Union Congress, a nominee of the Ministry for Tobago Affairs, and three members of the IDC (*Guardian* 31/05/1970). In 1978, however, the Council was abolished, and the IDC's board regained direct control of small business.

How successful were these two different experiments in ensuring effective participation for representatives of indigenous entrepreneurs? This is a difficult question, since personal interviews with representatives on the Cornwall Dairy Board in Jamaica and the Small Business Council in T&T reveal that these individuals were equally convinced that participation in the Corporation's decision-making structures secured benefits for small business. An important difference lies in the actual ability of representatives in the Jamaica and the T&T Corporations to make or influence decisions. In T&T, the tight reign over the IDC by central government meant that the Council was a mere formality while the Ministry exercised real decision-making power. Moreover, the fact that no small business association existed in T&T in the 1970s meant that so-called representatives on the Council were not truly representative. The charge has also been made that the small-business representative on the Council, Mrs Eileen Douglas, used her position to secure personal favours for her business ventures in garments (personal interview, former manager, Small Business Division, September 1992). When this situation is contrasted to the JIDC, with its decentralized decision-making and with farmers and small-business representatives on subsidiary boards, the conclusion of greater participation in Jamaica does seem to be apparent, and the association between goal realization and participation seems to be sustained.

IDCs, economic change and bureaucratic politics

The questions to be addressed in this section are, firstly, who were the bureaucrats in the JIDC and the T&TIDC during the 1970s? Secondly, to what extent did they share common interests with beneficiaries of economic change, and did they support or oppose the economic-change role of the IDC? To begin with the JIDC, a close look at the top-most bureaucrats in the 1970s reveals two distinct groups: older career administrative officers, or 'generalists' with ten or more years of service in the JIDC, and younger specialists, officers who were recruited in the 1970s to fill positions at the helm of the JIDC's technical units and subsidiaries.

The older 'generalists' included: Mr A. Lloyd Johnson, Personnel and Administrative Manager; Mr Carrol C. da Costa, Executive Director of the JIDC; Donald Evans, Research and Development Manager of the Food and Technology Institute; Mr Bertie Morris, Director of Training; and Roy Anderson and Lloyd Standing, Directors of Training. Five of these eight officers attended prestigious Jamaican colleges, and all were male, began their careers in the civil service, and were exposed to foreign training at some point in their civil service careers (personal interviews and personnel records of the JIDC).

The younger 'specialists' included: Fitzgerald Guthrie, Manager of the Toolmakers Institute; Donna Marsh, of the Toolmakers Institute; Normal Hislop, Manager of the Repairs and Maintenance Demonstration Unit; Errol Stephenson, General Manager of the National Tool & Die Company; and Charles French, Production Manager of the National Tool & Die Company. Most of these officers joined the JIDC during the 1970s. They all attended the University of the West Indies or the College of Arts, Science and Technology, had technical degrees or diplomas, were in their thirties, were almost all black, and, with one exception, almost all male (personal interviews and personnel records of the JIDC). Younger specialists shared with beneficiaries of change a working-class or peasant background, the same ethnic group, and a criticism of Jamaica's industrialization model of the 1960s.

In Trinidad and Tobago during the 1970s, one man held the reigns of power at the IDC. *At this time Eldon Warner was the T&TIDC, and the T&TIDC was Eldon Warner.* Warner was seconded from the civil service to the T&TIDC as Deputy General Manager in 1966, in preparation for the IDC's reorganization prescribed in the Third Five-Year Development Plan. He was also General Manager of the T&TIDC for a total of 16 years (1967–83). During this time, Warner personified the Corporation, and his presence on numerous government policy-making bodies was widely accepted as IDC participation. As well as being Chief Executive Officer of the IDC, Warner was Chairman of the Board of the Management Development Centre, and a board member of eight other state companies.

Warner's position as the undisputed head of the IDC was reinforced by the fact that, when compared to the Jamaican Corporation, the T&TIDC had fewer departments and fewer divisional heads to whom decision-making power was devolved. Because of Warner's central place in the IDC throughout the 1970s, the question of shared interests is best answered by closer examination of his background.

Warner was born in 1929, attended one of the top schools in Trinidad, St Mary's College. In 1949, he joined the civil service as a second-class clerk in the Colonial Secretariat. Warner was one of the early beneficiaries of the civil service training programme. Between 1951 and 1954, he read a BA in Politics Philosophy and Economics at St John's College, Oxford. In 1954, he was returned to the Colonial Secretariat, where he was promoted to Administrative Cadet. Between 1957–58, he served as a trainee economist with the IMF in Washington, and in 1958 he received an MA in Economics at Oxford University. Between 1970 and 1972, he studied a MSc in Management at the Massachusetts Institute of Technology. Between 1957 and 1961, Warner worked closely with Prime Minister Eric Williams as Economist in the Office of the Premier (1957–60) and Senior Economist in the Economic Planning Division of the Premier's Office (1960–61). In 1962 he was handpicked to act as Director of Finance & Economics in the Ministry of Finance, and in 1964, he was again handpicked to be Director of Personnel Administration. In 1966, he became Deputy General Manager of the T&TIDC (Curriculum Vitae of Mr Eldon Warner, T&TIDC 1978).

The appointment of Eldon Warner heralded a new era in the economic development of T&T. For the first time in the history of the IDC, the organization had a black General Manager. Warner's predecessor was David Weintraub, a Jewish-American of Austrian birth. Although Weintraub came 'strongly recommended to the Government of Trinidad & Tobago by Professor Arthur Lewis' (*Guardian* 11/6/1961) his appointment caused the government much embarrassment as the Opposition Democratic Labour Party made political capital of the fact that Weintraub, having been questioned by the McCarthy Committee of Un-American Activities, was branded a 'Communist' in the United States.

Warner's appointment was complemented by several other appointments: the first black Minister of Industry, Mr Overand R. Padmore; the first black Permanent Secretary in Ministry of Industry, Mr Edward Braithwaite; and the first black IDC Chairman of the Board, Mr Bernard V. Primus. Primus was a controversial figure who 'appeared as counsel for labour in several major disputes before [the] Industrial Court' (*Guardian* 23/3/1969). He was branded a 'rebel,' and in 1961 had been dismissed from the post of Research Economist in the IDC (*Guardian* 1/3/1969). By these appointments, the PNM sought to 'blacken' industry, the traditional bastion of whites, in an attempt to stave off the cries for 'Black Power' erupting on the streets of T&T. Furthermore, the PNM also warned manufacturers against discriminatory employment practices (*Express* 20/3/1970).

Warner was from a middle-class background. He was known to be sympathetic to the PNM's economic nationalism policy and, in some circles in the business community, he was viewed as a 'hot-headed radical' (personal interview with business representative, July 1992). Indeed, one of his first major decisions as General Manager in 1968 brought him into direct conflict with Shell Trinidad. Warner turned down Shell's application for pioneer concessions to undertake hardboard manufacturing. In a public statement in the *Sunday Guardian* of 17 June 1968, he condemned Shell for not acting in the national interest, citing as proof Shell's poor performance in plastics and furfural ventures. Not surprisingly, he was considered public enemy number one by Shell and other multinational corporations operating in Trinidad (*Guardian* 17/6/68).

To what extent did the specialists in Jamaica and Eldon Warner in T&T support the economic change policies of their respective IDCs? In the case of the specialists in Jamaica, personal interviews reveal that this group was favourably disposed to, and therefore supported, the Corporation's goals of economic change under Manley. The fact that they were young, black and largely politicized by the events of the 1960s, coupled with the JIDC's high profile and important role under Manley, have been offered to explain their commitment (personal interview with a former manager of JIDC, May 1992).

In the case of Eldon Warner in T&T, the evidence also suggests commitment to the government's programme of economic change. Warner was described in an interview by a close colleague as 'a natural PNMite. … He was pro-black and anti-colonial' (personal interview, ex-board member T&TIDC, September 1992). The same person was quick to point out that it was no accident that Warner became 'the blue-eyed boy' of the PNM and Prime Minister Eric Williams, since he mirrored the inherent contradictions of the party and the maximum leader. An ex-board member puts it this way: 'Warner was black, from humblish beginnings, appeared to be acting in the interest of black people, yet he was Oxford-educated and as close to the Trinidadian working classes as was the Mayor of Oxford' (personal interview, ex-board member T&TIDC, September 1992). The term 'Afro-Saxons' has been coined to describe the Warner factor in the political sociology of Trinidad and Tobago. The point, however, is that despite Warner's personal class contradictions, the evidence suggests that he supported the PNM's change goals for the IDC because of subjective factors. In short, there was evidence of bureaucratic politics.

The essential difference between Warner in T&T and the specialists in Jamaica was the centralization of power. It was in the hands of one man in the case of the former, and dispersed in the case of the latter. Similar to findings at the macro level, this difference suggests associations between broad-based politicization and greater change, and between centralized bureaucratic politics and lesser change.

General Conclusions

This chapter applied the change component of the framework of association at the macro level of the public sector, and at the micro level of the IDCs of Jamaica and T&T. The organizational variable—decentralization—was seen to be strongly associated with goal realization at both the macro and micro levels. Jamaica was characterized by more decentralized structures of economic decision-making in association with greater goal realization. T&T was characterized by centralized economic decision-making in association with lower goal realization. Similarly, the JIDC internal divisions enjoyed greater decision-making autonomy than the T&TIDC, and the JIDC also had greater success at realizing the goal of economic change in the 1970s.

The association between the policy environmental variable—participation—and goal realization established in development administration also seems to have been sustained, albeit with some qualification. While there was greater incorporation of University radicals and indigenous entrepreneurs into structures of economic policy formulation in Jamaica, the level of organization of the private sector also played a role in securing representation in decision-making structures. Moreover, at the macro and micro levels, participation was more broad-based in Jamaica than in T&T.

The association between the political environment variable—bureaucratic politics—and goal realization was only sustained with qualifications. Firstly, it was shown that shared interest is not sufficient for bureaucratic support for change goals. Secondly, it was broad-based bureaucratic politics caused by politicisation, rather than by bureaucratic politics *per se*, that was associated with goal realization. This was the case at both macro and micro levels.

Education, Social Change for Women and the Ministries of Education in Jamaica and Trinidad & Tobago

6

Introduction

The case study of the Ministries of Education is based on the assumption that educational attainment is a route to occupational mobility and women's occupational mobility is a good indicator of social change. Following from this assumption, the decision-making structures of the Ministries, the participation of women's interest associations in education policy formulation, and the subjective disposition of bureaucrats towards women's advancement through education become important focal points in explaining differences in social change between women in Jamaica and T&T, and between African and Indian women in T&T. Because the 1970s were the only period in which social change for women was adopted and pursued as government policy in the two countries, associations are explored mainly in this period. However, the fact that the governments in Kingston and Port-of-Spain indirectly addressed the condition of women through the education reforms of the 1960s, and that tacit endorsement was given to the goal of social change for women in the 1980s, also invites some analysis of these periods.

PART I:
Education Policy and Ministries of Education: The Setting

This discussion traces the evolution of education policy and the role of the Ministries of Education in Jamaica and T&T over the decades of the 1960s, 1970s and 1980s. It is important to set the backdrop for this discussion by recalling that, in the struggle for political independence, nationalists in both Jamaica and T&T identified education as a means of redressing class-based inequalities. Consequently, the creation of the Ministry of Education became a symbol of the new order and an expression of anti-colonialism.

Indeed, when the T&T Ministry of Education was created in June 1959 with the advent of the Cabinet/ministerial system of government, it was greeted with great hostility by its predecessor, the Department of Education. Because the Department of Education refused to wither away, in the transitory period, its staff, offices and even policies continued to exist, albeit separate from the new Ministry (interview with the Director of Planning, Ministry of Education, August 1992). One reason for the reluctance of the old functionaries to relinquish power was the importance of the Department of Education in the early 1950s under the stewardship of Roy Joseph. As part of the social development reform in the colonies during the 1950s, the Department of Education was allocated the largest share of expenditures for the three consecutive years preceding self-government in 1956 (GOTT Estimates of Revenue and Expenditure for the Year 1955, The colony of Trinidad & Tobago). Indeed, Campbell notes that 'one estimate from the Colonial Secretary was that about 20,000 new school places had been made available in the five years between 1950 and 1956' (1992: 62).

In Jamaica, the colonial Department of Education became the Ministry of Education in 1953 as a result of constitutional reforms that established a ministerial system. Compared to T&T, however, the transition seemed far less acrimonious. Indeed, after the initial grandiloquence associated with the Ministry's creation, the modus vivendi of the old colonial Department of Education permeated and soon dominated the new Ministry under a conservative PNP government.

By 1965, however, Education Acts were passed in both countries setting out the *raison d'être* of the new Ministry of Education. Under the respective Acts, the power of the Ministry was defined as coterminous to that of the Minister. Thus the respective Acts charged the Ministry of Education with the formulation, implementation and management of education. For example, Section 3, Act 8 of the Jamaican Education Act of 1965 defined the powers of the Minister/Ministry as follows:

a. To promote the education of the people of Jamaica and the progressive development of institutions devoted to that purpose;
b. To frame an educational policy designed to provide a varied and comprehensive educational service in Jamaica;
c. To secure the effective execution of the educational policy of the Government of Jamaica, and
d. To establish a co-ordinated educational system organised in accordance with the provisions of this Act. (GOJ Act No 8 1965: 1)

Under the PNM government in T&T, the Ministry of Education's staff, structure and scope of activities expanded dramatically in the 1960s as it set about formulating and implementing the 1968–83 education plan. The goal of the plan was to guarantee general education for all children up to age 14 in two stages, the Primary followed by Junior Secondary. The plan also aimed to eliminate the dreaded 11-plus examination, since all pupils would be guaranteed at least three years of free Junior Secondary education. The PNM's proposal was considered radical and incurred the anger of vested interests in education.

Because the goals of the Jamaican Ministry of Education under the JLP (1962–72) were less ambitious, the structure and size of the organization remained relatively unchanged. The 1966 New Deal for Education set out the government's education policy and, together with the Education Act of 1965, determined the role of the Ministry. Unlike the PNM in T&T, education policy in Jamaica of the 1960s aimed merely at devising a somewhat more democratic system for allowing entrance into the secondary school system; no promise was made of free education. To fulfil these modest objectives, a 1966 World Bank loan provided for the establishment of 50 junior secondary schools, four teacher-training colleges, the expansion of the College of Arts Science and Technology (CAST) and the Jamaica school of agriculture and the construction of 128 primary schools.

Despite these initiatives, adult education and the supervision of private schools remained outside the purview of the Ministry of Education in Jamaica. The Ministry's structure also remained relatively undifferentiated while its counterpart in T&T developed specialized structures for primary, secondary and post-primary school supervision. In addition, expenditure on education in Jamaica during the years 1960 to 1965 stood at 2.9 per cent of GDP, compared to 3.4 per cent for its counterpart in T&T (Finlay 1984: 122). Finlay concludes that: 'By the end of the decade of the sixties, developments [in education] were still minimal except in some specific areas' (1984: 46).

The 1970s were a period of fundamental change for both Jamaica and T&T. In Jamaica, the PNP government increased education expenditure to 5.4 per cent of GDP at current prices; the figure for T&T stood at 3.4 per cent. Manley's goals in education were contained the Ministry's policy paper, *The Education Thrust of the 1970s* (MOE 1972), and in subsequent policy statements. The net effect of the reforms of the 1970s was tantamount to free education from elementary to tertiary level. Consequently, the Organisation and Methods Division of the Ministry of Finance was asked to advise on the organizational development of the Ministry.

In T&T, the Ministry of Education also underwent significant organizational reform with an expanded role. The 1975 Prime Minister's proposals on education effectively set a new goal for education—the provision of free primary and secondary school education up to the fifth form. Although educational expenditures in GDP at current prices declined in the 1970s, this must be seen in the context of the oil boom during which total expenditure increased dramatically, and government expenditure on physical infrastructure and petroleum-related activities dwarfed all other categories of public-sector expenditure. The Ministry of Education establishment grew from 265 in 1963 to 16,819 in 1980 (GOTT Estimates of Expenditure, 1981).

To quote Miller (1989: 214), the 1980s were a period of 'retrenchment and reversals' in the Jamaican education system. Despite substantial cuts in education expenditure, the Ministry remained responsible for formulating policy and managing the system. Indeed, the Ministry's goals were reaffirmed in the amendment to the Education Act (Education Regulations of January 1981). Enabling the Ministry to undertake its tasks became the subject of a World Bank-sponsored administrative reform project. Under the Education Programme Preparation and Student Loan Project (World Bank IV), three studies were conducted on the Ministry of Education. In addition, in November 1989, a USAID-sponsored Primary Education Assistance Project (PEAP) was also conducted. Enhanced decentralization was one of the major objectives of these studies. Despite the fact that the Ministry's Regional Offices were closed in 1986, throughout the 1980s it was called upon to experiment with appropriated decentralized structures to achieve its goals in the face of limited resources.

Three factors dominated the education scene in T&T during the 1980s: skewed allocation of public finance in education, two new education plans, and the 1986 change in government. Despite falling revenues from the petroleum sector in the 1980s, approximately 12 per cent of total capital expenditures for the period 1983–86 was spent on education (GOTT Draft Development Plan 1983–86, Imperatives of Adjustment, Vol. II). While education represented the third highest area of public capital expenditure after state enterprises and housing, 70 per cent of this sum went into completing the Mt. Hope medical complex, a status project of the late Prime Minister; primary, secondary and teacher education were left significantly underfunded.

The 1985–90 Education Plan was formulated under the PNM government, and the 1989–92 Framework for the Education Plan was formulated under the new NAR government. The 1985–90 plan emphasized technical and vocational education. Coming in the wake of the 1984 report on technical vocational education and training in senior comprehensive schools, the plan also stressed curricular reform, the management of the school system, and educational facilities management in particular. Though formulated by the PNM, this plan was implemented under the NAR government. Accordingly, aspects of the plan were stressed or de-emphasized in keeping with the NAR's own philosophy on education. The Ministry of Education's Status Report on the Implementation of the 1985–90 Education Plan (MOE 1988) lists the changes made under the NAR.

The 1989–90 Framework established the parameters and goals for the Ministry in the interregnum between the end of the 1985 plan and the impending general election. The document stated that:

> The aim of our education plan is to develop citizens with the following: (i) the intellectual, moral and emotional capability to respond adequately and productively to the various challenges of life in a multi-racial, developing country and the changes which are being brought about rapidly in the economic foundations of civilization, particularly the challenges of science and technology. (Framework for an Education Plan 1989–92, MOE 1988: 3)

A more localized education policy planning and implementation structure was stressed for implementing these objectives.

The fall in government revenues associated with the NAR years in government made educational management at the Ministry of Education increasingly difficult. Ministry officials were continuously called upon to explore modalities of the government's cost-cutting proposals (personal interviews, August 1992). Consequently, the removal of the book and uniform grant by the NAR government in 1988 necessitated structural and functional internal adjustments within the Ministry. The proposal for an 'education surcharge' required extensive data collection on short notice, and the controversy surrounding the Minister's proposal to print textbooks locally (Annamunthado 1988) also demanded the attention of the Ministry's officials. The net result of these and other imaginative cost-cutting proposals of the NAR government was a reactive rather than a proactive Ministry.

Education and social change: The context of the inquiry

The battle between conservative forces wishing to maintain dualism, church-sponsored education and elitism in education, and progressive forces advocating secularism, democratization and equality of opportunity is a persistent theme in education research in Jamaica. Hence choices in education policy formulation and the manner in which education was administrated came to be interpreted in terms of the gains or losses for either side in this struggle.

This battle has its roots in the British Government's neglect of social welfare in the colonies; it was left to religious institutions to fill this gap. These religious institutions, of course, had their own hidden agenda, which ranged from maintenance of the status quo in the case of Catholic education, to challenging the status quo with regard to Hindus and, to a lesser extent, Muslims in T&T.

The battle between state and religious organizations in Jamaica was of much lower intensity than that which raged in T&T. Finlay suggests that this was so because 'many church leaders in Jamaica welcomed the handing over of schools to direct Government control since though they have been unquestionably the pioneers in all aspects of education, and notwithstanding the importance they attached to it, education was never the church's primary concern' (1984: 179). He contrasts the Jamaican situation to the 'unpleasant confrontations' that took place in T&T. Finlay's explanation, though incisive, merely touches on superficial differences between Jamaica and T&T. A more compelling explanation of the intensity of the church-state battle over education in T&T lies with the heterogeneous nature of the society, hence the PNM's multi-front battle with the Hindu, Anglican and Catholic churches. A second reason is, of course, the nationalism and anti-colonialism of the PNM and especially of Williams. For these reasons, changes in education policy formulation and administration were less conflict-ridden in Jamaica than in T&T. This context must be kept in mind when exploring associations between educational attainment for women in Jamaica and Indian women in T&T, and the specified attributes of the Ministry of Education.

PART II:

Educational Attainment for Women in Jamaica and Trinidad & Tobago, and Attributes of the Ministry of Education

Decentralization, the Ministry of Education and education policy formulation

In the development administration literature, the saliency of decentralization is premised on the assumption that vesting decision-making authority away from the political centre facilitates beneficiary participation and, therefore, change (see Chapter 3). In this study, the Ministry of Education, the Cabinet, and the Office of the Prime Minister are seen to constitute the political centre. Given this perspective, the question of decentralization is essentially one of the willingness of the centre to entrust decision-making authority to agencies, both governmental and nongovernmental, in the policy-making process. The fact that women in Jamaica experienced greater educational attainment between the 1960s and the 1980s suggests that there was also greater decentralization of decision-making authority from the political centre in Jamaica. This association is explored by mapping the network of organizations involved in education policy formulation in both countries, and by assessing the degree to which actual decision-making power was vested in structures not located at the centre. Three degrees of authority can be vested by the political centre: *devolution*, the highest stage of decentralization, followed by *delegation* and *deconcentration*. Table 6.1 presents the data on the relative degrees of decentralization in education policy formulation in Jamaica and T&T for the 1960s, 1970s and 1980s. The table shows that education policy formulation was consistently made at the centre in both Jamaica and T&T during the 1960s, the 1970s and the 1980s. Thus in the three periods, the Office of the Prime Minister, the Cabinet and the Ministry of Education were the sites for policy formulation. However, with regard to Jamaica, the table also shows that the centralization tendency was countered by an equally significant trend towards decentralization. Thus in Jamaica the authority to formulate aspects of education policy was vested in:

1. International development agencies in the 1960s and 1980s,
2. the Jamaica Teachers Association in the 1970s, and
3. Boards of Governors in all three periods (the 1960s, 1970s and 1980s).

With the exception of the 1980s, no such decentralizing tendency existed in T&T. Consequently, education policy formulation was more decentralized in Jamaica than in T&T.

Various factors explain why the tendency towards centralization was countered by decentralization in Jamaica. In the 1960s, centralization of decision making in the hands of then-Minister of Education Edwin Allen was largely a result of the personality and leadership style of the Minister (Nunes, undated). Centralization was also a reflection of historical processes beginning in the early 20th century and culminating with the creation of Ministry of Education in 1963 (Finlay 1984).

On the other hand, critical decisions on the direction of education were devolved to international development agencies because of the need for external funding (MOE Education Sector Survey 1977: 1). In addition to these loans there was a USAID technical assistance grant for Junior Secondary teacher training and curricular development to support the first World Bank loan of US$9.5 million. Because the JLP's education policy of the 1960s did not aim at ambitious reforms, it was left to international organizations such as the USAID to introduce a radical component into Jamaica's education policy.

Under the Manley government of the 1970s, the influence of international agencies on education policy formulation waned. However, the 1980s saw a reassertion of the power of international development agencies in education policy formulation. This was despite the fact that decision making was highly centralized under the Seaga government of the 1980s. Where decisions on education had cost implications, the

Table 6.1   *Decentralization of education policy formulation structures in Jamaica and T&T, 1960–90*

STRUCTURE & DEGREE OF AUTHORITY DECENTRALIZED	
Jamaica	Trinidad & Tobago
1960s	
Political Centre: Ministry of Education Office of Prime Minister & Cabinet (formulated policy)	
Education planning committee (advisory)	
Social Development Commission (advisory)	
Education and School Boards (delegation of authority to formulate aspects of policy)	
International development agencies (devolution of authority to formulate policy)	
Jamaica Teachers Association (influence)	
National Council on Education (advisory)	
Education Advisory Council (advisory)	

(Continued)

Seaga government was happy to devolve decision-making authority to international development agencies.

During this time, however, international agencies were more interested in funding 'projects' in education than they were in 'policies.' Whether or not projects were supported by an overarching policy framework became incidental. The following projects should be viewed against this background: the OAS's project on curriculum development, the USAID's family life education project, and the UNDP's pre-vocational studies project for grades 7–9 (MOE Annual Report of the Ministry of Education 1984–85). In the 1980s, central government devolved authority to formulate and fund decisions relating to projects in education. By the end of the 1980s, the Seaga government tried to remedy the disastrous effects of a decade without an education policy. Because the government could do no better than a feeble education programme within the Social Well-Being Programme, the 1980s effectively marked an end to education policy formulation.

Table 6.1   (continued)

STRUCTURE & DEGREE OF AUTHORITY DECENTRALIZED	
Jamaica	Trinidad & Tobago
1970s	
Political Centre: Office of Prime Minister, Ministry of Education & Cabinet (formulated policy)	Political Centre: Office of Prime Minister, Ministry of Education & Cabinet (formulated policy)
Regional offices of the Ministry (deconcentration of policy formulation authority, monitoring)	*Ad hoc* consultative bodies (advisory)
National Literacy board, Office of the PM, (delegated authority to formulate adult literacy policy 1972-4)	Ministry for Tobago (deconcentrated specific areas of policy formulation)
Jamaica Association for Advancement of Literacy (delegated authority to formulate and implement policy 1974-9)	National Institute for Higher Education (NIHERST) (advisory)
Social Planning Division of the National Planning Agency (monitor and advise)	Denominational school boards (some influence over policy formulation)
Education Advisory Council (advisory)	National Advisory Council (advisory)
Social Development Commission (advisory & implement adult literacy programme)	University (advisory)
Boards of Governors (devolution of areas of policy formulation)	Teachers associations (influenced policy)
Peoples National Party Women's Movement (PNPWM) (influenced policy formulation)	
International development agencies (delegated authority to formulate aspects of education policy)	
Jamaica Teachers Association (delegated authority to formulate policy)	

(Continued)

Table 6.1 *(continued)*

STRUCTURE & DEGREE OF AUTHORITY DECENTRALIZED	
Jamaica	Trinidad & Tobago
1980s	
Political Centre: Office of Prime Minister, Ministry of Education & Cabinet (formulated policy)	Political Centre: Cabinet, Ministry of Education & Office of Prime Minister, George Cambers 1981-86 and ANR Robinson 1986-91 (formulated policy)
International development agencies (devolution of authority to formulate policy)	Ministry of Education (policymaking)
Boards of Governors (delegated authority to formulate aspects of policy)	Tobago House of Assembly (influenced policy)
Teachers associations (Influence policy)	Women's League of the PNM (influenced policy)
Joint board of teacher education (delegated authority to formulate aspects of teacher education)	Denominational school boards (substantial influence over policy formulation)
	International development agencies (influenced policy)
	Ad hoc consultative bodies (advised on specific aspects of policy)
	University of the West Indies (advised on specific aspects of policy)
	Teachers associations (advised on policy)
	Servol (devolved authority to formulate aspects of policy)
	National Advisory committee (advised on policy)

Sources: Annual Reports of the Ministry of Education; National Plans; Annual Budget Speeches; personal interviews and Estimates of Expenditure for Jamaica and Trinidad & Tobago.

With regard to the second manifestation of decentralization, the Jamaica Teachers Association, it must be noted that this was a feature of the 1970s despite Manley's increasing centralization of education policy formulation into the Office of Prime Minister. Prior to the 1970s, teachers associations in Jamaica merely influenced education policy formulation from the outside. In the 1970s, the JTA's role expanded from simply influencing decisions in education to actual participation in formulation. It can be argued that Manley vested decision-making authority in the JTA as repayment for the union's support of the party while it was in political opposition throughout the 1960s.

Consequently, when the Prime Minister became disappointed with the slow pace of education reform in 1973, it was the JTA to which he turned to find an educator with a good track record as a manager to fill the post of Permanent Secretary in the Ministry of Education. The JTA recommended three names, one being then-Principal of Mico Teachers College Dr Errol Miller. Miller was accepted by the PNP government, and under his short but eventful tenure as Permanent Secretary (1973–74) almost all of the PNP's education reforms were implemented.

A second example of the JTA's role in policy formulation during the 1970s was the publication of the 1973 Handbook of School Management. The handbook was effectively a policy document on the role and functions of boards, principals and staff members in the school system. It was the result of a collaborative effort between the Ministry of Education and the JTA. The JTA was proud to claim that the union was given much latitude in finalizing the contents of this document (personal interview with JTA's President, June 1992).

As regards the decentralizing effect of Boards of Management, this feature of the Jamaican system was observed throughout the 1960s, 1970s, and 1980s. Finlay observes that:

> Jamaica has traditionally tended towards a very highly centralised form of government with powers of legislation covering as much as possible of the nation's and people's concerns. The Ministry of Education's administrative developments and current operations illustrate this trend. But structurally, there has also always been provision for decentralisation of authority. Hence ... supervision of schools by School Boards. (Finlay 1984: 181)

The Education Act and Education Code of 1965, the 1973 Handbook of School Management, and the 1980 Education Act designated the areas in which Boards had authority, and categorised the nature of their authority in terms of advice or decision making.

Throughout all three decades Parish/Education and Local/School Boards were delegated the authority to make decisions mainly in the following areas: appointments of principal and staff and termination/suspension of any member of staff, expenditure of grants, disciplinary matters, and controlling the use of school premises (Boich et al., MOE 1990: 5–29). However, in practice, real delegation of decision making was often threatened by the penchant of Board Chairpersons and Principals to centralize power into their own hands and take decisions in concert with politicians. The evidence presented in Table 6.1 suggests a persistent and significant trend towards decentralization of education policy formulation in Jamaica.

The table also shows that, in contrast, policy formulation in T&T was solidly centralized into the hands of the Prime Minister, Dr Eric Williams, during the 1960s and 1970s. During this time, all other structures, including international development agencies, had an advisory, implementation or influencing role. However, the 1980s saw a significant change to this state of affairs; for the first time, central government formally devolved decision-making authority to a nongovernmental agency, Service Volunteered for All (Servol).

Due to Williams' indelible stamp on education policy formulation in T&T, the following digression is necessary. Williams' interest in education stemmed from his experience as an educator, having served as Professor at Howard University in the 1940s. Moreover, as a nationalist, Williams was greatly troubled by the colonial structure and content of the education system. His education policies were first published in 1956 in the First Five-Year Development Plan 1958–62, subtitled the 'People's Charter for Economic and Social Development.' Between this time and December 1986, when the PNM eventually lost power, the Party's policy on education was further clarified in:

- the Cabinet Proposals on Education 1960
- the Second (1964–68) and Third (1969–73) Five Year Development Plans
- the 1965 Education Act
- the 1967–83 Draft Plan for Educational Development
- the Prime Minister's Proposals to Cabinet on Education 1975 and
- the Prime Minister's Further Proposals on Education 1975

Nation-building, social mobility and human resource development were the main goals of the education system contained in these documents. Secularism and equality of opportunity were the underlying philosophical tenets.

The fact that these goals remained consistent throughout the 1960s and 1970s is testimony to the undisputed centralization of education policy formulation in the hands of Dr Williams. Whereas Williams' control over education policy formulation was more covert in the period prior to 1975, Williams literally took over the education portfolio from the Minister of Education (the Hon. Carlton Gomes) in that year, and the *Prime Minister's Proposals on Education* (MOE 1975) became government's policy (personal interviews with ex-officials of the Ministry of Education, September 1992).

Indeed, Williams' hold over education policy formulation appeared to be so strong that, unlike Jamaica, international development agencies such as UNESCO and the World Bank exerted minimal influence. They were denied the opportunity to offer Trinidad & Tobago the philosophical and financial basis for education policies. Consequently, although UNESCO representatives took up office in the Ministry of Education between 1964 and 1966, influencing the 1964–68 Second Five-Year Plan and the 1967–83 Educational Development Plan, they remained critical of Williams' emphases in education and his heavy reliance on domestic sources of funding.

Interestingly, although at this time T&T was spending more on education than Jamaica, Jamaica was not criticized. Between 1960 to 1965, the T&T government spent an average of 3.4 per cent of its GDP on education, compared to Jamaica, which spent a mere 2.9 per cent for the same period (Finlay 1984: 122). Against this background, the UNESCO critique appears as a veiled search for influence and relevance.

Unlike international agencies, however, Denominational Boards mounted a successful challenge to Williams' control over the direction of education policy. Denominational educational bodies were key players in the education system of the Caribbean. At political independence, 13 denominational school boards dominated the education system in T&T. These were the Roman Catholic, Anglican, Presbyterian, Methodist, Moravian, Baptist, Sanatan Dharma Maha Sabha Hindu, Tackveeyatul Islamic Association, Kabir Panth Association, Arya Pratindhi Maha Sabha, Anjuman Sunnat Ul Jamaat, Trinidad Muslim League, and Seventh Day Adventists.

By 1960, denominational school boards owned and managed 355 schools compared to only 76 government schools. The Roman Catholic Church had the major share with 129 schools, followed by the Anglicans with 73 and the Hindus with 46 (CSO Digest of Statistics on Education 1967–68, 1970: 8–9). Williams's efforts to centralize education policy formulation were in fact a struggle to break the stranglehold of the denominational bodies, in particular the Catholic Church, on education.

In his struggle with the denominational boards, Williams gained the upper hand by appearing to compromise while still pursuing his agenda. More graphically, he took two steps forward and one step back (Campbell 1992:73). The fact that Williams often took a step backward for reasons of political expediency gave denominational bodies the impression that they had won a significant battle and retained control over their schools. This perception was both true and false. It was false in the sense that, Williams persisted in centralizing education policy formulation into his own hands, and refused to negotiate the goals of nation-building and human resource development for the education system. It was also true in the sense that, while Williams did not decentralize authority to denominational bodies, he granted them licence to make their own parallel policies—but on the condition that the state would only fund denominational boards if their 'policies' did not clash with those of the state.

State officials and denominational bodies were contained both by the political acumen of Williams and by the 1970s oil boom, which provided the material base to maintain a dual education system.

With Eric Williams' death in March 1981, the education policy of the new Chambers/PNM government fell under the influence of a widened cross-section of interests, including the PNM Women's League. In 1986, the PNM lost power after 30 years in office. Although the new NAR government paid lip-service to decentralization in education policy formulation, structures remained centralized, with the exception of devolution of decision making to Service Volunteered for All (Servol), a Catholic NGO, though the number of interests seeking to influence education increased even further. Hence the emergence of the Tobago House of Assembly, denominational boards and the Inter-American Development Bank as powerful actors capable of influencing education in the late 1980s.

Despite the centralization tendency in the Jamaican education system, the authority to formulate education policy and later education projects was decentralized to international development agencies in the 1960 and 1980s, to the Jamaica Teachers Association in the 1970s, and to Boards of Management throughout the entire 30-year period. In T&T, education policy formulation remained an activity of the centre. This was due largely to Eric Williams' influence over decision making in education and to his struggle with the denominational boards. The fact that the church and state in Jamaica reached an early compromise on the management of education (Finlay 1984) created the opportunity for a more decentralized system of decision making.

Because the struggle between church and state became a war of attrition in T&T, no such decentralized structures were developed; policy formulation remained centralized, and the ultimate prize became control over the centre. Stewart reaches a similar conclusion when she observed: 'Perhaps the word to describe the major changes in the school system proposed by the nationalists is "centralized," and herein lies the problem of denominational education in Trinidad' (1981: 192).

Women's interest associations and participation in education policy formulation

This discussion explores whether differences in educational attainment for women in Jamaica and T&T were associated with differences in the degree of participation of women's interest associations in education policy formulation. Before exploring this question, however, it is important to note that the principle of equality of opportunity which informed education reform in post-independence Jamaica and T&T effectively neutralized the potential action of women's associations in education. Moreover, to the extent that females took advantage of increased educational opportunities of the 1960s, by the 1970s women's educational attainment had improved and women's interest associations demonstrated little or no concern for this area. Consequently, while women's interest associations were present on education policy formulation bodies, their contributions seldom addressed questions of increased access for females or the curriculum's role in reinforcing the gender-based labour market segmentation that existed at political independence.

A second important point to note is that with the adoption of social change for women as government policy in Jamaica and T&T in the 1970s, powerful women's interest associations came to the fore. An interesting feature of this period was the roles played by the women's arms of the ruling political parties in Jamaica and T&T, and by women's interest units within the respective governments. While the very nature of their affiliation with the ruling political party questions their claim to be treated as 'interest associations' within the pluralist paradigm, their dominance, agitation and sometimes separate identity from the political party warrants their inclusion in this discussion.

Jamaica's powerful women's interest associations of the 1970s included the Peoples' National Party Women's Movement (PNPWM), the Committee for Women's Progress and the National Union for Democratic Teachers. The Women's Desk, and, after 1975, the Women's Bureau represented the institutionalized voice of women in public policy formulation. What were the concerns of these bodies in the 1970s, to what extent were they concerned with women's interests in education, and to what extent did they effectively institutionalize the voice of women in Jamaica's public policy formulation?

Assessments of the activities and achievements of these bodies in the 1970s (Blake 1984, Henry-Wilson 1989, Kaufman 1985) note victories in the areas of women's rights, income-generating projects and improvements in material conditions. No mention is made of achievements in the area of women's education. In the face of such silence, this research undertook a review of advocacies of these organizations reported in the *Gleaner* at the height of activities on woman power in Jamaica (1976–77). Here, too, the evidence suggests that they were primarily concerned with women's material conditions and their legal status; comparatively little attention was given to women's concerns in education. This is not surprising, since enrolment of female Jamaican students at the University of the West Indies almost equalled that of males by 1968, and by 1970, female enrolment was the highest for the English-speaking Caribbean (STATIN Statistical Yearbook of Jamaica, 1972–78).

However, to the extent that bodies such as the Women's Bureau and the PNPWM took up issues relating to women's legal and material conditions, the evidence suggests that they were proactive to the point of confronting the PNP establishment (Kaufman 1985). The evidence also suggests that they succeeded in raising the visibility of women in Jamaica and institutionalizing women's interests in Jamaica's policy formulation (Blake 1984, Henry-Wilson 1989). A comparison of the National Commission on the Status of Women in T&T and the Women's Bureau in Jamaica shows the former to have been temporary and ill-conceived, while the latter was a serious effort to institutionalize women's interests in public policy-making in Jamaica (Reddock 1988).

During the 1980s, however, the Women and Development Unit (WAND) of the University of the West Indies, and the Association of Women's Organizations in Jamaica have raised women's issues in education. Accordingly, WAND launched a regional effort with the aim of reversing institutionalized gender subordination in the Caribbean secondary schools curriculum. However, this effort has been hampered by the inherent logistic difficulties associated with regional cooperation ventures in the English-speaking Caribbean. Antrobus refers to the 'discouraging evidence of insularity … especially noticeable in those countries which command the greatest share of resources' (quoted in Yudelman 1987: 82). The effort has also been hampered by the persistence of the myth of gender equality in education. It is also too early to comment on the contribution of the Association of Women's Organisations to women's education in Jamaica during the 1980s, since this umbrella body was only established in 1988.

Similarly, in T&T, women's interest associations were also concerned with women's legal rights and economic conditions during the 1970s to the extent that they contributed to education policy, but their inputs were not informed by gender. The case of the Housewives' Association of T&T (HATT) demonstrates this point. HATT was perhaps the first working class women's association in the independence era of T&T. The association represented the interests of urban women of the working classes. Led by Hazell Brown, HATT in 1975 took up the issue of insufficient secondary school places for the children of T&T. However, despite its all female membership, at no point did HATT single out and identify the implications of limited access for the girls of the nation. Indeed, HATT inadvertently provided a platform for further undermining women in education by allowing Mr Osmond Downer, then president of the Secondary School Teachers' Association, to champion its cause. Downer was known for having publicly bemoaned the 'woman crisis in education.' He attributed the so-called crisis to 'too many female teachers' (*Express* 1/12/1976). Downer believed that: 'Boys like to feel that men should be in control, but in their schools women are dominant. In some schools even the principal and vice principal are women' (*Express* 1/12/1976).

However, the work of the Presbyterian church, Indian nationalist associations and the Federation of Women's Institutes constitute an important caveat to the general impression conveyed so far that women's interest associations were inactive in this area. In Part III which follows, the role of the Presbyterian Church and Indian nationalist associations in promoting Indian women's interests in education is discussed. For the moment, however, it is important to note that the Presbyterian Church and Indian nationalists influenced rather than participated in education policy formulation. It is also important to note that the ultimate aim of their actions was not to resolve a problem of gender but of racial inequality.

In 1977, Act No. 37 (the Federation of Women's Institutes Act of T&T) was passed to 'foster interest in and to ensure educational, cultural and civic development among the women of Trinidad & Tobago' (GOTT 1977). This act was essentially a paper tiger. The Federation was a loose and fluid association; with the exception of occasional statements in *ad hoc* education forums, it did not contribute to policy formulation in T&T. Indeed, the contribution of the Federation's representative, Margaret Brown, to the National Consultation on the 1985–90 Plan dealt largely with the special need of the handicapped in the education system; nothing was said about the problems of women (MOE Verbatim Reports of the National Consultation on the 1985–90 Education Plan, Ministry of Education 1985).

The 1980s were marked by a somewhat cosmetic attempt to institutionalize women's interests in public policy formulation through the ascendance of the Women's League of the PNM to power. In this period, the so-called 'kitchen cabinet' of the 1970s came into its own as four League members were allocated Ministerial portfolios, which included education. A review of the utterances and positions of 'kitchen cabinet' members contained in the press releases of the Ministry of Information, coupled with a review of the League's contribution to the 1985 National Consultation on Education, suggests that education for females was not addressed as a priority issue (Verbatim Report of the 1985–90 National Consultation on Education, Women's League contribution, MOE). Furthermore, during the 1980s, the National Commission, which also claimed to represent women's interests in T&T, merely took up issues of women's legal status. Even so, its temporary and *ad hoc* nature, located as it was within the Ministry of Labour with only one permanent support staff member, made it largely ineffective.

The findings suggest that questions of women's access to education, and gender bias in curriculum structure and content were not problematized nor addressed by women's interest associations in Jamaica and T&T. This was due to the principle of equality of opportunity that informed education reforms in the post-independence era. The fact that women enjoyed educational attainment despite the silence of interest associations can be attributed to the class-based principle of equality of opportunity informing education reforms. In a real sense, this finding is consistent with that of Bellew and King who conclude that:

> Intervention through programs targeted specifically to girls and women is neither the only nor necessarily the most cost-effective way by which a government can influence female education. Broad education policies matter. Even policies that seem entirely neutral with respect to gender can affect girls and boys differently. (1993: 319)

At first glance, these findings render the attribute 'beneficiary participation' incapable of explaining differences in educational attainment between women in Jamaica and T&T. However, the fact that women's interests figured more prominently in Jamaica and that women's interest associations were also institutionalized suggests that, while democratization is a sufficient condition for women's educational attainment, participation of interest associations, albeit in other areas affecting women, is a necessary condition. Against the background of this qualification, the participation variable does offer some explanation of differences in social change in the two countries.

Bureaucratic politics, male bureaucrats, female beneficiaries, and Ministries of Education

Since women's educational attainment in Jamaica and T&T was addressed within a wider problematic of democratization and underclass advancement, and since Jamaican women experienced more social change over the research period, an association is implied between social change in Jamaica and greater support of Jamaican Ministry of Education officials in favour of women's advancement. This has been termed bureaucratic politics. Because the 1970s were the high point of education reforms in Jamaica, the question of bureaucratic politics will be restricted to this era. Because the process of democratization commenced in T&T in the 1960s and culminated with the free education reforms of the 1970s, this discussion will span the 1960s and 1970s in T&T.

In a real sense, the education reforms in Jamaica of the 1970 were almost single-handedly implemented by the Permanent Secretary of the Ministry of Education at the time, Errol Miller. These reforms included the removal of the quota system for selection into the secondary school system, and its replacement with an open merit system based on performance. Reforms also included the conversion of the new Junior

Secondary Schools into five-year schools, and the introduction of free university education. The net result of such reforms is that public-sector expenditure as a percentage of GDP increased from 3.5 per cent in 1970 to 5.9 per cent in 1975. For the same period, public sector expenditure on education in T&T was in fact on the decline, from 3.9 per cent in 1970 to 3.1 per cent in 1975. So phenomenal was the expenditure commitment to education that, in 1974, the Ministry of Education was allocated and spent the largest public-sector disbursement (at current prices) of any Ministry in the independent history of Jamaica. Against this background, the question of the politics of public bureaucrats will be discussed in terms of the subjective disposition of the Ministry official who almost single-handedly implemented these reforms, Permanent Secretary Errol Miller.

The attribute 'bureaucratic politics' suggests that for the reforms of the early 1970s to have impacted so favourably on women, the implementor of the reforms, Permanent Secretary Errol Miller, was either committed to women's advancement, or to the PNP party which piloted these policies, or both. That is to say, he was not neutral. Indeed, the very fact that Miller was a political appointee and not a career civil servant implies an affirmative answer to the latter suggestion.

However, interviews with senior career civil servants in the Ministry of Education who served with Miller in the early 1970s, and with Miller himself, paint a more complex picture. Interviews reveal that Miller saw himself as an 'executive manager undertaking specific task-work' to implement education reform policies in the shortest time frame and with the least possible cost. After this task was completed he expected to return to his more substantive post as Principal of Mico Teachers' Training College. Having the luxury of not being a career civil servant, Miller flouted procurement and expenditure procedures and came into conflict with the Financial Secretary and the Civil Service Commission. Furthermore, Miller also came into conflict with the Prime Minister because of Manley's penchant for formulating and announcing new education policies before exploring their modalities with the administrative cadre of the Ministry. Miller recalls many such disagreements with the Prime Minister in 1974. He remembers disagreeing with Prime Minister Manley but being 'man enough' to speak his mind. He also recalls that after a 'man-to-man talk,' he and Manley reached a compromise resulting in mutual respect from both parties (personal interview with Errol Miller, June 1992).

Thus the evidence suggests that, though a political appointee, Miller's commitment was matched by his competence. Interviews with 1970s functionaries at the Ministry of Education found that while Errol Miller was resented for being a political appointee at the start of his career with the Ministry, he was considered at his departure to be more neutral than the previous Permanent Secretary. What follows is an account of a story cited by almost all of the Ministry officials who were interviewed. Miller's predecessor at the Ministry is said to have allowed then-Minister of Education Mr F. Glasspole to humiliate the Chief Education Officer by stripping him of his responsibilities and exiling him to a corridor of the Ministry for personal and political reasons. On becoming Permanent Secretary Errol Miller cleverly ended the CEO's exile by creating a new post of Education Planner in charge of Development. When asked about his motive behind this decision, Miller said:

> To treat one civil servant in that way is going to have everybody feeling insecure, whereas if I can show them that I have restored this man to a respectable job, and I had the capacity to do that, then I can motivate everyone to work and I did that against tremendous political opposition. (Personal interview with Errol Miller, June 1992)

The question of whether or not Miller's actions in piloting the reforms of the 1970s were based on a subjective commitment to social change for women remains to be explored. A useful starting point for exploring this question is Miller's 1969 PhD thesis entitled *Self-concept of Girls in Relationship to Physical and Social Intellectual Variables*. This thesis established Miller as having gender interests. It is one of the earliest works with a gender focus by a male scholar in the Caribbean social sciences. Despite his gender focus, however, Miller seemed unaware of the emerging 'gender bias' in education in the 1970s. This was largely because the reforms sought to redress class rather than gender inequalities, an objective to which Miller admitted being committed (personal interview, June 1992).

By the late 1970s, however, it became clear that women were taking advantage of increased education opportunities in Jamaica. By the late 1980s, this trend became an established pattern in which females markedly outperformed males. Although Miller was no longer Permanent Secretary by the 1980s, the impact of the 1970s education reforms on women was not lost on him. Consequently, Miller recognized that females were outperforming males in the education system, and as an

Independent Senator, he moved a motion to redress the imbalance in favour of males. The motion read as follows:

> Whereas there is an equal number of boys and girls in the primary school population ages 6–12, and whereas currently there is a wide disparity between the number of boys and girls entering high schools: Be it resolved that an equal number of places be provided each year for boys and girls. (Quoted in Miller 1990: 361)

Miller's motion was hotly debated in the Parliament and drew the ire of individuals, feminists and other associations within Jamaican society. Indeed, political scientist and newspaper columnist Carl Stone dismissed Miller's contentions as 'rubbish' (Stone 1989: 93), and John Haughton, General Secretary of the National Union of Democratic Teachers, accused him of 'advancing male chauvinist views under the guise of scientific investigation' (quoted in Miller 1990: 363). Therefore, while Permanent Secretary Errol Miller can take no direct credit for the educational advancement of Jamaican women, it can nonetheless be argued that the politicization of the Ministry of Education by Miller's appointment created the opportunities from which Jamaican females benefited.

With regard to Trinidad & Tobago, bureaucratic politics suggests that women's educational attainment was less significant either because Ministry of Education officials were less disposed to their advancement, or because they failed to support the education policies of the PNM. Previously, we noted the division between the traditionalists wishing to maintain elitism and dualism in education and the PNM wishing to widen access to education. A further point to note about traditionalists is that they were invariably men whose worldview was consistent with gender subordination through education.

In T&T, traditionalists occupied senior posts in the T&T Ministry of Education in the 1960s and during the period of the PNM's 'radical' programme of education reform in the 1970s. Perhaps the most important 'traditionalist' was Dr Charles Vernon Gocking. In 1961, Dr Gocking, a Queens Royal College (QRC) and Oxford University graduate, was handpicked by Eric Williams, also a graduate of QRC and Oxford University, to be Chief Education Officer (CEO) of the Ministry of Education. As the first local CEO, Gocking's appointment was initially heartily welcomed. However, it soon became apparent that Gocking represented the traditionalists in the T&T education system as he vehemently opposed Williams' readiness to open up the system (personal interview with Ministry officials, August 1992). When QRC graduate and Gocking's former student, Dr Ralph Romain, was appointed Permanent Secretary of the Ministry of Education, the Gocking-Romain team was said to have deliberately obstructed the over-ambitious policies of Williams and Minister of Education at the time, Donald Pierre. Though Gocking was of mixed blood and Romain was of African ancestry, they were said to be united in their opposition to the PNM's plan to open up the system to the sons and daughters of African slaves and Indian indentured servants. The two were also said to be particularly opposed to Donald Pierre. Pierre was a black Trinidadian and a solicitor who never attended secondary school; he achieved his qualification through private studies. Pierre was also born on the wrong side of town—Port-of-Spain South (personal interviews with Ministry officials, August 1992).

Although Gocking left the Ministry in 1966, he continued to express reservations over the direction and pace of education reforms (*Express*, 29/07/1975). Gocking also continued to influence education policy formulation in his capacity as advisor to the Minister of Education. As late as 1980, Gocking, then 72 years old and as conservative as ever, was Special Adviser to the Minister of Education. In a newspaper article of 27 September 1981, Augustus Ramrekersingh, Minister of Education under the 1991 PNM government, drew attention to the traditionalist underpinnings of Gocking's thinking. Dr Ralph Romain, Gocking's protégé and 'little black boy' as Gocking is known to have sometimes referred to him fondly, also continued to serve as Permanent Secretary in the Ministry of Education in the heyday of 1970s reforms. Dr Romain was only removed in the early 1980s, and Gocking's brother temporarily became Permanent Secretary of the Ministry.

Consequently, while Jamaican education reforms of the 1970s were implemented by Errol Miller—a political appointee committed to redressing class inequalities through education reforms—in T&T traditionalists lacking confidence in the government's reforms were called upon to manage the system. Not surprisingly, traditionalists advised against the phenomenal increase in school places and against the merging of elite schools such as QRC with the new state-run Junior Secondary and Senior Comprehensive Schools. Traditionalists were also insensitive to any argument for special provisions to increase school places for females. Moreover, they failed to recognize institutionalized gender barriers in the education system. The fact that PNM did not politicize the education bureaucracy but continued to rely on traditionalists such as Dr Gocking is indicative of the strength of traditionalists, the complexity of the system characterized by religious/ethnic differences, and the class biases of its political leader.

Consequently, it can be concluded that higher educational attainment for Jamaican women was associated with greater bureaucratic politics. However, bureaucratic politics was due to politicisation, and it sought to redress class rather than gender inequalities. In T&T, the lower education attainment of women was associated with lesser commitment of bureaucrats to the PNM's attempts to open up the system and redress class inequalities. Taking these qualifications into consideration, an association between bureaucratic politics and social change can be derived.

PART III:
The Ministry of Education, and Social Change for Indian and African Women in Trinidad & Tobago

Introduction

Because the findings on occupational mobility and educational attainment for Indian and African women in rural areas were generally consistent with national-level findings, associations are explored at the national level. This section considers whether differences in the educational attainment of Indian and African women in T&T between the 1960s and 1980s were associated with decentralization of education policy formulation, beneficiary participation and bureaucratic politics on the part of Ministry of Education bureaucrats.

Decentralization of education policy formulation

Was the Ministry of Education more inclined to decentralize aspects of education policy formulation in the 1980s than in the 1960s? The findings in Part II suggest an affirmative answer to this question. In Part II, it was revealed that education policy formulation remained largely centralized in the 1960s and 1970s. However, two interesting changes were observed in the 1980s. First, aspects of education policy formulation were devolved to Service Volunteered for All (Servol). Second, the Tobago House of Assembly (THA), the Inter-American Development Bank (IDB) and Denominational Boards exercised great influence over education policy formulation. The devolution of policy formulation authority to Servol in the late 1980s suggests that the system was becoming decentralized. The impact of the rise of influencing structures such as denominational boards on policy formulation is not as clear.

During the NAR's term in office, Servol, an NGO run by the Catholic church and largely funded by the Bernard van Leer Foundation of the Netherlands, received the authority to take decisions in the areas of vocational and pre-school education. Servol was started in 1970 following the 'black power uprisings' by Father Gerald Pantin—brother of the Archbishop of Trinidad & Tobago, Anthony Pantin, and of Clive Pantin who would be the Minister of Education under the NAR (1986–89). Through its Life Centres, Servol offered vocational training to the youth of depressed inner city and rural areas (*Guardian* 7/7/1985). Servol also specialized in pre-school education. Under the PNM, the Ministry of Education's relationship with Servol oscillated between open hostility and a grudging coexistence. That the relationship was never a happy one is not surprising, since Ministry officials were especially incensed by what was perceived as unreasonable demands, and by the fact that Servol duplicated services already offered by the Ministry (personal interviews with Ministry officials, August 1992).

With the appointment of Clive Pantin as Minister of Education in 1986, Servol became the reference point for the NAR government in formulating its vocational and pre-school education policy. Moreover, Servol functionaries were formally incorporated into policy formulation units within the Ministry. They were also granted unsupervised autonomy to:

(i) Develop and implement a training programme for pre-school teachers; and

(ii) To formulate a new programme for the administration of pre-schools. (National consultation on the sectoral plans for education: Projected targets for the period 1989–92, MOE 1989)

Many in the T&T education system found Servol's new power to be unacceptable. Such sentiment brought the negative reaction of the Association of Village and Community Councils of Penal, which refused to co-operate with Servol (*Express* 12/12/1990). Despite resistance from such associations, Servol became a powerful actor in education policy formulation during the period of the NAR government. But did devolution of decision-making authority to Servol decentralize education policy formulation in T&T? The evidence would seem to suggest otherwise. This was because, under the NAR, Servol was incorporated by the centre and soon became indistinguishable from the Ministry *per se*, thus begging the question of decentralization.

As regards the implications of increasing influence of the Tobago House of Assembly (THA), the Inter-American Development Bank (IDB), and the denomination boards for decentralization in education policy formulation, it should be noted that these structures rose to prominence in the 1980s, following the death of Eric Williams in 1981. In a bid to win legitimacy, the new PNM/Chambers government adopted a consultative decision-making style. This decision-making style continued under the succeeding Robinson/NAR government of 1986.

In 1982, the Tobago House of Assembly set out its own education policies in the Tobago Development Plan of 1981–90. This plan called for a:

> Layer of post-secondary schools, which Tobago had always lacked: a Teachers College, a Technical College, and finally what looked like a degree granting institution, namely a College of Arts, Science and Technology, possibly in association with the University of the West Indies. The Plan also called for changes in the curriculum of the secondary and primary schools, mostly in the direction of technical and vocational education of a type thought most relevant to Tobago: fishing, boat building and tourism. (Campbell 1992: 115)

When THA head A.N.R. Robinson became Prime Minister in 1986, many believed that the Assembly would be granted authority to implement this plan. However, this was not to be. Not only did central government fail to grant the Tobago House of Assembly the necessary authority to implement aspects of its plan, the government also failed to vest the THA with authority to formulate national education policy. As far as education in the 1980s was concerned, the THA was effectively an arm of government that supervised the implementation of national education policy.

Moreover, interviews with education lobbyists in the Tobago House of Assembly showed that, despite the fact that A.N.R. Robinson was Prime Minister, there was an increasing feeling that the same traditional forces which favoured Trinidad over Tobago and urban over rural education remained entrenched in the Ministry of Education. THA education lobbyists confess that, under a PNM government, such a situation would have been met with open confrontation. However, under the

Robinson government, education lobbyists within the Assembly chose instead to influence education policy by making direct, though informal, approaches to the Prime Minister. The upshot of this decision was that the THA was able to secure increases in education expenditure for Tobago without being formally incorporated into the policy formulation centre. Thus influence reinforced centralization but yielded results.

In the matter of the denominational bodies, it is important to note that in the 1960s and 1970s most denominational bodies avoided attempts at co-optation into a more structured policy advisory role, and chose instead to influence policy formulation through heated debates and threats in the national media. The early 1980s witnessed the increasing influence of denominational boards over education policy formulation as the new PNM/Chambers government capitulated under the weight of open confrontation with the boards.

In this period, denominational boards were able to influence two important policy outcomes. Firstly, boards lobbied for and achieved a retroactive increase in the Ministry of Education grants to Assisted Secondary schools. The PNM government agreed to the following: a basic increase of 42 per cent backdated to 1 January 1978 for all items of expenditure, except ancillary staff and practical subjects which were provided for under separate items of expenditure; to provide a minimum of three watchmen per school; to refund the National Insurance commitment of the boards; and to introduce new payments for Technical Drawing, Art and Craft. Secondly, the Sanatan Dharma Maha Sabha (SDMS) won a victory by preventing the government from implementing its plan to take over assisted schools. The government's plans were contained in the 1981 Bruce Committee Report which recommended national ownership and joint management of all national schools.

In the closing years of the 1980s, the influence of school boards persisted. On this occasion, however, it was due to the change in government and the fact that the new Minister, Clive Pantin, was once an administrator in the school board system. As a school board system administrator, Pantin had often come into open conflict with the Ministry of Education under the PNM. As Minister, he experimented with institutional forms aimed at decentralizing education policy formulation. The School Board Report of 1987, which advocated increased power for the school boards, should be viewed against this background.

Thirdly, in the mid- to late-1980s the Inter-American Development Bank had a noticeable influence over education policy. The late-1980s was a period in which the NAR government experienced extreme revenue shortfalls. Not surprisingly, the government allowed the World Bank to set policy priorities in return for funding. Consequently, while the government's education policy emphasized developments through community colleges, the Inter-American Development Bank chose instead to problematize and fund primary education. Thus, for a total sum of US$55 million (GOTT Loan Contract Document, March 26, 1987: 5), the NAR's policy priorities were derailed. The Bank's programme aimed to 'improve the quality of primary education and, thereby, to provide a sound basis for attainment of universal secondary education of good quality' (GOTT Loan Contract Document, 26 March 1987: Annex A).

Because external actors such as the Inter-American Development Bank preferred to interact with a small group of government representatives, their influence in policy formulation produced a centralizing rather than a decentralizing effect.

In conclusion, the evidence presented above suggests that, while the devolution of decision-making authority to Servol centralized Ministry's policy formulation role, the increasing influence of powerful interests served to decentralize the system and reduce the power of the Ministry in the 1980s.

Indian women's interest associations and participation in education policy formulation

Part II of this chapter revealed that, throughout the research period, women's interest associations in Jamaica and T&T largely neglected women's issues in education. However, the case of Indian women in T&T proved to be an exception. It was noted that both the Presbyterian Church and Indian nationalist associations articulated Indian women's interests in education, and they sought to influence policy outcomes in this general direction. No similar associations existed for black women in T&T. The inquiry below explores the implied association between educational attainment and the participation of interest associations in education policy formulation.

The problem of low literacy levels among Indian women was first addressed by the wives of Canadian Presbyterian missionaries as part of a wider problem of low literacy levels among Indian indentured labour in T&T. Indeed, as late as 1921, only 62 out of every thousand Indian women were literate, while 179 out of every thousand Indian males (and 697 out of every thousand for other ethnic groups) were literate (Harewood 1974: 114). Harewood's research reveals that in the 1943–46 period, Indian women in Trinidad had the highest illiteracy rates among both males and females in the British West Indies; 66 per cent of all Indian females aged 10 years and over were illiterate; for the same period, only 37 per cent of Indian males aged 10 years and over were illiterate. In Barbados only 8 per cent of females were illiterate; in Jamaica 21 per cent of females were illiterate; and in British Guyana, also with a large Indian population, only 59 per cent of Indian females were illiterate.

An important point discerned from these works is that Indian women's education was strongly advocated by Presbyterians as part of a deliberate policy of training literate Indian women to either be the wives of mission teachers and Catechists, or to be future teachers themselves. In this regard, Hamel-Smith notes that 'Sarah Morton herself observed that of the 83 girls who had attended the Home she had established, 16 had married Catechists and all, except three, had married suitable men. The Canadian Mission clearly understood that to establish a self-perpetuating missionary outpost, conversion of women to Presbyterian norms of culture and family rearing was essential' (1984: 5). Since Canadian mission teachers were Presbyterians, this meant that Indian female teachers were expected to convert to the Presbyterian faith. In return, they were guaranteed liberation from the traditional roles of Indian women as agricultural labourers, wives and mothers, and entry into respectable employment. This is one reason why teachers' training colleges were attached to Presbyterian girls' colleges.

Dr Mahase gives some personal insights to this situation with the comment that her 'early education began in the Presbyterian School at a time when the options open to women were few; in fact most women were only able to be wives and homemakers. The girls in the Presbyterian system could become primary school teachers.

When it became clear that Indians were accepting Presbyterian education but resisting conversion (Samaroo 1983), the motive for Indian women's education in the independence era shifted from the provision of converted teachers to the production of an elite cadre of females for top positions in T&T. The fact that this cadre was almost all Indian is not surprising because of the Indian legacy of Presbyterian schools, their location in Indian catchment areas, and the fact that under the 1960 Concordat, school principals were free to select 20 per cent of their form-one admissions from the pass list. The cumulative effect of these factors was that, by 1992, six of the nine prominent Indian women to figure in the *Who's Who of T&T* were former pupils of the oldest Presbyterian girls' secondary school in Trinidad, Naparima college. None of the 54 non-Indian women also figuring in the *Who's Who of T&T* had attended a Presbyterian girls' college. The six Naparima college graduates were: Gladys Gafoor, lawyer and judge; Valere Laila, psychologist and high commissioner; Radhica Saith, business executive and wife of the Acting Prime Minister in 1992; Dr Patricia Mohammed, sociologist and women's activist; Dr Anna Mahase, educator and school principal; and Her Excellency Aalayhar Hassanali, teacher and the wife of the President of the Republic of Trinidad & Tobago.

The history of Presbyterian involvement in education in Trinidad has been inextricably linked with mobilization, advocacy and organization for the education of Indian women. By the 1980s, the Presbyterian Church had established itself as a force to be reckoned with in the field of education. In terms of numbers of schools and enrolment the Presbyterian Church ranked fourth behind the government, Roman Catholic, and Anglican schools, in that order. Between 1964 and 1972, the Presbyterian Church educated an average of 35,000 students per year at the primary and secondary level; approximately 49 per cent were females. But it was in the late 1980s that Presbyterian achievements in Indian women's education peaked as a succession of distinguished female Indian scholarship winners were produced.

The question to be addressed at this juncture is, in view of the centralized nature of education policy formulation in T&T, was the Presbyterian Church success in the area of Indian women's education associated with increasing participation in education policy formulation? Table 6.1 suggests that the Presbyterian and other denominational school boards influenced rather than participated in policy formulation in the 1980s. To complete this picture, it is also important to note that a few Presbyterian individuals such as Dr Anna Mahase and Rev. Cyril Paul were co-opted into important policy formulation bodies within the Ministry of Education and the government in general. Dr Mahase served as a member of the board of the Archibald Vocational Institute, the Advisory Council for the establishment of the College of Arts and Sciences at UWI St Augustine, School for Blind Children, and Vice President of the Assisted Secondary Schools Principals Association of Trinidad & Tobago. She was also a member of the Caribbean Examination Council (CXC) and member of the Board of Governors of NIHERST, the National Institute of Higher Education, Research, Science and Technology (*Guardian* 29/10/1991).

It can be argued that while Dr Mahase's incorporation into such structures was based on her track record as an educator, she was also perceived as representative of Presbyterian Church and, therefore, Indian women's interests.

Education for the toiling Indian masses of Trinidad (both male and female) was an important plank in the philosophy of Indian nationalist associations such as the Sanatan Dharma Maha Sabha and the Arya Samaj. This discussion deals mainly with the Maha Sabha due to its contribution to education expansion for Indians in T&T in the post-World War II era (Campbell 1992). Because the strength of the Indian nationalist argument often rests on the politics of numbers, associations such as the Maha Sabha seemed equally committed to the education of Indian girls and boys. Thus despite the perception of cultural barriers to women's education in the Indian community, the evidence suggests that the politics of numbers prompted nationalist associations to be equally committed to the education of the Indian woman (Table 6.2).

Table 6.2 shows that Hindu education boards were no less committed to educating girls than boys. In fact, the table shows that the Hindu schools were comparable to government schools in their enrolment rate for girls. The population of government schools was usually black and of working-class backgrounds, whereas the upper classes, the browns and whites, opted for private or assisted schools. Burnham's study, *Education and Social Change in Trinidad & Tobago* (1992), puts this finding into context. He argues that not even the conservative Maha Sabha could escape the modernizing tendency that characterized Indian nationalist associations in the diaspora and cites Vertovec's 1987 research to substantiate this argument.

Did Indian nationalist associations such as the Maha Sabha participate in education policy formulation, and was participation greater in the 1980s? To answer these questions it is important to note that, unlike the Presbyterians, the PNM government resisted giving the Maha Sabha's representatives access into the corridors of education decision-making. Indeed, Campbell notes that 'in his election campaign in 1956 Williams referred to the Maha Sabha schools as political cells of the People's Democratic Party, his Indian political opposition' (1992: 82).

There is no evidence to suggest that the NAR government was more amenable to incorporating the Maha Sabha into policy formulation.

Table 6.2   *Enrolment of girls and boys in primary and secondary school in T&T by religious denomination and government schools*

Year	Sex	Government	Roman Catholic	Hindu
1957	Boy	15 317	25 264	6 539
	Girl	14 851	24 992	6 213
	Total	30 168	50 256	12 752
1967	Boy	25 819	32 695	10 971
	Girl	25 580	33 384	10 438
	Total	51 399	66 079	21 409
1972	Boy	29 822	31 954	11 327
	Girl	28 277	33 026	10 671
	Total	58 099	64 980	21 998
1984	Boy	23 863	23 146	8 490
	Girl	22 163	24 995	8 361
	Total	46 026	48 141	16 851

Note: The 1984 figures are only for primary school enrolment.

Sources: CSO A Digest of Education Statistics, for the years 1962–62, 1967–68 and 1971–71; CSO Report on Education Statistics, 1983–84.

In its 'politico-religious' role (Burnham 1992), the Maha Sabha responded to exclusion by excessive and direct confrontation. All efforts were made to flout the Ministry's recruitment and appointments policy. Against government policy, the Maha Sabha adamantly campaigned for Indian teachers to be appointed to Indian schools, and for greater opportunities for Indians within the education bureaucracy (*Express* 15/8/ 1982). Moreover, the Maha Sabha used the threat of school closure as its ultimate bargaining weapon (*Express* 20/8/1982).

Maha Sabha confrontation yielded the desired results. The PNM appeared beaten as it gave in to the successive demands of the organization. Thus, without being incorporated into decision-making structures, the Maha Sabha was influencing policy outcomes. Indeed, as late as 1981, when other denominational boards were willing to hand over the full management of schools to the government due to a lack of funds, the Maha Sabha stood alone in forcing the PNM government to retreat over its nationalization proposals contained in the Bruce report (*Guardian* 5/6/1981).

In addition, the Maha Sabha's advocacy also forced the government to address the problem of urban bias in education. This bias was consistently interpreted as an anti-Indian bias. Hence Maha Sabha Secretary General Sat Maharaj's contribution to the National Consultation on the 1968–83 Education Plan, where he charged that 'there has been a deliberate plot over the past 15 years to make the acquisition of a good education by children of Hindus unattainable' (Verbatim Report of the National Consultation on the 1968–83 Education Plan, MOE 1969).

The proof of Maharaj's anti-Indian charge was demonstrated by the comparison of statistics with Tobago, which was also agricultural but with a large black population. Maharaj showed that Tobago, with a lower population density than Caroni had three secondary schools offering 1,428 places, while Caroni had three secondary schools offering 1,624 places. He therefore argued that 'Tobago children will be twice better off than the children of agricultural workers of Caroni who are predominantly Hindu.' Maharaj was even more provocative when concluding that 'we have oil money to assist all our Caribbean neighbours but none for our Hindu brothers and sisters in Caroni' (Verbatim Report of the National Consultation on the 1968–83 Education Plan, MOE 1969).

The government responded positively to the Maha Sabha's anti-Indian charge in education. By 1988, Caroni had nine secondary schools offering 10,914 places; Tobago had four secondary schools, offering 2,816 places (CSO 1991, Annual Statistical Digest 1989, Tables 62–64, 64–66). Thus the Maha Sabha succeeded in redressing the anti-rural/anti-Indian bias in the distribution of education places in T&T.

In conclusion, it is clear that the Maha Sabha did not conform to the expected pattern of interest associations in the participation literature of development administration. It was not formally incorporated into structures of decision making and sometimes behaved more as a political party than a pressure group. In spite of, or perhaps because of, this modus operandi, the Maha Sabha was able to influence important decisional outcomes which resulted in increases in the number of school places for Indian boys and girls. Thus the Maha Sabha presence had a decentralizing effect on education policy formulation in the 1980s.

As regards the flip-side of this story, the association between black women's lower educational attainment and lower participation in education policy formulation, it must be noted that, in the post-independence history of T&T, no interest associations articulated the problems of black women in education or in any other sphere of policy making. The PNM Women's League, the Housewives Association, and the National Joint Action Committee (NJAC) all stopped short of formulating an ideology that defined black women as an underclass with special needs. The PNM Women's League spoke for all women, and the Housewives Association was oblivious of gender and race. As a black nationalist interest association, the NJAC only recognized one point of differentiation, that of the white hegemonic economic structure and its allies versus the oppressed 'black' masses. 'Black' therefore became an undifferentiated and unspecified category, sometimes including both men and women, Indians and Africans, but relevant only in as far as it represented the antithesis of the white oppressors. Such a philosophy seemed incapable of aggregating or advocating the interests of black women.

Bureaucratic politics, the Ministry o,˜ Education and Indian women's educational attainment

This final section considers the association between increasing educational attainment for Indian women and bureaucratic politics on the part of Ministry of Education officials in favour of this group. This question is explored by first identifying the incidence of Indian and Indian female bureaucrats in the Ministry of Education. This is based on the assumption that, in a plural society such as T&T, Indian bureaucrats in general and Indian female bureaucrats in particular are more likely to be sympathetically disposed to the educational accomplishments of Indian women. Secondly, it will be considered whether the actions of bureaucrats actively promoted the interests of Indian women in education.

The memoirs of Dr Winston Mahabir, first Minister of Health in independent T&T, offers an interesting point of entry for this discussion. Mahabir (1975) revealed that although he was considered by Williams for the position of Minister of Education in the 1956 Cabinet, he was eventually appointed to Health because:

Table 6.3   *Percentage of Indians and Indian female officers by functional categories in the T&T Ministry of Education, 1956–80*

| | | Categories | | | |
Year	Race/sex	Execu-tive	Admin/ Account	Secre-tarial	Clerical
1956	Indian	20	—	18	11
	Indian female	2	—	18	4
1971	Indian	21	12	13	11
	Indian female	—	—	11	3
1980	Indian	6	21	11	33
	Indian female	—	8	11	17

Notes: Because the Ministry's classifications changed as the Ministry grew over time, the same functionaries are not captured in each period. Thus the 1956 civil list is divided into the following functional areas: Executive (Director, Deputy and Assistant Directors of Education, Supervisors, Principal Officers, all officers and supervisors of the Inspectorate, School Feeding and Extension Services Department); Admin/Accounting (Administrative Secretary); Secretarial (Secretaries, Steno-secretaries and Typists), and Clerical (Senior, First and Second-class clerks).

The 1971 list is divided into Executive (Permanent Secretary, Economists, Educational Liaison Officers, Examinations Officers and Administrative Officer II to V); Admin/Accounting (Administrative Assistant Accountants and Audit Assistants); Secretarial (Secretaries, Clerk Stenos; Typists) and Clerical (all clerks).

The 1980 list is divided into Executive (Permanent Secretary, Chief Education Officer, Directors, Administrative Officer II to V, Economist I, and Examinations Officer); Admin/Accounting (Administrative Assistant, Accountants, and Audit Assistants); Clerical (all clerks).

Sources: GOTT Civil Lists 1956, 1971 and 1980.

> Williams responded to pressure not to place an Indian in the Ministry of Education, since the Department of Education was already infested with Indians! (Mahabir 1975: 44)

Much has been said about the under-representation of Indians in the civil service of T&T (Ryan 1991: 65–71). Table 6.3 attempts to establish the representation of Indians and Indian women at the executive, administrative/accounting, secretarial and clerical functional areas of the Ministry of Education for the years 1950, 1970, 1980 and 1990. The Civil List of 1956, 1971 and 1980 constitutes the sampling frame for identifying Indian functionaries. Because the list for the late 1980s was not published at time this research was conducted, the 1980 data were updated with a list of all permanent appointments made to the Ministry of Education between 1985 to 1990. The Service Commissions Department prepared this list at the request of the author. The somewhat crude technique was used of identifying Indian functionaries by names; the margin of error of this approach has not been determined. Since it is more likely for an Indian to have a Christian name than for a non-Indian to have a Hindu or Muslim name, despite the rise of black Islam in Trinidad, it can reasonably be concluded that this approach may under-represent rather than over-represent Indians in the bureaucracy.

Data presented in this table must be interpreted carefully since no comparison is made with other races or especially women of other races in the bureaucracy. Nonetheless, between 1956 and 1980, the number of Indians in general and Indian women in particular in the Admin/Accounting and Clerical categories of the Ministry's staff has increased significantly. The Service Commission's list of permanent appointments to the Ministry between 1985 to 1990 suggests that this trend continued in the Admin/Accounting category and that significant improvement was seen in the Executive category. Thus in the area of executive appointments, by 1990 the Permanent Secretary of the Ministry was Indian, two of the three Research Officers appointed in this period were Indian (one male and one female); one of the two Administrative Officers V appointed was an Indian male, 12 of the 34 Curriculum Officers were Indian (only 2 of whom were female), and one of the two Education Liaison Officers was an Indian male.

Whether or not Indian bureaucrats at the Ministry in the 1980s acted in the interest of Indian females is a difficult issue to consider. It requires evidence of non-rational and therefore non-neutral actions in favour of Indian females on the part of Indian bureaucrats. This question is explored by examining the popular perceptions of the actions of Ministry of Education bureaucrats in T&T, and through interviews with top bureaucrats, past and current, in the Ministry of Education, interviews with ex-Ministers of Education, and discussions with teachers in government Junior Secondary, Senior Comprehensive and Secondary Schools.

By the 1980s, the examination pass record of the new Junior Secondary and Senior Comprehensive state schools built in the previous decade had proved to be disappointing when compared to the traditional board-managed 'prestige' schools. Against this background, parents scrambled for limited places in 'prestige' schools and a popular perception soon developed that the system, with the complicity of the Ministry of Education bureaucrats, discriminated against African children in favour of the children of upper-class Indian and White families. While this perception remained dormant for most of the 1980s, in 1988 the Pandora's box was opened when calypsonian Weston Rawlins (Cro Cro) sang the calypso 'Corruption in Common-Entrance' and won the National Calypso Monarch Final Competition. Corruption in Common-Entrance gave vent to the popularly-held belief that, in the allocation of secondary school places, talented black children were denied limited places in prestige schools—'Yuh chile could be bright like a bulb and from Laventille [a black working class area], Forget Holy Name Convent and Bishop Anstey [prestige schools]' (*Express* 2/6/1988). In this calypso, Cro Cro publicly identified the much-revered Dr Anna Mahase as a school principal practising such discriminatory practices.

In a plural society like T&T, the calypso 'Corruption in Common-Entrance' sparked off a debate in which the perspectives of contributors were closely associated with their race. Ten Hindu Associations—the Hindu Women's Organisation, Indian Review Committee, Caribbean Hindu Centre, Indian Museum Committee, Hindu Seva Sangh, Dharmaprach, Hindu Parchar Kendra, Vedanta Society, Society for the Promotion of Indian Culture, Edinburgh Hindu Temple and the Wilkinson Street, El Dorado, Cultural Group—publicly condemned the calypso as 'racists,' 'insulting to Indians' and called for Indians to boycott subsequent shows in which Cro Cro was billed to perform (*Express* 20/2/1988).

Ministry of Education officials who were interviewed recounted the pressure they came under when, in the heat of the debate, they were accused of giving principals of prestige schools unlimited access to Common Entrance pass lists. Principals were alleged to have personally selected students from these pass lists to fill the 20 per cent discretionary quota and to influence the selection of the 80 per cent mandatory quota (personal interviews, August 1992). They also recalled that 'a well-argued letter' in the *Express* of March 15, 1988 by Dr Randy Peters caught the attention of several Members of Parliament and resulted in pressure being put on the Minister of Education to reveal the relationship between Ministry of Education officials and 'prestige' school principals, viz. the pass list (personal interviews, August 1992). Dr Peters' letter stated the following:

> Let Ms. Mahase reveal what criteria she used to allocate her 20% and what is the final ethnic composition of this batch. And let those who after all this, still grumble about racialism based on the preponderance of East Indian names, analyse the distribution of disposable income among the various ethnic groupings that constitute our society. (*Express* 15/3/1988)

Several Ministry of Education officials interviewed attributed the questioning of their probity to what was referred to as 'the blatantly pro-Indian actions' of the Chief Education Officer (1985–90) and later Permanent Secretary (1990) and his brother the Curriculum Officer (1985–90), and to the naivety of the Minister of Education (1986–89) 'who allowed himself to be led'. Ministry Officials told of the Chief Education Officer's personal involvement in matters as 'petty' as the appointment of clerks and cleaners, his motive being to increase the Indian presence at the Ministry (personal interview, August 1992).

The Chief Education Officer (CEO) was described as ambitious, a supporter of the ruling NAR and openly 'pro-Indian' (personal interviews, August 1992). Indeed, the NAR Minister of Education, who worked with the CEO when he was appointed Permanent Secretary of the Ministry, tells the story of how he was deliberately economical with information so that certain decisions could be taken in the interest of Indian schools and Indian functionaries within the Ministry. The Minister reveals that this tactic was only curbed when a threat was issued 'to break open his skull' with an empty soft-drink bottle which stood on the desk after a lunch break (personal interview with ex-Minister of Education, August 1992).

Taken together, these findings point to a more significantly Indian-conscious presence at the Ministry of Education in the 1980s. When seen against the background of the renaissance of Indian cultural identity taking place in T&T in the 1980s and the jostling of ethnic groups for limited resources in post-oil-boom T&T, events at the Ministry of Education appear to be a microcosm of wider societal politicization. Given that the Indian population outnumbered the African population by the late 1980s, and given that blacks traditionally dominated the civil service, the politicization of the education bureaucracy and indeed the public service in the 1980s seemed a natural outcome. Whether this contributed to the advancement of Indian women is questionable. However, the fact is that politicization was associated with educational attainment and social change for this group in the 1980s.

With regard to the flip side of the story, bureaucrats' subjective disposition towards black females, Ministry of Education officials interviewed by this writer suggested that this also occurred. Indeed, it was revealed that, in the 1960s and 1970s, it was common practice for the Ministers of Education to call upon bureaucrats to 'see what they could do' for the children (girls and boys) of constituents or friends. It was explained that the problem of the 1980s was that, as more and more parents asked for special political favours, fewer access channels existed for blacks or Indians who were not 'big-shots' (personal interview, August 1992). When seen against the background of diminishing state resources in the 1980s, the resurgence of ethnicity in T&T, and the NAR's ascendance to power in 1986, a situation arises where the boundaries of race, class and gender seem to collapse.

General Conclusions

In Part II, it was shown that differences in educational attainment between women in Jamaica and T&T were associated with differences in the organization variable—decentralization. In Part III, differences in educational attainment between Indian and African women were also found to be associated with decentralization. The Ministry of Education in Jamaica displayed a greater propensity to decentralize decision-making authority than the T&T Ministry of Education. In T&T in the 1980s, the period in which Indian women achieved the greatest educational attainment, the Ministry of Education also exhibited a greater propensity to decentralize decision making.

As regards the environmental variables—participation and bureaucratic politics—associations were only established and differences explained with some qualifications. In the case of beneficiary participation, the degree of institutionalization of women's interest associations, the extent of participation in other areas of policy formulation, and the strength of the interest association (e.g., the T&T Maha Sabha) were all found to be associated with educational attainment. Similarly, the political environmental variable, bureaucratic politics, was qualified in the sense that both the Permanent Secretary of the Ministry of Education in Jamaica and the experience of the bureaucrats of the T&T Ministry of Education in the 1980s demonstrated that politicization rather than bureaucratic politics *per se* was associated with increased educational attainment, and therefore social change as well.

7 The Theory and Practice of Development Administration: Postscript and Notes into the 21st Century

Introduction

This chapter concludes the study with a summary of the associations found in the 1960–90 segment of the study. These associations will be examined further in the second part of the chapter, which spans the period 1990–98. Conclusions on the theory and practice of development administration will be drawn and observations made on their implications for the 21st century.

Public Bureaucracy and Economic Growth: The Associations

The study found associations between the realization of economic growth goals and the organizational attribute (administrative capacity-building). It was found that, compared with Trinidad & Tobago, Jamaica, which achieved a higher economic growth, also invested more in administrative capacity-building. Moreover, such efforts were generally supported by a government committed to administrative development, initiated in a consociational environment between the Civil Service Association and the government of the day, and such efforts made systematic and institutionalized use of foreign technical expertise. In contrast, the government in Trinidad & Tobago viewed public bureaucrats as a veritable fourth estate and thus showed little commitment to administrative development. The Civil Service and later the Public Service Associations responded with hostility and refused to be co-opted into any efforts of capacity building. Furthermore, because of the evidence of aversion to foreign expertise, the government of the day neglected to co-ordinate or institutionalize this administrative development function, though it did make reluctant use of foreign consultants.

The two environmental variables (autonomy and facilitative policy content) showed only a qualified association with goal realization. The political environment variable—autonomy from the political centre—was only able to explain differences in growth goal realization during the 1960s; in the 1980s, it was control, not autonomy, that was associated with economic growth. This point was clearly brought out in the comparative study of the Industrial Development Corporations in Part II of Chapter 4. The Jamaica IDC, which had a better record of realizing set growth goals in the 1980s, was found to be more closely controlled by the Seaga government. The characteristics of the 1980s management climate, which determined closer control, were the involvement of external funding agencies, the centralization of economic policy-making, and the implementation of macroeconomic management policies. Thus, autonomy did not appear to be universal in its coverage and the qualification emerged that, given the management climate of the 1980s, it is closer control, not autonomy, that was associated with goal realization.

Interestingly, when discussing autonomy from the political centre, we encountered the superior associational value of the facilitative policy content. It was shown in Chapter 4 that, in the 1980s, the degree to which the policy environment was facilitative was more closely associated with economic growth than autonomy was. Therefore, when this attribute was actually considered, it was found to be capable of explaining the differences in growth goal realization between Jamaica and T&T. However, there was one important qualification. Contrary to the neo-liberal arguments considered in Chapter 3, facilitative economic policies were found to be a manifestation of a different *type* and not of a lower *level* of state interventionism. Consequently, while it can be concluded that facilitative policies are associated with goal realization it does not follow that lower state interventionism is also similarly associated. In fact, the experience of Jamaica in the 1980s suggests just the opposite. Thus Seaga's economic growth strategy, which aimed to facilitate increased private-sector involvement, also required a greater degree of interventionism from the state. The state was called upon to finance, administer and monitor its new facilitative function, all activities with high associated costs.

Taking these qualifications into account, it was concluded in Chapter 4 that the realization of economic growth goals was indeed associated with administrative capacity-building, to a limited extent with autonomy from the political centre, and also with facilitative policy content.

Public Bureaucracy and Economic Change: The Associations

In Chapter 5, differences in economic change between the two countries were found to be associated with the second organizational attribute of decentralization. Indeed, Jamaica, with greater economic change in the 1970s, also had more decentralized economic decision-making structures. This was true at both national level and at the micro level of the IDC case study. In Jamaica, there were more levels of structures in economic decision-making to which a higher degree of decision-making authority was vested. On the other hand, T&T was characterized by excessive centralization, both at the macro level of national economic policy-making agencies and at the micro level of the IDC case study. Thus few decision-making structures existed in T&T and the PNM government seemed less willing to vest authority in any other agencies.

While the policy environment attribute (participation) was generally found to be associated with differences in economic change, important qualifications were also apparent. First, the length of term in office of the government initiating change was found to be a good predictor of willingness to incorporate the advocates and beneficiaries of change. Thus the new Manley government incorporated both groups and the old PNM government in T&T introduced economic change as a 'within-input,' and only selectively admitted bureaucrats and technocrats into decision-making centres. In this regard, while both large and small businesses gained entry to the Jamaican system, they were virtually excluded in T&T.

The second qualification was that it was not participation *per se*, but broad-based participation, that was found to be associated with economic change. Third, the more organized and centralized the interest associations (as were private-sector organizations in Jamaica), the greater their participation in economic policy formulation. The more fragmented they were (as in the case of T&T), the lesser the participation. Thus, it was concluded in Chapter 5 that it was not beneficiary participation *per se* that was associated with economic change. Rather, qualifications revolved around the major issues of whether the government spearheading change was newly elected or not, the range of interests incorporated into the policy formulation process, and the organization and development of economic interest associations.

As regards the political environmental variable of bureaucratic politics, this, too, was subject to qualified confirmation. First, the basic premise of this variable—that shared interests between bureaucrats, the beneficiaries of change, and politicians spearheading change is a predictor of bureaucratic support for change policies—was challenged by experiences in T&T. Second, it was not bureaucratic politics *per se* but *activated* bureaucratic politics in the form of *politicization* that was, in fact, associated with economic change. Furthermore, it was a broad-based, inclusive type of politicization that occurred in Jamaica, and which was associated with change. In T&T, politicization was exclusionary and restricted to a small elite group of bureaucrats. This was associated with a lower level of economic change. Therefore it was concluded in Chapter 5 that economic change was associated with decentralization, and that participation and bureaucratic politics also had qualified associations.

Public Bureaucracy and Social Change: The Associations

Differences in educational attainment between women in Jamaica and T&T were found to be associated with differences in the degree to which education policy formulation structures were decentralized. Table 6.1, which compared the structures and extent of decentralization in education policy formulation in the two countries, illustrated the greater decentralization of Jamaica, as compared to T&T. In T&T, education policy formulation was characterized by extreme centralization occasionally punctuated by *ad hoc* consultations. This led to a situation in which direct and informal representation was made to the political centre, reinforcing the country's tendency towards centralization.

However, differences were not so easily explained by the policy and political environment variables. Indeed, in the latter segment of this chapter, beneficiary participation almost appears inapplicable since women's interest associations were virtually inactive in women's education issues in both countries. Nonetheless, higher educational attainment for women in Jamaica was found to be associated with a higher visibility and greater activity of women's interest associations in areas other than education. It was also found to be associated with higher institutionalization of women's interest associations in the policy-making process in general. Findings from the longitudinal part of the study on differences in educational attainment of Indian and African women in T&T contributed further support to the findings from Chapter 5. The Maha Sahba's role in T&T education policy formulation demonstrated that the strength of demand articulation can effectively transform influence into participation and create a decentralizing effect.

As regards bureaucratic politics, in both the comparative and longitudinal sections of the study an association was found between politicization of the bureaucracy and higher educational attainment for women. Therefore, the essential difference between top bureaucrats spearheading education reforms in Jamaica and T&T was that bureaucrats in Jamaica were politically committed to change, while in T&T, top posts in the Ministry of Education were occupied by neutral career professionals or by conservatives opposed to change. In T&T during the 1980s, increased educational attainment for Indian women occurred in a highly politicized atmosphere affecting both the Ministry and society in general.

Taking these qualifications into account, it was concluded in Chapter 6 that the goal of social change was associated with decentralization, and that beneficiary participation and bureaucratic politics had qualified associations.

Conclusions

Taken together, the conclusions in Chapters 4, 5 and 6 suggest that the research question can be answered in terms of the variables of association presented in the framework. While qualifications were important and added new dimensions for consideration, they did not refute the basic essence of the attribute under consideration. One important finding, however, was the greater explanatory power of the two organizational attributes: administrative capacity-building with regard to growth goals, and decentralization with regard to change.

POSTSCRIPT

Introduction

In this postscript, the findings of the 1960–90 study are re-examined further. Our purpose is to determine whether the associations found at that time continue to explain the performance of development bureaucracies in the 1990s. Consistent with the ends-means approach of this study, development goals of the 1990s will first be established. This will be followed by an assessment of the extent to which goals have been achieved. We will then seek to explain goal realization in terms of the associations found in the 1960–90 study.

Development Goals in the 1990s

Economic growth through a radical programme of structural adjustment has been a dominant development goal of the 1990s in both Jamaica and T&T. In Jamaica, PNP Ministers who were once advocates of democratic socialism have had no choice but to accept the new realities of adjustment upon assuming office in 1989. Under the leadership of the late Michael Manley, and later P.J. Patterson, the PNP concerned itself with restarting the engine of economic growth by continuing the export-led development strategy of the Seaga government. Privatization, financial-sector reform and trade liberalization were the policy instruments for effecting the new policy. In addition, for the first time, questions about societal values were put on the agenda by the PNP and made central to the realization of economic growth. National pride, customer service, quality, and social partnership are some of the underlying values emphasized by the PNP.

Despite claims to the contrary, social change for underclasses was not a central goal of the PNP government in the 1990s. While this question preoccupied the minds of the party's left, especially at times of general elections, social change was merely to be addressed through economic growth and prosperity—typical neo-classical solutions. Not surprisingly, throughout the 1990s, discussions about the empowerment of underclasses such as women and the poor were conducted in terms of employment opportunities offered by the market rather than through welfare policies and agencies in education or health. This is so despite the existence of PNP social-welfare interventions such as the Human

Resources Development Program, the Social and Economic Support Fund, the Jamaica Social Investment Fund, and the Poverty Alleviation Program. In real terms, the PNP government of the 1990s de-emphasized social change programs in education, health and housing. Public expenditure in these areas fell by a staggering 32 per cent between 1988 and 1993 (Handa and King 1997).

At the start of the 21st century Jamaica finds itself with the PNP still in power, policy direction is once more shifting to incorporate issues of social change. It is against this background that the new Growth with Equity programme should be viewed. It is also against this background that the theme of the 1997 Budget Presentation of Prime Minister Patterson—Education: Pathways to the Future—should be noted. In a real sense, this shift in focus represents the triumph of lobbying efforts by nongovernmental voluntary organizations, women's interests association, teachers associations and the organized private sector. It is also a policy reaction to the orgy of violence that has consumed the under-funded and under-staffed school system in Jamaica.

In contrast, T&T finds itself consumed by politics of social change in the 1990s. For the PNM and UNC governments, whose tenures in office are from 1991–95 and 1995–2000, respectively, the question of social change for the country's dominant East Indian population has become a major populist goal to be pursued. In the 1990s, this concern was first put on the agenda by the Manning-led PNM government with the establishment of the Centre for Ethnic Studies in St Augustine, Trinidad in 1992. Manning had hoped that questions of the disempowerment and under-representation of the East Indian population in strategic sectors and public agencies could be addressed in dispassionate policy terms—what he called 'facts minus emotion and bias.' However, this was not to be. What appeared to be a weak affirmative action initiative by the Afro-Trinidadian-dominated PNM was soon overtaken by the processes of cultural renaissance, politicization and ethnic consciousness that were taking place in the East Indian community during the 1980s. Not surprisingly, this movement came to fruition in 1995 when, for the first time in the independent history of T&T, an East Indian-dominated political party fought and won a general election on a platform of justice and social change for East Indians. More general concerns of empowerment for the country's unemployed, poor or self-defined disadvantaged Muslim community were at best subsumed under the ethnic argument, or worse, ignored.

The PNM's defeat at the polls was not only indicative of East Indian nationalism, it stood as testimony to the disenchantment of the party's native constituency—urban Afro-Trinidadians—over issues of economic reform. This brings us to the second goal of stabilization and economic growth, which also loomed large in the 1990s. If social change dominated the populist agenda, then stabilization and growth dominated the official policy agenda in the 1990s. At the end of the 1980s, the fall in the real price of oil on the world market threw the T&T economy into a spiral of decline—living standards fell, unemployment increased, and professionals migrated to greener pastures abroad. The PNM, and later the UNC, aimed to halt the slide by reducing public-sector expenditure levels through privatization, in particular the commercialization of public utilities. Growth was to be achieved through structural adjustment policies in which the non-traditional export sector was expected to take a lead role. This was a continuation of the NAR's policies of the late 1980s. As in Jamaica, structural adjustment constituted the context in which growth was to be pursued in T&T. Unlike Jamaica, however, issues of growth often found themselves relegated to second place as superstructural issues of race and identity dominated the debates of the day.

Achievement of Development Goals in the 1990s

Jamaica's experience at achieving economic growth goals in the 1990s can be recorded as a success story. The evidence suggests that this outcome can be attributed to the strategies for growth under the structural adjustment programme. Between 1990 and 1995, the Jamaican economy grew by 2.9 per cent (World Development Report 1997). While growth was recorded throughout the entire 1990s, it was especially concentrated in 1989 and 1990, 4.5 per cent and 5.3 per cent respectively (Handa & King 1997). The areas of growth were in agricultural production for domestic consumption and in the manufacturing sector for export (World Development Report 1997). Consequently, by 1993, 65 per cent of total exports were comprised of manufactured goods, and food comprised only 14 per cent of total imports. Between the 1980s and 1993 the percentage of manufactures in total exports grew by 3 per cent and the percentage of imported food fell by 6 per cent (World Development Report 1997).

In terms of social change, the PNP's approach to this issue through economic policy seemed to have been successful. Hence the unusual phenomenon in which the period of greatest adjustment in the early 1990s was associated with social change indicators such as low unemployment, closure of income inequality gaps, and employment creation especially for women and rural communities. Such findings challenge Latin American and Asian experiences where neo-liberal adjustment policies have been found to exacerbate inequalities. While extraneous variables such as remittances from abroad have been offered as some explanation of this phenomenon, the point is that the PNP's policies resulted in substantial employment creation in the manufacturing sector, especially garment manufacturing in the Free Zones, and in the agricultural sector in particular. Women were major beneficiaries of these policies.

Indeed, the cumulative effect of the PNP's policies on women can be seen from the debates and discussions that marked the celebration of International Women's Day in 1998. Discussions during this time were conducted largely in terms of the accomplishments of women in the labour market. This is especially significant since, for the first time, an effective separation has been made between educational attainment, employment opportunities and women's empowerment. The 1998 STATIN report, which constituted the reference point for these discussions, led many to argue that it was now time for discriminatory employment policies in favour of men (see *Jamaica Gleaner*, 'Jobs for the boys and men,' 12/3/98). This can be explained in part by the general de-emphasis of educational attainment in Jamaica in the 1990s, coupled with the realities of low-skilled labour requirements for the export-led economy.

In T&T, the UNC's success at the polls coupled with its subsequent consolidation of power upon assuming office have led many to conclude that the goal of social change had been realized. A survey of the two main newspapers at that time suggests, that at the popular level, many observers were convinced that the case for social change in the East Indian community rested largely on the symbolic value of an East Indian Prime Minister, an East Indian Deputy Prime Minister and an East Indian-dominated Cabinet.

On the other hand, a more cautious group of East Indian politicians, businessmen and professionals drew attention to the dominant socio-economic position held by the old white plantocracy and the Syrian-

Lebanese community in T&T. For them, the triumph over the Afro-centric PNM was but one victory on one front; other battles had to be fought to ensure that East Indians remained a culturally distinct but upwardly mobile social class. Those holding this view focused on the education system. They argued for the preservation of equality of access in the system, for the greater autonomy of School Boards, and for proportionate opportunities for East Indian children if mobility and cultural integrity were to be achieved (see *Guardian*, 'Educational Opportunity for Hindus must be: Frank Rampersad,' 16/3/92). Despite the fact that such demands ran counter to the popular perception that the system was already biased in favour of East Indians, they won the argument in the education reform debates of the 1990s in T&T. Thus, the 1990s witnessed significant social change for East Indians as the arena of politics fell under their control, and as the structure of the education system seemed set to allow for mobility and cultural integrity.

With respect to the economic goals of stabilization and growth, the evidence of the 1990s suggests that, while some small measure of stabilization did occur, growth through structural change eluded T&T. The unemployment rate, which stood at 20 per cent in 1990, declined by only a small margin to 17.2 per cent in 1995 (Central Statistical Office 1995). Similarly, T&T's external debt profile improved, though only minimally. In 1989, this figure stood at 53.9 per cent of GNP, in 1994 it was 47 per cent of GNP, but by 1995, this figure had increased again to 52 per cent (World Development Reports 1997, 1996 and 1991). While the Jamaican economy grew by 3.6 per cent between 1985 and 1995, in T&T growth was -1.7 per cent. Between 1990 and 1995, only a marginal average annual growth rate of 1 per cent was recorded for T&T; for Jamaica this figure stood at 2.9 per cent for the same period (World Development Report 1997). In terms of sectoral growth in the economy for the period 1990 to 1995, the average annual growth rate in agriculture was 1.3 per cent, industry was 0.2 per cent and services -0.1 per cent (World Development Report 1997). Unlike Jamaica, which was able to mount a strong export-led manufacturing drive, in T&T the much anticipated structural adjustment did not come. Hence, with the exception of an increase in services, petroleum-related activities continued to dominate industrial production and the T&T economy. Consequently, while value-added in the manufacturing sector stood at 18 per cent in Jamaica in 1995, in T&T the figure was 9 per cent for the same year (World Development Report 1997). These figures suggest an economy in limbo, basically unchanged from the previous decade and with seething social problems from a persistently high unemployment rate. In short, despite the large-scale privatization programmes and financial-sector reforms to take place in this period, we cannot say that the goal of economic growth has been achieved.

Development Bureaucracy and Economic Growth in the 1990s: The Associations

To what extent did the associations established in the 1960–90 segment of the study also hold true in the decade of the 1990s? To recall, the organizational variable—administrative capacity-building—was found to have strong correlations with goal achievement in the area of economic growth. Given Jamaica's higher growth rate in the 1990s, one should also expect to find a higher incidence of administrative capacity-building.

At first glance, T&T's experimentation with administrative reform in the 1990s calls this association into question. For the first time in its independent history, T&T appeared to be confronting the issue of administrative capacity-building through a large-scale administrative reform programme in the public services during the 1990s. The first step in this direction was the creation of a Ministry of the Public Service in the Office of the Prime Minister in 1991. Management expert and University lecturer Gordon Draper, who was to lead the administrative reform programme, headed the Ministry. Draper had been a member of the last administrative reform effort under the PNM in the 1980s—the Dumas Committee. In defending the introduction of administrative reform in Parliament, Minister Draper noted that what was different about the new programme was the new-found political will to reform (Commonwealth Secretariat 1995). The UNC government taking office in 1995 appears to have sustained the commitment to administrative reform, as seen from the fact that the Green Paper 'Towards a New Public Administration' (1996) was one of its first clear policy statements.

Under the PNM, the new programme had several aims: to make government more efficient, to make management in the public service more effective, to provide quality service with the aim of customer satisfaction, to improve financial and information management, and to develop policy analysis and co-ordination capacity in the public service. Agency-specific and function-specific implementation strategies were employed. In the case of the agency-specific strategy, key departments and ministries (e.g. the Ministry of Education and Health) were targeted for strengthening and reform, while the function-specific strategy sought to improve systems common to all public agencies.

Despite these efforts, however, close comparison of the administrative reform programmes in Jamaica and T&T reveals important differences and suggests that the Jamaican programme was deeper, more strategic in its implementation, and met with greater acceptance and success. The situation in T&T is partly explained by the Public Services Association's opposition to government, noted in the earlier part of this study. PSA opposition to government persisted into the 1990s. The PSA bitterly opposed more controversial reform measures such as the assignment of some Public Services Commission's executive powers to Permanent Secretaries. The PSA also opposed reorganization in the Ministries of Education and Health, and threatened to shut down the public service if aspects of the reform were not reversed. In fact, the failure of the PNM at the polls was due, in part, to the industrial unrest that ensued in the public sector during 1995. The Jamaica Civil Service Association also opposed aspects of the reform programme. However, the Association's history of corporatist engagement with the PNP government in particular, coupled with the PNP's consultative approach, resulted in a situation where the Association's consent was even sought and obtained when the government could not meet targeted salary increases. The Jamaican situation can be explained by the ripeness of structural adjustment, the fact that the Civil Service had little choice but to accept dominant realities under SAP, and of course, the presence of radical and labour elements in government.

But perhaps the most significant differences between the two reform programmes lie in the depth and sophistication of the programme in Jamaica. While administrative reform in T&T was interpreted mainly in terms of systems improvement and mild administrative reform, in Jamaica an administrative revolution was taking place. Two features—human resource audit and retrenchment—were central to Jamaica's administrative revolution.

In T&T, both the PNM and UNC governments undertook superficial damage limitation measures by redeploying staff, encouraging early retirement, and separating long-term, temporary and contract staff. However, no comprehensive human resources audit of the public service was undertaken, and the proposed job evaluation exercise was neither comprehensive nor completed. In contrast, the extensive human resource audit and job evaluation exercise in Jamaica (the Point Factor Evaluation System) constituted the basis for wide-scale retrenchment, which was embarked upon simultaneously with selective recruitment (Fast Tract Recruitment). Hence, within the first half of the 1990s, the size of Jamaica's public service was reduced from 49,808 to 38,000 through retrenchment. Of the 38,000 positions that existed by 1994, 10,000 were vacancies to be filled by specialized and multi-skilled human resources (*Jamaica Herald* 16/3/94). The supply of labour was to come from Jamaicans abroad, expatriates from other countries such as Nigeria, and, very often, retired military officers. Central to the government's ability to attract and retain new staff was a new and attractive compensation package. The administrative reform programme aimed to revise all civil servants' salaries to 80 per cent of the market value on a phased basis, and senior public servants were to be the first beneficiaries of this provision as their jobs were assigned a higher value in the job evaluation schema.

For the government in Port-of-Spain, salary increases did not constitute a strategy in its toolkit of reform options. The government had inherited a public-services wages debacle arising from the NAR's unilateral cessation of Cost of Living Allowances (COLA) and a 10 per cent reduction in public servants' salaries. Reluctantly, in 1992 the PNM government kept its election promise to restore COLA and salary increases, and settled its debt to public servants in the form of bonds and compulsory time off. The issue of salary increases as a motivational strategy was a luxury that the PNM could ill afford with a TT$2.2 billion debt to public servants. Even where the government attempted to recruit high-skilled top managers, as in the case of the Tourism and Industrial Development Company (TIDCO) Chief Executive, the public outcry and Opposition questions time in Parliament suggested that T&T was not prepared for a meritocratic system in which strategic posts attracted commensurate compensation.

Furthermore, it must be said that, while the PNM and later the UNC merely tinkered with existing public-service capacity-building structures such as the O&M and Personnel Departments and Central Training Unit, in Jamaica new structures were brought into existence, and a deliberate effort was made to bring in new blood at the leadership level. In Jamaica, the Public Sector Efficiency and Reform Directorate was established and headed by Dr Garnett Brown. The Management Institute for National Development was also brought into existence to integrate and co-ordinate training agencies in the public service. To further invigorate public service, a new head of the civil service who was known to be achievement-oriented was recruited from outside. In short, the findings above provide further evidence of the association between administrative capacity-building and economic growth.

With regard to the two environmental variables—autonomy and facilitative policy content—a similar pattern of associations found in the 1960–90 research also appears in the 1990s. Regarding the issue of autonomy, during the 1990s, central government in both Jamaica and T&T sought to keep a tight reign on strategic public-sector agencies. Despite the emphasis paid to accountability, professionalism and managerialism, the political centre dictated policy direction, often in an undemocratic manner, and sought to influence aspects of managerial autonomy in key areas such as personnel. This was especially so in T&T under the UNC, with the first-time government preoccupied with personnel issues like recruitment and promotion in strategic public-sector agencies such as TIDCO. Indeed, the managerial autonomy of the Personnel Department, the Public Services Commission, the Statutory Authority Services Commission, and even the Police Services Commission were openly infringed upon as the new government engineered the removal of an entire crop of senior officers and used their influence to replace them with others who displayed their loyalty and trustworthiness. Thus, the 1990s ushered in a new era in which the bureaucratic ideals of neutrality and meritocracy, held high by the old Afro-Saxon bureaucrats, were challenged as never before in the independence history of T&T.

In Jamaica, autonomy was also circumscribed in the 1990s as politicians often encroached into the decisional space of managers. Unlike in T&T, however, interference was more in the area of strategic policy concerns than with personnel issues of appointments and dismissals. The financial sector, in particular, attracted the attention of government, and the PNP maintains close control in an effort to forestall crisis and avert insolvency. This government agency, Finsac, has recently become a dreaded watchdog, if not the bulldog, of financial-sector institutions with public equity. This has also been the experience of the apex public-sector agency, Jampro. Such experiences invite the conclusion that the more strategic the agency for the success of the adjustment programme, the lesser the autonomy of managers, and the greater the level of political interference through mechanisms of regulation and control. The resignation of Jampro's Chief Executive Officer and two Vice-Presidents in June 1994 is indicative of how the political centre (in this case, the Chairman of the Board) can intervene and change the policy direction of a public company. The conflict and the eventual resignations revolved around the Chairman's concern that Jampro favoured foreign investors over domestic. The CEO who took over following these resignations, seemed more amenable to the interests of domestic investors.

With respect to the final variable—facilitative policy content—it must be noted that in both Jamaica and T&T, the governments made it clear that the role of the state was no longer that of producer; a new role of facilitator and regulator was instead adumbrated. In a real sense, the scale of the divestment to occur in the utilities, mineral sectors, tourism and manufacturing in both countries in this era suggests that development bureaucracies had found a new *raison d'être*. The important differences between Jamaica and T&T are made apparent, however, when the respective agencies earmarked to facilitate private-sector investment—Jampro and TIDCO—are compared.

As in Chapter 4, we find that while in the 1990s Jampro's portfolio was dominated by activities such as information dissemination to potential investors, TIDCO was busy building tourism facilities on the beaches of Maracas in Trinidad and constructing sewer plants in Bon Accord and Buccoo in Tobago. A review of Jampro's activities in the 1990s under the New Industrial Plan reveals that there was no such project in Jamaica. Rather, private-sector investment in similar tourism-development ventures was facilitated by Jampro. In conclusion, the experience of the 1990s demonstrates a pattern of association similar to that of the 1960–90 years of the study.

Development Bureaucracies and Social Change in the 1990s: The Associations

With regard to the association between decentralization, participation, and bureaucratic politics and social change, a few observations are made regarding the situation in T&T, where social change was defined in ethnic terms and was achieved in the 1990s.

The Ministry of Education, and education policy in general, is an important arena for understanding these changes. With respect to decentralization, the variable most strongly associated with social change, a close examination of the debates in education planning in the 1990s reveals that East Indian interest associations fought and won the battle to preserve the decentralized School Board system. This period was also characterized by participation in education policy formulation through a broad-based consultative process. The event that precipitated the debates of the 1990s was the 1994 publication of a research report by the Centre for Ethnic Studies entitled 'A study of the secondary school population in T&T: Placement patterns and practices.' The findings of this report confirmed previously held suspicions that the denominations School Board, with its right to determine 20 per cent of student intake, had altered the balance of power in the interest of East Indian and white students from upper-class homes; Afro-Trinidadian females with similar or better scores were found to be the greatest casualties of this system.

The general conclusion drawn from the report was that School Board autonomy over recruitment, placement and transfer provided disproportionate educational opportunities to racially specific groups. The fact that the report's release was timed to coincided with the National Consultation on Education suggests that the PNM was preparing to take control over what appeared to be a dysfunctional system (interviews with ex-Cabinet Ministers, July 1997). However, two factors prevented this course of action. The first was the strong opposition of interest associations, including Catholic and East Indian associations, to any attempts to reform the system. Indeed, the Maha Sabha called for a national referendum if School Board rights guaranteed under the Concordat were to be revised. The second was that, although the PNM was concerned with the discriminatory implications of the School Board system, it was also persuaded of the effectiveness of decentralization as a superior implementation strategy in areas of social policy. Consequently, to the delight of participating interest groups, the outcome of the forum was a new education policy that deepened decentralization in education as never before in the history of T&T.

With regard to the environmental variables—bureaucratic politics and participation—a pattern similar to that of the 1980s could be observed in the 1990s. The decade of the 1990s witnessed increased participation by East Indian interest associations in education policy-making. This was aided by the wider processes of mobilization and politicization that were taking place in T&T. What was different about this period, however, was that the interest associations participating in education policy formulation appeared to have developed beyond the old-style Maha Sabha. They tended to be umbrella institutions, more formally constituted than the Maha Sabha, and headed by individuals with relatively higher education levels. In the 1990s, issues of bureaucratic politics in the Ministry of Education also came to a head when the female Afro-Trinidadian Permanent Secretary of the Ministry was removed and replaced with a male East Indian officer.

One final comment that must be made at this juncture is that, as the goal of social change for the East Indian population of T&T dominated the populist agenda in 1990s, the question of advancement for East Indian women as a distinct group was subsumed in the new movement. Thus the only female member of the UNC with an independent populist following was dubbed a 'loose canon' and summarily banished into political wilderness. While in the field of education the statistics continue to show high performance levels for East Indian females, this is not reflected in the new political dispensation dominated by male East Indian Ministers and heads of parastatals; business also takes on a similar configuration. In conclusion, the findings of the 1990s are similar to those of the 1980s, showing an association between the specified development administration variables and social change. However, on this occasion, change took on an ethnic hue.

The Practice of Development Administration in Jamaica and Trinidad & Tobago: Some Notes into the 21st Century

As the Caribbean nations of the Commonwealth move into the 21st century, they do so in a context of economic restructuring, incorporation into the internationalization of criminality, and considerable challenges to the nationhood project launched in the early 1960s. Given this context, it is imperative that the role and function of administration be re-examined and discussed. In both Jamaica and T&T, the respective governments in power towards the close of the 20th century already hinted at the direction of development administration. Are they on the right track? What difficulties lie ahead with the implementation of their programmes? What are their chances of success and the threats in their environment?

At the start of the 21st century, the PNP government in Jamaica is charting a course for development administration based on a new type of performance-oriented managerialism with accountability. This new thinking seems to be based on the premise that 16 years of the administrative reform programme is sufficient to reap returns. Consequently, development bureaucracies are now expected to initiate social partnerships with NGOs, the private sector, and international development agencies. In doing so, they and their officers are to be held accountable if targets are not achieved. This new thinking was heralded by the Citizen's Charter launched in December 1994.

The Charter as it was conceived was tantamount to institutionalizing the Ombudsman function throughout the public service, as all participating agencies were required to render quality service that was responsive to the needs of clients and social partners. By 1996, it became clear that the accountability essential to the success of the Charter could only be enforced if each unit and functionary were assigned clear goals and objectives. By early 1998, government had developed a set of punitive sanctions for failure to achieve goals and objectives. In effect, all participating public agencies are now being asked to execute a contract with central government for services to be provided. Failure to provide such services will attract penalties such as wage freezes and withholding of funds; surpassing targets is to be rewarded by 'special recognition and remuneration.' This new vision for the future strives to reconcile issues of social change with the dominant model of economic growth. This is particularly important as the PNP confronts and redresses the poverty-related causes of 'political tribalism' in the garrison communities of contemporary urban Jamaica.

In T&T, the programme of the UNC government—Public Administration for the 21st Century (P.A.-21)—is anchored with notions of mobilizing and motivating of the population towards the goal of efficiency and service. For the UNC, the challenge of the 21st century is to create a 'total quality nation' in which professional standards and efficiency are precipitated by the winds of change sweeping through the country. Under P.A.-21, it was envisioned that a 'new type of public administration' would set an example for civil society by becoming 'a symbol of patriotism and national pride' (GOTT Green Paper 1996: 7). In short, a total quality public administration is expected to lead a total quality nation. It was further envisioned that the public service and civil society will demonstrate a work ethic and organizational behaviour 'based on competence, performance, productivity, quality and high standards, service to the public/customers' (ibid.). While the underlying goal informing P.A.-21 is economic growth, social change through increased participation by the East Indian community is implied as a necessary condition for goal attainment.

Jamaica and T&T are now following two fundamentally different models for development administration. Their origins lie in the conditions specific to each country, as do their chances of success or failure. Consequently, while the Jamaican model assumes material reward as the maximum motivator, in T&T higher-order needs of belonging and high achievement constitute the bedrock of the model.

The theoretical superiority of the T&T model is, however, undermined by the fact that the mobilization ideology articulated by the UNC for high achievement and total quality in both the bureaucracy and the wider society has, so far, failed to include the non-East Indian population. Indeed, the UNC's reaction to what they perceive as 40 years of East Indian exclusion has led to a situation in which the consolidation of representation is the current development politics. Who should be mobilized, around whose national goals, how these goals benefit ethnically defined communities, and who should implement them are questions that now dominate the development administration agenda in T&T.

On the other hand, the negative implications of the neo-MBO and pseudo-Taylorite Jamaican model seem to be offset by the location of this model within a framework that views development as a social partnership between the state, the private sector, civil society organizations, international capital and international development organizations. This model is advanced by middle-class interests from a standpoint of a social consensus involving constituencies that are still in conflict in T&T and other parts of the Caribbean. T&T's reliance on mobilization in the context of ethnic polarization suggests that, unless the benefits of selective mobilization in the public service outweigh the costs of alienating non-East Indian bureaucrats, then it is conceivable that, at best, low motivation or, at worse, sabotage, will characterize the T&T public service in the 21st century.

One possible solution to this problem may be to exploit the motivational value of performance-based reward systems for specific categories of public servants, as proposed in Jamaica. This, however, may not be possible given the absence of any such precedent in the administrative-reform experience of T&T. Moreover, given the throes of ethnic conflict in which the society now finds itself, it is inconceivable that any argument for selective reward enhancement will be interpreted as anything but discriminatory.

Jamaica seems to be entering equally dangerous waters at the start the 21st century. Unless serious consideration is given to motivating middle to lower ranks around non-monetary reward as was done in the old days of democratic socialism, the full benefits of the administrative reform program may not be realized. Unlike their T&T counterparts, Jamaicans, with their homogenous culture, can be rallied around patriotism, i.e., performance management may not be the only motivator. So far, this question has been addressed through the PNP's emphasis on societal values. This, however, is not enough. The PNP, or indeed any successor government, must find creative ways to motivate public servants around themes that draw from goals of social change and redistribution.

Finally, as economic growth continues to be the main development goal to dominate the policy agenda in Jamaica and T&T at the outset of the 21st century, the imperatives of change cannot be ignored. How can these two be reconciled? What is the relationship between development bureaucracies implementing growth and change goals and what are the fiscal implications? For the first time, the 1990s ushered in an era in which economic growth was precipitated by economic change, which in turn precipitated social change for groups such as women in Jamaica. Can this situation be sustained? Given the 1998 crisis of Jamaica's garment sector, the criticism that Jampro attracted with the 1998 publication of the infamous Kurt Salmon report, and the country's mounting debt burden, questions about the sustainability of the Jamaican growth model become even more significant (*Observer* 12/4/98). In T&T, a quaint situation has emerged in which economic growth preoccupies the formal policy agenda while social change dominates the populist agenda. Resources deployed in support of the latter have had an inverse impact on the former. The challenge for T&T in the 21st century is more demanding than P.A.-21. It is a challenge to harness the potential of rebirth occasioned by social change to achieve structural adjustment and sustainability. Central questions that must occupy the mind of any astute Caribbeanist are: what bureaucratic structures will make this possible, who should head them, and what socio-political system is required for success?

Two further issues follow from this point. First, the pre-eminence of economic growth on the policy agenda has marked an end to party politics and signalled a new era of policy continuity and political managerialism in the Commonwealth countries of the Caribbean. In Jamaica, old-style socialists recruited into government have turned their creative energies to managing aspects of the adjustment program with vigour and commitment. The difference between the JLP and PNP has simply become an issue of acronyms. In T&T, the UNC has also had no alternative but to continue and, indeed, to deepen many of the PNM's and NAR's economic programmes. The UNC's excursions into the politics of ethnic redress can potentially render T&T an exception in the current era of managerialism and policy continuity.

Secondly, the end of conviction politics in the 1990s also seems to spell an end to gender politics. In both Jamaica and T&T, social change for women is no longer on the agenda. Despite our findings in the previous chapter that women can benefit from certain policies even when they are not the targeted beneficiaries, the absence of gender-focused policy making in Jamaica and T&T is cause for concern. This observation is, however, more applicable to T&T than to Jamaica. In Jamaica, gender concerns have been more popularized by the activities of the Bureau of Women's Affairs. The problem with the Jamaican situation, however, is that popularization may lead policymakers to conclude that women's emancipation has been achieved. Indeed, the counter-ideology that men, not women, are the underclass in Jamaica is potentially more dangerous than T&T's failure to address gender questions altogether.

Implications for the Theory of Development Administration: Some Notes into the 21st Century

The uncertain future of Public Administration makes the problems of Development Administration pale into insignificance. Nonetheless, at the outset of the 21st century, as Development Studies retreats even further, it is imperative that the questions on bureaucracy's attributes for development be confronted with new zeal and answered satisfactorily. The current answers put forward by the World Bank, with its neo-liberal thinking, cannot be accepted in isolation from 40 years of development administration theorization, that preceded the new orthodoxy. What is required now is that a future course for development administration be charted in the waters of converging variables and recurring themes. This study has demonstrated the utility of such an approach. Its findings confirm the theoretical integrity of development administration as a discipline, and offers research and theory-building directions for the 21st century.

Perhaps the most important of such findings is that organizational variables are more closely associated with bureaucratic performance than are environmental variables. This suggests a bright future for the normative/consultancy perspective in development administration, as possibilities exist for enhancing performance through strategies such as administrative capacity-building and decentralization. The commitment of the World Bank to reform and reorganization is not misplaced. Its practice of fine-tuning bureaucracy's structures and functions are also not misplaced in the search for improved performance levels. This finding supports the organizationalist perspective in development administration. It also supports the view that a science of public administration may yet emerge if wider comparative application can confirm the supremacy of organizational control attributes over environmental variables. One environmental variable considered and rejected in this study is that of size. Given the location of the case study in the Commonwealth Caribbean, rejection of this factor is further proof of the emerging universality of explanation.

What this study has also shown is that development administration should not be cautious in making claims about causal relationships between bureaucratic characteristics and the realization of development goals. This is not only a methodologically sound concern, and the recent experience of Jamaica reveals that new public-sector management practices are predicated on the assumption that strategic development bureaucracies have specific goals to achieve for which they must be held accountable. Therefore, it is a legitimate concern to seek to establish the relationship between attributes of bureaucracy and performance.

Similarly, by confirming the assumption that the attributes of development bureaucracy vary according to the nature of the development goal, the research points to a wide and sometimes changing scope for development administration. This finding, in particular, suggests that the current preoccupation with public-sector management and best practices is no substitute for a comprehensive development administration focus. This is because empirical reality teaches that best practices and new management strategies differ from country to country and, sometimes, between sectors in countries. The real challenge is to make sense of such differences through a development administration framework. Such a framework should relate best practices to the nature of development goals, and complement the focus on organizational practices with political and policy environment determinants.

Of equal importance are the findings from T&T that reveal the mobilization value of identity (gender and race) and its implications for bureaucratic politics and the effective management of change. This touches on the fledgling discourse of postmodernism in public administration and on motivational theory in general (Fox & Miller 1995). It also reopens the question on the utility of bureaucratic neutrality and raises issues about good governance and representativeness. Thus, questions of subjectivity in administration, which were formally viewed as traditional, prismatic behaviour, are now legitimately part of the postmodern discourse in public administration. Whether deviant or conformist, the potential of identity must be explored in future works of development administration.

Finally, through the environmental variables—participation and facilitative policy content—insights were offered into transactions between development bureaucracies and interest groups. Certain characteristics of these groups were found to be important—e.g., the extent of their organization and institutionalization. The normative implications of this finding need to be examined further in order to build capacity in nongovernmental organizations to influence public policy in developing countries. This is an important emerging area for research and action in development administration.

This study has shown that development administration is not dead. It may have had an expectant past, and it certainly has had a handicapped present, but its maturity and future are to be found in a dynamic process of theory building around recurring themes spanning from Fred Riggs to the World Bank.

Appendices

Table A1.1 *Percentage share of public administration in Jamaica's GDP, 1966–89*

Year	% Share	Year	% Share
1966	7.4	1979	13.2
1969	9.2	1980	14.0
1970	8.4	1981	14.2
1971	8.3	1982	15.2
1972	9.0	1983	14.2
1973	10.2	1984	11.9
1974	11.6	1985	10.4
1975	12.6	1986	9.7
1976	14.2	1987	9.0
1977	14.8	1988	8.9
1978	13.6	1989	8.3

Notes: As defined by the Statistical Institute of Jamaica, 'Public Administration' includes both central and local government agencies. Share in GDP represents actual expenditure, (capital and recurrent) on central and local government agencies; the parastatal sector is not captured by these statistics.

Sources: Statistical Yearbook, 1987 and 1989.

Table A1.2a Jamaica: Percentage and number of employed labour force in public administration, 1960s to 1990s

Year	%	Number	Total employed labour force
1968	10	55,300	572,200
1969	10	62,400	624,400
1972	11	67,300	598,200
1973	11	69,600	637,500
1976	14	122,000	871,700
1980	14	133,800	975,400
1985	10	101,700	1,035,000
1986	9	94,700	1,062,400
1987	8	88,200	1,060,200
1988	8	74,100	871,800
1989	8	69,000	881,100

Sources: Statistical Abstracts of Jamaica, 1967 and 1976 and 1980; The Labour Force Report 1989; and Statistical Yearbook, 1974 and 1979.

Table A1.2b Trinidad & Tobago: Percentage and number of employed labour force in public administration, 1960s to 1990s

Year	%	Number	Total employed labour force
1965	7	25,426	358,800
1968	8	29,238	363,800
1970	8.5	31,420	366,200
1975	10	39,241	395,800
1977	10.5	45,440	430,800
1979	11	53,114	447,300
1985	9.5	37,000	392,100
1986	10	40,000	390,500
1987	10	37,800	372,300
1988	10	36,600	371,600
1989	10	36,400	366,000
1990	10	39,600	374,100
1991	10	40,100	401,000

Sources: The National Income of Trinidad & Tobago 1981–91; and Comparative Analysis of the Growth of the Public Service Establishment and the Growth in the Labour Force and Population During the Period 1960-1980. (*Note:* Public administration is defined in the above sources as central and local government services.)

Table A1.3   The English-speaking Caribbean: A profile

Country	Population in 1995	Size in sq km
Anguilla	7,019	0.12
Antigua/Barbuda	67,000	0.44
Barbados	260,000	0.43
Belize	211,000	22.96
Dominica	72,000	0.75
Grenada	92,000	0.34
Guyana	826,000	214.97
Jamaica	2,500,000	11
Monsterrat	12,000	0.13
St Lucia	160,000	0.62
StKitts/Nevis	41,000	0.36
StVincent/Grenadines	110,000	0.39
Trinidad/Tobago	1,300,000	5

Country	Per Capita (US) 1995	Status	Growth rates 1985–95
Anguilla	na	Colony	na
Antigua/Barbuda	6,770	Ind 1981	2.5
Barbados	6,560	Ind 1966	0
Belize	2,530	Ind 1981	5.0
Dominica	2,800	Ind 1978	4.3
Grenada	2,630	Ind 1974	na
Guyana	530	Ind 1966	0.4
Jamaica	1,510	Ind 1962	3.6
Monsterrat	na	Colony	na
St Lucia	3,130	Ind 1979	na
StKitts/Nevis	4,760	Ind 1983	4.7
StVincent/Grenadines	2,140	Ind 1979	4.5
Trinidad/Tobago	3,770	Ind 1962	-1.7

Key: na – not available; Ind – Independence

Sources: World Development Report 1996 and 1997.

Table A2.1 Foreign ownership of assets by sectors in the T&T economy in 1976

Sector	Total assets (TT$000)	Ownership (%)		State
		Foreign	Local	
Sugar	193,189	—	16	84
Petroleum	2,358,129	73	1	26
Food, drink & tobacco	247,681	35	53	12
Textiles, garments & footwear	49,800	32	68	—
Print., publish. & paper conversion	47,169	47	35	18
Wood & related products	34,876	6	68	26
Chemicals & non-metallic	108,567	42	58	—
Assembly-type & related	158,218	57	43	
Electricity & water	464,057	—	—	100
Construction	285,429	3	97	—
Distribution	836,725	9	91	—
Transport, storage & commun.	317,458	4	8	88

Notes: The CSO calculates ownership by dividing total sectoral assets by foreign-owned, local privately-owned, and state-owned assets for each sector.

Sources: Central Statistical Office, unpublished data.

Table A2.2 Percentage of males and females working in industrial groups by administrative area in T&T, 1960

Admin. area	Agri- culture	Min- ing	Manu- facture	Con- struction	Com- merce	Public utilities[*]	Ser- vices
Urban: San Fernando							
Male	1.6	7.9	25.1	16.5	19.8	9.1	19.4
Female	0.3	0.8	11.8	1.2	20.8	2.4	62.2
Urban: Port-of-Spain							
Male	1	1	17	8	25	13	34
Female	0.1	0.2	17	0.3	22	3	57
Rural: Caroni							
Male	44	0.7	21	11	7	8	8
Female	52	0.1	8	2	11	1	46
Rural: Tobago							
Male	36	0.3	8	23	6	8	18
Female	19	—	12	5	14	2	48

[*] Transportation, communication, electricity and water.

Source: The T&T Census Bulletin No. 6 'Working Population by Sex and Type of Worker' 1962, GOTT.

*Table A2.3 Ethnic distribution of T&T's population by
administrative areas 1960–80*

Areas	African	Indian	European	Mixed	Other
1960	43.3	36.5	1.9	16.3	2.0
Port-of Spain	57.8	9.0	3.5	23.5	6.3
San Fernando	47.2	25.8	3.3	20.8	2.9
Arima	34.9	15.4	0.7	44.7	4.2
St George	48.3	26.5	2.7	20.4	2.1
Caroni	14.5	69.9	0.5	14.2	0.9
Nariva/Mayaro	35.5	47.2	0.5	14.9	1.8
St Andrew/St David	41.2	33.8	0.3	23.4	1.4
Victoria	28.6	60.4	1.3	9.0	0.7
St Patrick	42.4	42.2	1.3	12.9	1.2
Tobago	92.9	1.3	0.8	4.5	0.5
1970	42.8	40.1	1.2	14.1	1.6
Port-of Spain	38.4	10.4	2.2	22.0	5.9
San Fernando	48.1	28.1	2.4	18.4	2.8
Arima	33.0	15.8	0.5	47.5	3.0
St George	50.8	26.5	1.9	18.7	1.9
Caroni	20.1	72.2	0.3	6.5	0.6
Nariva/Mayaro	31.6	32.6	0.1	9.3	1.6
St Andrew/St David	41.8	59.0	0.2	31.7	0.9
Victoria	28.5	6.1	2.2	8.0	0.7
St Patrick	40.6	47.6	0.5	10.0	1.1
Tobago	94.4	1.5	0.6	2.8	0.4
1980	41.0	40.8	0.9	16.4	0.9
Port-of Spain	57.3	11.8	1.5	26.4	3.1
San Fernando	45.1	28.9	2.1	22.1	1.7
Arima	34.5	20.9	0.3	42.9	1.4
St George	73.2	14.8	0.3	11.2	0.6
Caroni	50.6	25.3	1.7	21.2	1.2
Nariva/Mayaro	20.0	71.1	0.2	8.2	0.4
St Andrew/St David	28.7	54.3	0.4	16.3	0.4
Victoria	37.3	38.3	0.1	23.9	0.4
St Patrick	27.0	62.6	0.6	9.4	0.4
Pt Fortin	32.2	55.5	0.2	11.6	0.5
Tobago	93.7	1.6	0.4	3.6	0.6

Note: Population distribution is for the total non-institutional population.

Sources: 1970 and 1980s statistics derived from Abdulah 1984: 53. 1970 statistics extracted from The Annual Statistical Digest 1979, 1982, Table 12: 13.

          Appendices

*Table A2.4   Labour force by occupation and sex, in Jamaica and
          T&T, 1985*

JAMAICA

Occupation	Sex	
	Male	Female
Professional, technical, executive, managerial	43	57
Clerical & sales	32	68
Self-employed & independent	66	34
Service	25	74
Craftsmen, production process, operating	84	15
Unskilled manual labourers	66	34
Not specified	32	68
Total	53	46

TRINIDAD & TOBAGO

Occupation	Sex	
	Male	Female
Professional & technical	52	48
Administrative, executive, management	76	24
Clerical & related	30	90
Service & sales workers	51	49
Labourer, process worker, craftsman	85	15
Worker in transp., construct. & communication	96	4
Farmer, fisherman	79	21
Not stated	100	—

Sources: Jamaican statistics derived from Miller 1990. T&T statistics derived
from Labour Force Report 1989, Central Statistical Office, GOTT.

Table A2.5 Percentage of total male and female population working in industrial groups by administrative area in T&T, 1980

Admin. area	Agri-culture	Min-ing	Manu-facture	Con-struction	Com-merce	Public utilities[*]	Ser-vices
Urban: San Fernando							
Male	1.5	19	7	16	18	10	24
Female	0.6	4	4	2	23	4	60
Urban: Port-of-Spain							
Male	1	1	11	16	17	35	29
Female	0.1	1	9	5	22	8	52
Rural: Caroni							
Male	23	3	11	24	8	8	16
Female	13	4	11	6	20	3	39
Rural: Tobago							
Male	0.4	8	2	36	9	6	25
Female	0.1	2	2	13	29	6	44

* Transportation, communications, electricity, water.

Sources: Population and Housing Census 1980 Volume VIII, Income, Table 2, 1987, Central Statistical Office, GOTT.

Table A2.6 Percentage change in occupations of females in T&T, by ethnic group, 1960–90

Occupations	All ethnic groups	African	Indian	Mixed	Other
Professional & technical	5.8	5.8	7.8	4.7	3.9
Admin, exec. & managerial	-9	-0.5	-1.5	-0.8	-0.9
Clerical	17.9	18.3	22.8	13.2	2.0
Sales	0.4	0.7	1.4	-2.9	-4.6
Farmers & fishermen	-12.1	-5.3	-37.0	-5.4	-2.7
Production & related	-4.01	-5.7	-0.1	-4.6	-0.3
Transport & eqpt operators	-1.1	-1.0	-0.2	-2.1	-1.3
Construction workers	-1.0	-0.9	-1.6	-0.5	-0.3
Craftsmen N.E.C.	6.0	7.0	5.8	4.2	1.9
Service workers	-14.8	-22.1	-1.0	-9.6	-1.6
Other N.E.C.	3.8	4.0	3.5	3.8	4.3

Source: Reddock 1991: 217.

Table A5 Selection from list of top-T&T public servants serving concurrently on boards of key statutory companies and corporation whilst also retaining substantive posts, 1979

Mr Eldon Warner
1.	National Agro Chemicals Ltd	Member
2.	National Gas Co.	Member
3.	T&T National Petroleum Marketing Co.	Member
4.	Iron and Steel Co.	Member
5.	Point Lisas Industrial Port Development Co.	Member
6.	Trinidad Bagasse Products Ltd	Member
7.	Management Development Centre	Vice-Chairman
8.	International Marketing Corporation	Member
9.	Allied Inn Keepers of T&T	Member

M.H.N. Adams
1.	T&T Port Contractors	Executive Chairman
2.	Pt Lisas Corporation	Member
3.	T&T Electricity Commission	Member
4.	National Insurance Board	Member
5.	National Housing Authority	Chairman
6.	Namucar	Member

Mr Frank Barsotti
1.	Caroni Limited	Chairman
2.	Forres Park Limited	Chairman
3.	Orange Grove Nation Company	Member
4.	T&T Development Finance Company	Chairman
5.	T&T Export Credit Insurance Co.	Chairman

Mr Sam Martin
1.	National Gas Co.	Member
2.	Iron Steel Co.	Member
3.	Pt Lisas Corporation	Member
4.	Trinidad Nitrogen Co.	Member

Mr Unus Baksh
1.	Shipping Corporation of T&T	Member
2.	Workers Bank of T&T	Member
3.	Caribbean Investment Corporation	Member
4.	Caribbean Development Bank	Member

Mr George H. Legall
1.	T&T National Petroleum Marketing Co.	Member
2.	Trinidad-Tesoro Petroleum Co.	Member
3.	Fertilisers of T&T	Member

Richardson Andrews
1. Orange Grove National Co.   Chairman
2. T&T Telephone Co.   Member
3. Port Authority   Member

Mr Bashrath Ali
1. National Gas Co.   Member
2. Trinidad Bagasse Products   Member
3. Industrial Development Corporation   Member

Note: The complete list from which the above 8 were extracted contains 61 entries of public servants serving on Boards. Those not mentioned here served, in the main, on only one or two Boards concurrently.

Source: Public Servants on Boards of Management of Statutory Boards and Companies in Which the Corporation Sole has Shares. The Corporation Sole, Ministry of Finance, GOTT, 1979.

*Table A6.1   Highest level of educational attainment of female
              population 5 years and above in African- and Indian-
              dominated rural administrative areas, T&T, 1960*

| | Rural administrative area | |
	Caroni	Tobago
Total female population	36,894	13,930
No education		
Number	8,328	187
%	22	1
Primary		
Number	26,824	12,513
%	73	90
Secondary		
Number	1,640	1,194
%	4	8
University		
Number	16	34
%	0	0.2

Source: Census Bulletin No.15, Central Statistical Office, GOTT, 1962.

*Table A6.2   Highest level of educational attainment of female
              population 5 years and above in urban administrative
              areas, T&T, 1960*

| | Urban administrative area | |
	Port-of-Spain	San Fernando
Total female population 5 yrs +	44,782	17,922
No education		
Number	1,127	839
%	2.5	5
Primary		
Number	31,479	12,982
%	70	72
Secondary		
Number	11,300	3,774
%	25	21
University		
Number	163	63
%	0.3	0.3

Table A6.3 *Highest level of educational attainment of female population 5 years and above in Indian- and African-dominated rural administrative areas, T&T, 1980*

	Rural administrative area	
	Caroni	Tobago
Total female population 5 yrs +	60,681	17,579
No education		
Number	5,620	101
%	9	0.5
Kindergarten & primary		
Number	38,361	12,100
%	63	68
Secondary		
Number	15,838	5,060
%	26	29
University		
Number	330	89
%	0.6	0.5

Note: The difference between total female population 5 years & > (column 2) and the summation of kindergarten—primary, secondary, and university population (columns 3, 4 & 5) is reflected in the categories 'not stated' and 'other' educational level in the Census data from which this table is derived. These figures are largely insignificant and therefore not captured in this table.

Sources: Population and Housing Census 1980, Volume 11, Table 6. Central Statistical Office, 1983, GOTT.

Bibliography

Books and Journal Articles

Adam, C., Cavendish, W. & Mistry, P.S. (1993) *Adjusting Privatization.* London: Ian Randle Publishers.

Adamolekun, L. (1989) 'Public Sector Management Improvement in Sub-Saharan Africa: The World Bank Experience'. In Balogun, M.J. & Mutahaba, G. (eds) *Economic Restructuring and African Public Administration.* Colorado: Kumarian Press.

Adamolekun, L. & Rowlands, L. (eds) (1979) *The New Local Government System in Nigeria: Problems and Prospects for Implementation.* Ibadan: Heinemann.

Ahiram, E. (1966) 'Distribution of Income in Trinidad-Tobago and Jamaica'. *Social and Economic Studies* 15 (2) 103-20.

Allahar, A.L. (1989) *Sociology and the periphery theories and issues.* Toronto: Garamond Press.

Ambursley, F. & Cohen, R. (eds) (1983) *Crisis in the Caribbean.* Kingston: Heinemann Books.

Annamunthodo, W. (1988) *Plunderers and Our Children. The Printing of Textbooks Locally in Relation to Open Government and One Love.* Trinidad: The Public Affairs Committee of T&T.

Auty, R. (1988) 'Trinidad & Tobago: Windfalls in a Small Parliamentary Democracy'. In Gelb, A. (ed.). *Oil Windfalls. Blessing or Curse?* Oxford: World Bank Research Publishers, Oxford University Press.

Ayub, A.M. (1981) *Made in Jamaica. The Development of the Manufacturing Sector.* Baltimore: Johns Hopkins University Press.

Baker, R. (ed.) (1992) *Public Administration in Small and Island States.* Connecticut: Kumarian Press.

Bamberger, M. (1991) 'The Importance of Community Participation'. *Public Administration and Development* 11 (3) 281-284.

Barclay, L-A. (1991) 'Industrial Policy and the State in T&T'. MSc Thesis, St Augustine, Department of Economics, University of the West Indies.

Barnett, L. (1977) *The Constitutional Law of Jamaica*. Oxford: Published for the London School of Economics and Political Science by Oxford University Press.

Barrett, I. (1985) 'The Ombudsman in Jamaica'. *Social and Economic Studies* 34 (1) 59-75.

Bartilow, C. (1986) 'Public Administration under Democratic Socialism in Jamaica'. MSc Thesis, Mona, Jamaica: Department of Government, University of the West Indies.

Bauer, P.T. (1972) *Dissent on Development*. London: Cox & Wyman.

Beckford, G. & Girvan, N. (eds) (1983) *Development in Suspense*. Kingston: Friedrich Ebert Stifung.

Bellew, R.T. & King, E.M. (1993) 'Educating Women: Lessons from Experience'. In King, E.M. & Hill, M. (eds) *Women's Education in Developing Countries. Barriers, Benefits, and Policies*. Baltimore: Published for the World Bank, John Hopkins University Press. 285-322.

Benedict, B. (ed.) (1967) *Problems of Smaller Territories*. London: University of London/Athlone Press.

Berman, P. (1980) 'Thinking about Programmed and Adaptive Implementation: Matching Strategies to Situations'. In Ingram, H. & Mann, D. (eds). *Why Policies Succeed or Fail*. London: Sage Yearbooks in Politics and Public Policy, Vol.8.

Beyle, T.L. & Lathrop, G.T. (eds) (1970) *Planning and Politics: Uneasy Partnership*. New York: The Odyssey Press.

Bjorkman, J.W. (1979) *Politics of Administrative Alienation in India's Rural Development Programs*. Delhi, Ajanta Publications.

Blake, H. (1984) 'Jamaica Case Study'. In Gordon, S. (ed.). *Ladies in Limbo. The Fate of Women's Bureaux. Six Case Studies from the Caribbean*. London: Women and Development Programme, Human Resources Development Group, Commonwealth Secretariat.

Boneo, H. (1983) *Government Control over Public Enterprises in Latin America*. International Centre for Public Enterprises in Developing Countries, Monograph Series, No. 9, Ljubljana: ICPE.

Boyd, D. (1988) *Economic Management, Income Distribution, and Poverty in Jamaica*. New York: Praeger.

Braibanti, R. & Spengler, J.J. (eds) (1961) *Tradition, Values and Socio-Economic Development*. Durham, N.C.: Duke University Press.

Bray, M. (1992) 'The Organization and Management of Ministries of Education in Small States'. In Baker, R. (ed.). *Public Administration in Small and Island States*. Connecticut: Kumarian Press.

Bryant, C. & White, L. (1982) *Managing Development in the Third World*. Colorado: Westview Press.

Bryant, C. (1980) 'Organizational Impediments to Making Participation a Reality: Swimming Upstream in AID'. *Rural Development Participation Review* 1 (3) 8-10.

Burnham, P. (1992) 'Education and Social Change in Trinidad & Tobago'. Unpublished Report, Ministry of Education, Trinidad & Tobago.

Caiden, N. & Wildavsky, A. (1974) *Planning and Budgeting in Poor Countries*. New York: John Wiley.

Campbell, C. (1992) *Colony and Nation. A Short History of Education in Trinidad & Tobago*. Kingston, Jamaica: Ian Randel.

Chakravarty, S. (1991) 'Development Planning: A reappraisal'. *Cambridge Journal of Economics* 15 (1) 5-19.

Charlton, C. (1991) 'Investment Patterns and Economic Growth in Jamaica: 1981-1988'. MA Research Paper. The Hague, Institute of Social Studies.

Cheema, S.G. & Rondinelli, D.A. (eds) (1983) *Decentralization and Development: Policy Implementation in Developing Countries*. Beverly Hills: Sage.

Commonwealth Secretariat (1995) *Current Good Practices and New Developments in Public Service Management. A Profile of the Public Service of Trinidad & Tobago*. Ontario: Commonwealth Association for Public Administration and Management.

Conyers, D. (1981) 'Decentralization for Regional Development: A Comparative Study of Tanzania, Zambia and Papua New Guinea'. *Public Administration and Development* 1: 107-20.

Copestake, J. (1996) 'NGO-state collaboration and the new policy agenda-the case of subsidized credit'. *Public Administration and Development* 16: 21-30.

Courier, The (1990) 'Barbados. Basking in Economic Sunshine'. September-October 11-28.

Crichlow, M.D. (1988) 'Agricultural Policy and the Development of a Small Holding Stratum in Jamaica, 1930-1980'. PhD Thesis, Binghamton: Graduate School of the State University of New York.

Dahl, R. (1947) 'The Science of Public Administration'. *Public Administration Review* 7 (1) 1-11.

Dahl, R. (1961) *Who governs? Democracy and Power in an American City*. New Haven: Yale University Press.

Davies, O. (1984) 'Economic Transformation in Jamaica: Some Policy Issues'. *Studies in Comparative International Development* 19 (3) 40-58.

Dimock, M. (1949 'Government Corporations. A Focus of Policy and Administration'. *The American Political Science Review* 43 (5) 899-921.

Dwivedi, O.P. & Nef, J. (1982) 'Crises and Continuities in Development Theory and Administration: First and Third World Perspectives'. *Public Administration and Development* 2: 59-77.

Farrell, T.M.A. (1984) 'In Whose Interest. Nationalization and Bargaining with the Petroleum Multinationals: The Trinidad & Tobago Experience'. Mimeograph, St Augustine: University of the West Indies.

Farrell, T.M.A. (1986) 'The Caribbean State and its Role in Economic Management'. In Davies, O. (ed.). *The State in Caribbean Society*. Mona: University of the West Indies.

Farrell, T.W. (1989) 'The IMF and the Trinidad & Tobago letter of Intent'. *Asset* 7 (2) 8-19.

Finlay, A.A. (1984) 'Recent Educational Changes and Developments in Jamaica and their Implications for Administration'. PhD Thesis, Ann Arbor, Michigan: Columbia Teachers College.

Fisseha, Y. & Davies, O. (1981) 'The Small-Scale Manufacturing Enterprises in Jamaica: Socio-Economic Characteristics and Constraints'. *Rural Development Series*, Working Paper No.16, Michigan: Michigan State University.

Fox, C.J. & Miller, H.T. (1995) *Postmodern Public Administration. Towards Discourse*. London: Sage.

Francis, F. (1979) 'The Evolution of Development Planning in Trinidad & Tobago'. MSc Thesis, Department of Economics, Trinidad & Tobago, St Augustine: University of West Indies.

Fry, G. (1986) 'The British Civil Service Under Challenge'. *Political Studies* 34 (3) 533-55.

Gable, R.W. (1975) *Development Administration Background Terms, Concepts, Theories and a New Approach*. Washington D.C.: USAID.

Garcia-Zamor, J-C. (1970) 'Development Administration in the Commonwealth Caribbean'. *International Review of Administrative Sciences* 36 (3) 201-14.

Garcia-Zamor, J-C. (1977) *The Ecology of Development Administration in Jamaica, Trinidad & Tobago, and Barbados*. Program of Development Financing, Organization of American States.

Garner, M.R. (1983) 'The Relationship Between Government and Public Enterprise'. In Reddy, G.R. (ed.). *Government and Public Enterprise. Essays in Honour of Professor V.V. Ramanadham*. London: Frank Cass.

Garrity, M. & Picard, L.A. (1996) *Policy Reform for Sustainable Development in the Caribbean*. Brussels: International Institute of Administrative Science Monographs.

Ghai, Y. (1977) 'Law and Public Enterprise in Tanzania'. In Ghai, Y. (ed.). *Law in the Political Economy of Public Enterprise. African perspectives.* Uppsala: Scandinavian Institute of African Studies.

Ghai, Y. (ed.) (1990) *Public Administration and Management in Small States: Pacific Experiences.* London: The Commonwealth Secretariat.

Girvan, N. (1971) *Foreign Capital and Economic Underdevelopment in Jamaica.* Mona, Jamaica: Institute of Social and Economic Research.

Girvan, N. et al. (1991) *Rethinking Development.* Mona: The Consortium Graduate School of Social Sciences, University of the West Indies.

Glaessner, P. (1992) 'Genesis of the Administrative Reform Programme in Jamaica'. In Ryan, S. & Brown, D. (eds) *Issues and Problems in Caribbean Public Administration Vols. I & II.* St Augustine, Trinidad: Department of Government, Univeristy of the West Indies.

Gleaner Publishing Company, The (1987) *The Jamaica Directory of Personalities 1985-1987.* Kingston: The Gleaner Publishing Company.

Gray, E.A. (1983) 'State Power and Forms of Political Opposition in Post-Colonial Jamaica 1962-72', PhD Thesis, Ann Arbor: University of Michigan, University Microfilms International.

Griffin, K. (1981) 'Economic Development in a Changing World'. *World Development.* 9 (3) 221-226.

Grindle, M. (1997) 'Divergent Cultures? When Public Organizations Perform Well in Developing Countries'. *World Development* 25 (4) 481-95.

Gross, B. (1967) *Action Under Planning.* New York: McGraw-Hill.

Hamel-Smith, A. (1984) 'Primary Education and East Indian Women in 1900-56 Trinidad'. Paper Presented at the Third Conference on East Indians in the Caribbean. St Augustine, Trinidad: University of the West Indies.

Hamilton, B.L. (1964) *Problems of Administration in an Emergent Nation: A Case Study of Jamaica.* New York: Praeger.

Handa, S. & King, D. (1997) 'Structural Adjustment Policies, Income Distribution and Poverty: A Review of the Jamaican Experience'. *World Development* 25 (6) 915-30.

Hansen, M. (1985) 'Management Improvement Initiatives in the Reagan Administration: Round Two'. *Public Administration Review* 45 (3) 441-46.

Hanson, A.H. (1964) 'Government Organisation for Government Enterprise'. In Moodie, G. (ed.).

Harewood, J. (1974) *The Population of Trinidad & Tobago.* World Population Year, CICRED Series.

Hassard, J. & Parker, M. (eds) (1994) *Towards a New Theory of Organizations.* London: Routledge.

Heady, F. (1970) 'Bureaucracies in Developing Countries'. In Riggs, F.W. (ed.) *Frontiers of Development Administration*. Durham, N.C.: Duke University Press.

Heady, F. (1979) *Public Administration. A Comparative Perspective*. New York: Marcel Dekker.

Heaver, T. (1986) 'Protest Movements in Jamaica and their Impact on Change 1938-1968'. MSc Thesis, Mona, Jamaica: Department of Government, University of the West Indies.

Henry, N. (1989) *Public Administration and Public Affairs*. New Jersey, Prentice-Hall.

Henry-Wilson, M. (1985) 'Institution-Building and Development. A Case-Study of the Ministry of National Mobilization and Human Resource Development Established in Jamaica, January 1977'. MSc Thesis, Mona, Jamaica: Department of Government, University of the West Indies.

Henry-Wilson, M. (1989) 'The Status of the Jamaican Woman, 1962 to the Present'. In Nettleford, R. (ed.) *Jamaica in Independence*. Kingston, Jamaica: Heinemann Publishers.

Hirschmann, D. (1981) 'Development or Underdevelopment Administration? A Further "Deadlock"'. *Development and Change* 12 (3) 459-79.

Hondale, B.W. (1981) 'A Capacity Building Framework: A Search for Concepts and Purpose'. *Public Adminstration Review* 41 (5) 575-80.

Hood, C. & Schuppert, G.F. (eds) (1988) *Delivering Public Services in Western Europe*. London: Sage.

Hood, C. (1990) 'Public Administration: Lost an Empire, Not Yet Found a Role?' In Leftwich, A. (ed.) *New Developments in Political Science. An International Review of Achievements and Prospects*. Hants, England: Edward Elgar Publishing.

Hyden, G. (1983) *No Shortcuts to Progress. African Development Management in Perspective*. London: Heinemann Educational Books.

Ilchman, W.F. (1965) 'Rising Expectations and the Revolution in Development Administration'. *Public Administration Review* 25: 329-414.

Indiresan, P.V. (1990) *Managing Development*. New Delhi: Sage Publications.

Islam, N. (1993) 'Public Enterprise Reform: Managerial Autonomy, Accountability and Performance Contracts'. *Public Administration and Development* 13 (2) 129-52.

Jaeger, A.M. & Kunungo, R.N. (eds) (1990) *Management in Developing Countries*. London: Routledge.

Jain, R.B. (ed.) (1989) *Bureaucratic Politics in the Third World*. Delhi: Gitanjali Publishing House.

James, V. (1993) *Caribbean Survival Strategies: The Competitive Practices of Indigenous Capitalist*. St Augustine: Department of Economics, University of the West Indies.

Jefferson, O. (1972) *Post-War Economic Development of Jamaica*. Mona, Jamaica: Institute of Social and Economic Research.

Jones, E. (1968) 'The Role of Statutory Boards in the Political Process of Jamaica 1955-65'. MSc Thesis, Mona, Jamaica: Department of Government, University of the West Indies.

Jones, E. (1970) 'Pressure Group Politics in the West Indies. A case study of Colonial Systems: Jamaica, Trinidad and British Guiana'. PhD Thesis, Manchester: University of Manchester.

Jones, E. (1975) 'Tendencies and Change in Caribbean Administrative Systems'. *Social and Economic Studies* 24 (2) 239-56.

Jones, E. (1976) 'Bureaucracy as a Problem-solving Mechanism in Small States: A Review in terms of the Current Literature'. In V. Lewis (ed.) *Size, Self-determination and International Relations: The Caribbean*. Mona, Jamaica: Institute of Social and Economic Research.

Jorgensen, J.J. (1990) 'Organizational Life-cycle and Effectiveness Criteria in State-owned Enterprises: the Case of East Africa'. In Jaeger, A.M. & Kanungo, R.N. (eds) *Management in Developing Countries*. London: Routledge.

Jun, J.S. (1976) 'Reviewing the Study of Comparative Administration: Some Reflections on the Current Possibilities'. *Public Administration Review* 36 (6) 641-47.

Kaufman, M. (1985) *Jamaica Under Manley. Dilemmas of Socialism and Democracy*. London: Zed.

Kemp-Hope, R. (1983) 'The Administration of Development in Emergent Nations. The Problem in the Caribbean'. *Public Administration and Development* 3 (1) 49-59.

Kernaghan, W.D.K. & Dwivedi, O.P. (eds) (1983) *Ethics in the Public Service*. Brussels: International Institute of Administrative Sciences.

Kersell, J. (1987) 'Government Administration in a Small Microstate: Developing the Cayman Islands'. *Public Administration and Development* 7: 95-107.

Kersell, J. (1985) 'The Administration of Government in Bermuda'. *Public Administration and Development* 5: 373-84.

Khan, J. (1982) *Public Management: The Eastern Caribbean Experience*. Leiden: Royal Institute of Linguistics and Anthropology.

Khan, M.M. (1985) 'Rural Development Programs in Bangladesh'. In Garcia-Zamor, J-C. (ed.) *Public Participation in Development Planning and*

Management. Cases from Africa and Asia. Colorado, Boulder: Westview Replica Edition.

Kiggundu, M.N. (1990) 'Managing Structural Adjustment in Developing Countries: An Organizational Perspective'. In Jaeger, A. & Kanungo, R. (eds) *Management in Developing Countries.* London: Routledge.

King, E.M. & Hill, M. (1993) *Women's Education in Developing Countries. Barriers, Benefits, and Policies.* Baltimore: Published for the World Bank, John Hopkins University Press.

King, J. (1967) *Economic Development Projects and their Appraisal.* Baltimore: John Hopkins Press.

Kitching, G. (1989) *Development and Underdevelopment in Historical Perspective.* London: Routledge.

Kitchen, R. (1992) 'Administrative Reform in Jamaica: A Component of Structural Adjustment'. In B. Smith (ed.) *Progress in Development Administration. Selected papers from Public Administration and Development 1981-1991.* West Sussex: John Wiley & Sons.

Konig, K. (1997) 'Three Worlds of Public Administration Modernization'. Roundtable of the International Institute of Administrative Sciences' Quebec City.

Korten, G. (1985) 'A Participatory Approach to Irrigation Development in the Philippines'. In Garcia-Zamor, J-C. (ed.) *Public Participation in Development Planning and Management. Cases from Africa and Asia.* Colorado, Boulder: Westview Replica Edition.

La Palombara, J. (ed.) (1963) *Bureaucracy and Political Development.* N.J.: Princeton University Press.

Lee, E. (1988) 'Land Reform and the Process of Agrarian Change in Jamaica (1972-1980): An analysis of the Project Land Lease Programme'. MA Research Paper. The Hague: Institute of Social Studies.

LeFranc, E. (1989) 'Petty Trading and Labour Mobility: Higglers in the Kingston Metropolitan Area'. In Hart, K. (ed.) *Women and the Sexual Division of Labour in the Caribbean.* Kingston, Jamaica: Consortium Graduate School of Social Sciences.

Leftwich, A. (1994) 'Governance, the State and the Politics of Development'. *Development and Change* 25 (2) 363-86.

Leftwich, A. (1993) 'Governance, Democracy and Development in the Third World'. *Third World Quarterly* 14 (3) 605-24.

Lehmbruch, G. (1979) 'Consociational Democracy, Class Conflict and the New Corporatism'. In P.C. Schmitter & G. Lehmbruch (eds) *Trends towards Corporatist Intermediation.* London: Sage.

Leonard, D.K. (1987) 'The Political Realities of African Management'. *World Development* 15 (7) 899-910.

Lesson, P.F. & Nixon, F.I. (1988) 'Development Economics and the State'. In Lesson, P.F. & Minogue, M.M. (eds) *Perspectives on Development. Cross-disciplinary themes in Development Studies*. New York, Manchester University Press.

Levy, O. (ed.) (1973) *Personalities Caribbean*. Kingston: Personalities Caribbean, Ltd.

Levy, O. (ed.) (1979) *Personalities Caribbean*. Kingston: Personalities Caribbean, Ltd.

Lewis, G. (1968) *The Growth of the Modern West Indies*. New York: Monthly Review Press.

Leys, C. (1969) *Politics and Change in Developing Countries*. Cambridge: Cambridge University Press.

Lijphart, A. (1975) 'The Comparable-Case Strategy in Comparative Research'. *Comparative Political Studies* 8 (2) 158-177.

Lindblom, C. (1975) 'The Sociology of Planning: Thought and Social Interaction'. In Bornstein, M. (ed.) *Economic Planning, East and West*. Cambridge: Ballinger Publishers.

Lindenberg, M. (1989) 'Making Economic Adjustment Work: The Politics of Policy Implementation'. *Policy Science* 22 (3-4) 359-94.

Lowi, T. (1964) 'American Business, Public Policy, Case Studies and Political Theory'. *World Politics*, 16 (4) 677-715.

MacDonald, B.S. (1986) *Trinidad & Tobago: Democracy and Development in the Caribbean*. New York: Praeger.

Mahabir, W. (1975) *In and Out of Politics*. Port-of-Spain: Inprint Caribbean.

Manley, M. (1982) *Jamaica. Struggle in the Periphery*. London: Third World Media Ltd.

Mascarenhas, R.C. (1993) 'Building an Enterprise Culture in the Public Sector: Reform of the Public Sector in Australia, Britain, and New Zealand'. *Public Administration Review* 53 (4) 319-28.

Mathur, B.P. (1977) *Public Enterprises in Perspective*. Bombay: Orient Longman.

McClelland, D. (1964) 'The Achievement Motivation in Economic Growth'. In Novack, D. and Lekachman, R. (eds) *Development and Society: the dynamics of economic change*. New York: St Martin's Press.

McGregor, E. Jr (1983) 'The Public Service Problem'. *Annals of the American Academy of Political and Social Science* 46 (March) 61-76.

Meckstroth, T.W. (1975) 'Most Different Systems and Most Similar Systems: A Study in the Logic of Comparative Inquiry'. *Comparative Political Studies* 8 (2) 132-57.

Mehmet, O. (1978) *Economic Planning and Social Justice in Developing Countries*. London: Croom Helm.

Meillassoux, C. (1970) 'A Class Analysis of the Bureaucratic Process in Mali'. *Journal of Development Studies* 6 (2) 97-110.

Midgley (1986) 'Community Participation: History, Concepts and Controversies'. In Midgley et al.

Midgley, J., Hall, A., Hardiman, M. & Narine, D. (eds) (1986) *Community Participation Social Development and The State*. London: Methuen & Co.

Miller, E. (1969) 'Self-concept of Girls in Relationship to Physical and Social Intellectual Variables'. PhD Thesis, Mona, Jamaica: University of the West Indies.

Miller, E. (1989) 'Educational Development in Independent Jamaica'. In Nettleford (ed.) *Jamaica in Independence*. Kingston, Jamaica: Heinemann Publishers.

Miller, E. (1990) *Jamaican Society and High Schooling*. Mona, Jamaica: Institute of Social and Economic Research.

Mills, G.E. (1966) 'Education and Training for the Public Services in the West Indies'. *Journal of Administration Overseas* 5 (3) 155-66.

Mills, G.E. (1971) 'Public Administration in the Commonwealth Caribbean: Evolution, Conflicts and Challenges'. In T. Munroe & R. Lewis (eds) *Readings in Government and Politics of the West Indies*. Kingston, Jamaica: The Herald.

Mills, G.E. (1977) 'Conflict between Ministers, Civil Servants'. In S. Ryan (ed.). *Issues and Problems in Caribbean Public Administration*. Mona, Jamaica: University of the West Indies.

Mills, G.E. (1990a) *A Reader in Public Policy and Administration*. Mona, Jamaica: Institute of Social and Economic Research.

Mills, G. (1990b) 'The English-speaking Caribbean'. In V. Subramaniam (ed.) *Public Administration in the Third World*. London: Greenwood Press.

Moharir, V.V. (1991) 'Capacity Building Initiative for Sub-Saharan Africa'. *Public Enterprise* 11 (4) 235-45.

Montgomery, J.D. (1986) 'Bureaucratic politics in Southern Africa'. *Public Administration Review* 46 (95) 407-13.

Montgomery, J.D. (1988) *Bureaucrats and People. Grassroots Participation in Third World Development*. Maryland: Johns Hopkins University Press.

Murray, D.J. (1977) 'A Problem in the Administrative Development of Small Island States'. In Sharma, S.K. (ed.) *Dynamics of development: An international perspective. Volume one: General, political and administrative*. Delhi: Concept Publishing.

Murray, D.J. (1981) 'Microstates: Public Administration for the Small and Beautiful'. *Public Administration and Development* 1 (3) 245-56.

Murray, D.J. (1985) 'Public Administration in the Microstates of the Pacific'. In E. Dommen and P. Hein (ed.) *States, Microstates and Islands*. London: Croom Helm.

Nelson, J. (1988) 'The Political Economy of Stabilization: Commitment, Capacity, and Public Response'. In Bates, R.H. (ed.) *Towards a Political Economy of Development. A Rational Choice Perspective*. California: University of California Press.

Norton, H. (1969) *The Role of the Economist in Government Policy-making*. Berkeley, California: McCutchan Publishing.

Nunes, F.E. (1974) 'Towards a Classification of Caribbean Business Organizations'. In Nunes, F.E. & Draper, G. (eds) *Notes on Organization and Change in the Caribbean. Introductory Readings in Organizational Theory and Behaviour*. Mona, Jamaica: Institute of Social and Economic Research.

Nunes, F.E. & Draper, G. (eds) (1974) *Notes on Organization and Change in the Caribbean. Introductory Readings in Organizational Theory and Behaviour*. Mona, Jamaica: Institute of Social and Economic Research.

Nunes, F.E. (1976) 'The Nonsense of Neutrality'. *Social and Economic Studies* 25 (4) 347-65.

Nunes, F.E. (1990) (reprint) 'The Declining Status of the Jamaican Civil Service'. In Mills, G.E. (ed.) *A Reader in Public Policy and Administration*. Mona, Jamaica: Institute of Social and Economic Research.

Nunes, F.E. (undated) 'Policy and Decision-making. A Case Study of the 70/30 Education Regulation: Policy-making, Reactions and Consequences'. Jamaica: Administrative Staff College, General Management Course Teaching Material, No. GM/C3/69.

OEDC (1966) *Government Organisation and Economic Development*. Paris: OECD Publications.

Panitch, L. (1979) 'The Development of Corporatism in Liberal Democracies'. In Schmitter, P.C. & Lehmbruch, G. (eds) *Trends Towards Corporatist Intermediation*. London: Sage.

Pantin, D. (1990) 'Prospects for the Foreign Direct Investment Export Model in Jamaica and the Caribbean'. *Latin American Perspectives* 64 (17) No. 1: 55-72.

Parris, C. (1976) 'Political Dissidence in Post-independence Jamaica and Trinidad: 1962-72'. PhD Thesis, New York: Graduate Faculty of Political Science of the New School for Social Research.

Parris, C.D. (1976) *Capital or Labour? The Decision to Introduce the Industrialization Act in Trinidad & Tobago*. Working Paper No. 11, Mona: Institute of Social and Economic Research.

Paul, S. (1982) *Managing Development Programs. The Lessons of Success.* Colorado: Westview Press.

Pempel, T. & Tsunekawa, K. (1979) 'Corporatism Without Labour? The Japanese Anomaly'. In Schmitter, P. & Lembruch, G. (eds) *Trends Towards Corporatist Intermediation.* London: Sage.

Peters, G. (1990) 'The Necessity and Difficulty of Comparison in Public Administration'. *Asian Journal of Public Administration* 12 (1) 3-28.

Peters, G. (1991) 'Government Reform and Reorganization in an Era of Retrenchment and Conviction Politics'. In Farazmand (ed.) *Handbook of Comparative and Development Public Administration.* New York: Marcel Dekker.

Post, K. (1978) *Arise Ye Starvelings. The Jamaican Labour Rebellion of 1938 and its Aftermath.* The Hague: Martinus Nijhoff.

Pressman, J.L. & Wildavsky, A. (1973) *Implementation.* Berkeley, California: University of California Press.

Price, R.M. (1975) *Society and Bureaucracy in Contemporary Ghana.* Berkeley, California: University of California Press.

Przeworski, A. & Teune, H. (1970) *The Logic of Comparative Social Inquiry.* New York: John Wiley.

Puthucheary, M. (1978) *The Politics of Administration. The Malaysian Experience.* Oxford: Oxford University Press.

Pye, L. (1963) 'The Political Context of National Development'. In Swerdlow, I. (ed.).

Raadschelders, B.J. (1992) 'Definitions of Smallness: A Comparative Study'. In Baker, R. (ed.) *Public Administration in Small and Island States.* Connecticut: Kumarian Press.

Reddock, R.E. (1980) 'Industrialisation and the Rise of the Petty Bourgeoisie in Trinidad & Tobago'. MA Research Paper, The Hague: Institute of Social Studies.

Reddock, R.E. (1988) 'Commentary: The Quality of Life'. In Ryan, S. (ed.) *The Independence Experience 1962-1987.* St Augustine: Social and Economic Studies.

Reddock, R.E. (1991) 'Social Mobility in Trinidad & Tobago'. In Ryan, S. (ed.) *Social and Occupational Stratification in Contemporary Trinidad & Tobago.* St Augustine: Institute of Social and Economic Research.

Rice, E. (1988) 'Public Administration in Post-socialist Eastern Europe'. *Public Administration Review* 52 (2) 116-24.

Riggs, F. (1963) 'Bureaucrats and Political Development'. In La Palombara, J. (ed.) *Bureaucracy and Political Development.* N.J.: Princeton University Press.

Riggs, F. (ed.) (1971) *Frontiers of Development Administration*. Durham, N.C.: Duke University Press.

Riggs, F. (1991) 'Public Administration: A Comparativist Framework'. *Public Administration Review* 51 (6) 473-77.

Robinson, A.N.R. (1987) *Transition and Reconstruction in Independence: Trinidad & Tobago a Third World Challenge*. St Augustine, Trinidad: Institute of International Relations, University of the West Indies.

Rondinelli, D. (1983) 'Implementing Decentralization Programmes in Asia: A Comparative Analysis'. *Public Administration and Development* 3 (3) 181-207.

Rondinelli, D. (1987) *Development Administration and U.S. Foreign Aid Policy*. Boulder, Colorado: Lynne Rienner.

Rondinelli, D., Nellis, J.R. & Cheema, G.S. (1984) *Decentralization in Developing Countries: A Review of Recent Experience*. Washington, D.C.: The World Bank.

Rondinelli, D. & Nellis, J.R. (1986) 'Assessing Decentralization Policies in Developing Countries: The Case for Cautious Optimism'. *Development Policy Review* 4: 3-23.

Ryan, S. (1972) *Race and Nationalism in Trinidad & Tobago: a Study of Decolonization in a Multiracial Society*. Toronto: University of Toronto Press.

Ryan, S. (ed.) (1977) *Issues and Problems in Caribbean Public Administration*. Mona: University of the West Indies.

Ryan, S. (1989) *Evolution and Reaction. A study of Parties and Politics in Trinidad & Tobago, 1970-1981*. St Augustine: Institute of Social and Economic Research.

Ryan, S. (1991) 'Social Stratification in Trinidad & Tobago'. In S. Ryan (ed.) *Social and Occupational Stratification in Contemporary Trinidad & Tobago*. St Augustine: Institute of Social and Economic Research.

Ryan, S. & Brown, D. (eds) (1992) *Issues and Problems in Caribbean Public Administration Vols. I & II*. St Augustine: Trinidad, Department of Government, Univeristy of the West Indies.

Samaroo, B. (1983) 'Education as Socialization: Form and Content in the Syllabus of Canadian Presbyterian Schools in Trinidad from the late 19th Century'. Unpublished mimeograph.

Sandoval, J.M. (1983) 'State Capitalism in a Petroleum-based Economy: the Case of Trinidad & Tobago'. In F. Ambursley & R. Cohen (eds) *Crisis in the Caribbean*. Kingston: Heinemann Books.

Schahczenski, J. (1992) 'Development Administration in the Small Developing State: A Review'. *Public Administration and Development* 10(1) 69-80.

Schmidt, M. (1982) 'Does Corporatism Matter? Economic Crisis, Politics and Rates of Unemployment in Capitalist Democracies in the 1970s'. In Lehmbruch, G. & Schmitter, P. (eds) *Patterns of corporatist policy-making*. London: Sage.

Schmitter P. (1979) 'Modes of Interest Intermediation and Models of Societal Change in western Europe'. In Schmitter, P. & Lehmbruch, G. (eds) 1979 *Trends Towards Corporatist Intermediation*. London: Sage.

Schuyler, G.W. & Veltmeyer, H. (eds) (1988) *Rethinking Caribbean Development*. Halifax: International Education Centre.

Sebastien, R. (1982) 'State Sector Development in Trinidad & Tobago: 1956-1982'. *Tribune* 2 (1) 42-84.

Seers, D. (1972) 'The Prevalence of Pseudo-Planning'. In Faber, M. & Seers, D. (eds) *The Crisis in Planning*. London: Chatto and Windus for Sussex University Press.

Senior, O. (1972) *The Message is Change. A Perspective on the 1972 General Elections*. Kingston: Kingston Publishers in association with McGraw-Hill.

Sherwood, F. (1971) 'The Problem of the Public Enterprise'. In Riggs, F. (ed.) *Frontiers of Development Administration*. Durham, N.C.: Duke University Press.

Shivji, I. (1973) *The Silent Class Struggle*. Dar-es-Salaam: Tanzania Publishing House.

Smith, B.C. (1988) *Bureaucracy and Political Power*. Sussex: Wheatsheaf Books.

Srinivas, K.M. (1990) 'Holistic Strategies for Worker Dis-Alienation in Developing Countries'. In Jaeger, A.M. & Kanungo, R.N. (eds) *Management in Developing Countries*. London: Routledge.

Stephens, E. & Stephens, J. (1986) *Democratic Socialism in Jamaica*. London: Macmillan.

Stewart, S. (1981) 'Nationalist Educational Reforms and Religious Schools in Trinidad'. *Comparative Education Review* (June) 183-201.

Stone, C. (1989) *Carl Stone on Jamaican Politics, Economics and Society*. Jamaica: The Gleaner Company.

Thomas, C.Y. (1974) *Dependence and Transformation. The Economics of the Transition to Socialism*. New York: Monthly Review Press.

Thomas, C.Y. (1984) *The Rise of the Authoritarian State in Peripheral Societies*. New York: Monthly Review Press.

Thomas, C.Y. (1988) *The Poor and the Powerless. Economic Policy and Change in the Caribbean*. New York: Monthly Review Foundation.

Tisdell, C. & Fairbairn, T.I. (1983) 'Development Problems and Planning in a Resource-poor Pacific Country: The Case of Tuvalu'. *Public Administration and Development* 3 (4) 341-59.

UN Economic Commission for Asia and the Far East (UNECAFE) (1971) *Some Problems of Plan Implementation in the Second Development decade.* Bangkok, Thailand: UNECAFE.

UN Economic Commission for Asia and the Far East (1955) *Economic Development and Planning in Asia and the Far East.* Bangkok, Thailand: UNECAFE.

UN Institute for Training and Research (UNITAR) (1969) 'Status and Problems of very Small States and Territories'. New York: United Nations.

UN Institute for Training and Research (UNITAR) (1971) 'Small States and Territories, Status and Problems'. New York: United Nations.

United Nations (INTERPLAN) (1969) *Appraising Administrative Capability for Development.* New York: United Nations.

UN Public Administration Division of Economic and Social Affairs Department (UNPAD) (1968) 'Comparative Analysis of the Distinctive Public Administration Problems of Small States and Territories'. New York: United Nations.

United Nations (1966) 'The Administration of Economic Development Planning; Principles and Fallacies'. New York: United Nations.

United Nations (1951) Handbook of Public Administration. New York: United Nations.

Uphoff, N. (1985) 'People's Participation in Water Management: Gal Oya, Sir Lanka'. In Garcia-Zamor, J-C. (ed.) *Public Participation in Development Planning and Management. Cases from Africa and Asia.* Colorado, Boulder: Westview Replica Edition.

Verma, S.P. & Sharma, S.K. (eds) (1984) *Development Administration.* New Delhi: Indian Institute of Public Administration.

Walinsky, L.J. (1963) *The Planning and Execution of Economic Development: a nontechnical guide for policy-makers and administrators.* New York: McGraw-Hill.

Walker, J.A. (1996) 'From Riggs to the World Bank: Recurring themes in the study of Development Administration'. *Indian Journal of Public Administration* 42 (2) 119-31.

Walker, J.A. (1997) 'Trade liberalization and state-owned enterprise performance in Most Different Systems. A comparative study of Jamaica and Nigeria'. Roundtable of the International Institute of Administrative Science, Quebec City.

Waterson, A. (1963) 'Planning the Planning under the Alliance for Progress'. In Swerdlow, I. (ed.) *Development administration. Concepts and problems*. Syracuse, N.Y.: Syracuse University Press.

Waterson, A. (1965) *Development planning: Lessons of Experience*. Baltimore: John Hopkins Press.

Waterson, A. (1972) 'An Operational Approach to Development Planning'. In Faber, M. & Seers, D. (eds) *The Crisis in Planning*. London: Chatto and Windus for Sussex University Press.

Wiarda, H.J. & Kline, H.F. (eds) (1990) *Latin American Politics and Development*. Boulder: Westview Press.

Widdicombe Jr, S. (1972) *The Performance of Industrial Development Corporations. The Case of Jamaica*. New York: Praeger Special Studies.

Wijeweera, B. (1992) 'Public Administration in the Small Developing State: a Critique of the Theory'. *International Review of Administrative Sciences* 58 (3) 391-402.

Witter, M. & Kirton, C. (1990) *The Informal Economy in Jamaica. Some Empirical Exercises*, Working Paper No. 36. Mona: Institute of Social and Economic Research.

World Bank (1978) *The Commonwealth Caribbean. A World Bank Country Economic Report*. Baltimore: John Hopkins University Press.

World Bank (1982) *Jamaica: Development Is ·:es and Economic Prospects*. Washington, D.C.: The World Bank.

World Bank (1988) *Country Economic Report on Trinidad & Tobago*. Washington, D.C.: The World Bank.

World Bank (1995) *Bureaucrats in Business: The Economics and Politics of Government Ownership*. New York: The World Bank.

World Bank (1997) *World Development Report*. Washington, D.C.: The World Bank.

World Development Report (various years). Oxford: Oxford University Press.

Wunsch, J.S. (1991) 'Sustaining Third World Infrastructure Investments: Decentralization and Alternative Strategies'. *Public Administration and Development* 11 (1) 5-23.

Yudelman, S. (1987) *Hopeful Openings. A Study of Five Women's Development Organizations in Latin America and the Caribbean*. Connecticut: Kumarian Press.

Newspaper Articles

Jamaica

Jamaica Gleaner
28/1/1970, PSOJ Calls for Federation of Unions.
29/7/1979, Duncan Replies to Opposition Charge.
24/11/1980 JIDC 30th Anniversary Gleaner Supplement.
6/10/1982, Civil Service Lost over 2,000 Workers.
27/10/1982, Southern Processors Ltd. Sold for $1.5m.
7/7/1985, JIDC, Private Sector Side by Side.
19/3/1985, JIDC at Work Under National Industrial Plan.
2/12/1989, Staff Exodus at Jampro.
12/3/98, Jobs for the Boys and Men.

Jamaica Herald
16/3/1994

Observer
12/4/98, Garment Industry in Trouble.

Trinidad Guardian
22/10/1987, Jamaica Changing Entrepreneurial Landscape.

The Toronto Star
5/9/1992, Michael Manley now Believes in Capitalism.

Trinidad & Tobago

Express
3/4/1968, Report Suggests Wider Powers.
6/4/1968, We Can't Take Mr Wyeth's Report Too Seriously – IDC.
2/3/1969, IDC to Sink $240,000 in Plastics Firm.
20/3/1970, O'Halloran Warns Manufacturers: Gentlemen, Stop Discrimination.
7/6/1975, Retail Business Gets Lion's Share of Loans from IDC.
29/7/1975, Ex-CEO sees Government's Junior Secondary Move as Political.
2/12/1975, Big Civil Service Shake-up.
1/12/1976, Too Many Female Teachers Says Union. Bad Effect on Male Students, Claims STATT.
6/5/1978, Julien on 8 Boards for his Brains.
26/7/1981, Warner to Head NEC?
27/11/1981, Crisis in the Secondary School System.
15/8/1982, Education Board Member: Selection of Supervisors a Scandal.
20/8/1982, Sabha Board of Education Delivers an Ultimatum.

11/12/1982, Crisis in SBA, Group Locked Out.
3/5/1984, IDC Appoints New General Manager.
13/3/1986, Government Ignoring Performance of Private Sector.
30/2/1987, Overdue Loans to IDC $3m.
4/5/1987, PM: Nation Can't Live by Oil Alone.
11/7/1987, Export or Perish 11/7/1987.
20/2/1988, Hindus Want Action Against Cro Cro.
2/3/1988, Free Expression a Calyposinan's Right.
15/3/1988, Cro Cro's Vision Accurate. Another View by Dr Randy Peters.
21/5/1988, US Investor to Take Look at T&T.
6/12/1988, Scotland: IDC's Small Business Programme not Properly Evaluated.
26/2/1989, The One-Stop-Shop – A Brief History.
26/2/1989 Sunday Express IDC 30th Anniversary Supplement
12/12/1990, Hands Off our Schools.

Mirror
22/1/1965, Minister Never Prepared to Delegate Authority.
20/3/1966, Of Red Tape and Political Football. The IDC Must Stand on its Own Legs.

Guardian
4/9/1959, Foreigners Preferred.
9/6/1961, Incompatible Men at IDC 9/6/1961.
11/6/1961, DLP Queries Weintraub's Position.
30/8/1963, Small Plant Could Handle Steel Needs.
23/3/1963, IDC to Push Local Processing of Food.
17/10/1965, I Don't Care Department – That is What Our Businessmen Call the IDC.
25/5/1966, Shake-up for IDC.
22/9/1966, Dhanny Quits IDC.
17/6/1968, IDC Describes Shell Bagasse Claim as Untrue.
9/12/1968, IDC to Move Ahead with 45 New Posts.
4/12/1968, Maharaj Charges IDC Only Aids Capitalists.
1/3/1969, Primus Now Chairman of IDC.
23/3/1969, New Faces on IDC Board.
3/10/1969, Carry On Steve!
31/5/1970, Small Business Council.
2/12/1970, Opposition Attack on Public Servants.
7/9/1975, Trinidad's Coming Industrial Boom.
5/12/1977, Cabinet Agrees to Recast IDC's Role.
7/5/1978, Keep the Mauvais Langue Down.

5/6/1981, Ministers Meet School Boards.

19/2/1984, Another Exercise in Futility. That's the Enquiry into Public Service.

5/3/1985, Move to Expedite Decision-making Process at IDC.

24/5/1985, IDC Now Putting More Emphasis on Small Business.

7/7/1985, Servol – 15 years of Dedicated Service.

23/8/1987, Battle to the End.

28/3/1988, IDC Outlines Plan to Help Small Business.

23/4/1989, Nine Thousand, Six Hundred Likely for VTEP.

29/10/1991, School Principal at Age 28.

16/3/92, Educational Opportunities for Hindus Must Be: Frank Rampersad.

Official Documents

Jamaica

Central Planning Unit (CPU)
Technical Assistance Newsletters 1960-69.

Government of Jamaica (GOJ)
Act, No. 8 of 1965, The Education Act, Laws of Jamaica, 1965.

Act No. 7 of 1990, The Jampro Act, the Jamaica Promotions Corporation (Jampro) Act, 1990.

Act No. 13 of 1952, The Jamaica Industrial Development Corporation Act, 1952.

Annual Budget Speeches for the years 1960-92.

Commonwealth Development and its Financing – Jamaica 1964. London, Commonwealth Economic Commission, Her Majesty's Stationery Office.

Education: Pathways to the Future. Budget Presentation 1997.

Emergency Production Plan 1977-78, 1977.

Estimates of Expenditure (1960-90).

First Five Year Independence Plan 1963-68, 1962.

Going for Growth – Medium Term Economic Programme, 1988.

Growth with Equity, Opening and Closing Budget Presentations 1994/95.

National Plan for Jamaica 1957-67, 1958.

National Census, 1960.

National Physical Plan 1970-90, 1971.

Second Five Year Plan 1970-75, 1971.

Social Well Being Programme, 1988.

Ten Year National Plan for Jamaica 1957-67, 1957.

Third Five Year Plan 1978-82, 1978.

The National Development Planning Function, August 1972. Memorandum to all Permanent Secretaries from the Office of the Prime Minister, Ref. No. 010.10.

World Bank\GOJ Human Resources Facility, World Bank Roundtable Meeting, Conference Paper No.2. 1984

World Bank\GOJ, Human Resource Facility, Roundtable Meeting 5-7 February, 1985.

Hansard

Budget Debate Presentation by the Prime Minister, Hon. Edward Seaga, 1981.

Budget Debate Speech by Michael Manley, edited from the Hansard, 1974

Jamaica Industrial Development Corporation (JIDC)

A Review of the JIDC 1956-64, published in 1966.

Annual Reports of the Jamaica Industrial Development Corporation, 1960-88 (excluding 1975 and 1976).

Financial Statements of the Jamaica Industrial Development Corporation 1960-88 (excluding 1973).

Jamaica Industrial Development Corporation News 1 (1) August 1984.

Memorandum by the General Manager, JIDC on Jamaica Woolens Ltd., 1962.

Ministry of Education (MOE)

Annual Reports of the Ministry of Education (various years).

Boich, J. et al. The Study of School Administration. Consultants, Ministry of Education and the World Bank, World Bank IV Project, 1990.

Miller, W. & Ross, M. (eds), Education Sector Survey, 1977.

The Education Thrust of the 1970s, 1972.

Ministry of Industry (MOI)

Address to the Jamaica Manufacturers Association by the Minister of Industry, Commerce and Tourism on the occasion of the Industrial Development Corporation's 25th anniversary, 1977 Kingston, Jamaica: Ministry of Industry, Commerce and Tourism, Government of Jamaica.

Cabinet Submission of the Minister of Industry and Commerce, Hon. Dogulas Vaz, MIC 34/5/109, 1984. Kingston, Ministry of Industry and Commerce.

Letter from Mr Martin V. Dagata, Ag. Director of USAID to the Minister of Industry and Commerce, the Hon. D. Vaz, 26 April 1985. Kingston, Jamaica.

Memo to the Permanent Secretary of the Ministry of Industry and Commerce, from the Financial Secretary 13/1/84, Kingston, Ministry of the Industry and Commerce.

Memo to the Minister of State from the Permanent Secretary, MOI, 26 May 1987.

Personal Records of the JIDC Establishment, 1960-82.

Remission of Debt Charges due from the JIDC. Ministry of Trade and Industry File No. 42/7/13, January 1967, Kingston, Government of Jamaica.

Ministry Papers (MP)

Capital Development Fund – Annual Reports 1979 and 1980, Ministry Paper No. 81, 1980.

Developments in Industry, Ministry Paper No. 38, 1967.

Economic and Social Planning in Jamaica, May 1972. Ministry Paper No. 10, 1972.

Establishment of a Frozen Foods Processing Plant. Ministry of Trade and Industry, File No. 35/6/04, January, 1967.

Income Tax Amendment Law, Ministry Papers 15 to 18, as appended to the 1969 Annual Budget, 1969.

Jamaica Woolens Ltd, Ministry Paper No. 57, of 1962, 1962.

Review of Industry, Ministry Paper No. 38 of 1967, 1967.

National Planning Agency/The Planning Institute of Jamaica (NPA)/(PIOJ)

Distribution of Income in Rural and Urban Areas, 1979.

Economic and Social Survey of Jamaica 1976, 1981, 1989 and 1990. Kingston, National Planning Agency and The Planning Institute of Jamaica.

Statistical Institute of Jamaica (STATIN)

Labour Force Report 1973, 1974, 1989, 1990 and 1998.

Statistical Abstracts (various years).

Statistical Yearbook of Jamaica (various years).

Trinidad & Tobago

Central Bank (CB)

Handbook of Key Economic Statistics 1955-1985, 1989.

Central Statistical Office (CSO)

An Analysis of Government Revenue and Expenditure 1966-71, 1978.

Annual Statistical Digest 1966, 1989, published 1967 and 1991, respectively.

Census of Population 1960, Census Bulletin Nos. 6, 15, 20 and 12, 1962.

Census of Population 1960, Income Report, Census Bulletin Publication No. 44, 1977.

Digest of Education Statistics 1962-63, 1966-67, 1967-68, 1971-72, published 1965, 1969, 1970 and 1974, respectively.

Labour Force Report (various years).

National Income of Trinidad & Tobago 1966-85, 1987.

National Income of Trinidad & Tobago 1981-91, 1993.

Population and Housing Census 1980 Volumes II and VIII, 1987.

Quarterly Economic Report (January - June 1990), 1991.

Report on Education Statistics 1983-84, and 1987-88, published 1986 and 1990, respectively.

Review of the Economy, 1989.

Social Indicators, 1975.

Statistics at a Glance, 1995.

Government of Trinidad & Tobago (GOTT)

Administrative Improvement in T&T. United Nations Office of Technical Cooperation Terminal Report Project No. TRI/71/509, 1976.

Act No. 11 of 1958, The Industrial Development Corporation Act, 1958.

Act No. 37 of 1977, The Federation of Women's Institutes Act of Trinidad & Tobago.

Act No. 19 of 1989, The Voluntary Termination of Employment Act, 1989.

Act No. 4 of 1995, The Tourism and Industrial Development Company of Trinidad & Tobago Ltd. Vesting Act.

Annual Budget Speeches 1960-93.

Civil Lists of the Government of Trinidad & Tobago, 1956, 1971 and 1980.

Comparative Analysis of the Growth of the Public Service Establishment and the Growth in the Labour Force and Population During the Period 1960-80.

Dolly Report – Report of the Working Group on the Organization and Streamlining of the Public Service Practices and Procedures in T&T – Chairman C. H. Dolly, 1969.

Draft Development Plan 1983-86, Vol.I and II, subtitled – The Imperatives of Adjustment, 1983.

Draft Medium Term Economic Programme 1989-91, 1988.

Draft Public Sector Investment Programme 1989-91, 1988.

Draft Medium Term Macro Planning Framework 1989-91, 1988.

Estimates of Expenditure (various years).

Estimates of Revenue and Expenditure for the Year 1955, The colony of Trinidad & Tobago, 1956.

Final Report of the National Commission on the Status of Women, 1978.

First Five Year Development Programme 1958-62, 1961.

Growth of the Establishment and Percentage Salary increases for selected Public Officers 1965-80, 1980.

King Report, 1958

Lee Report – Report to the Hon. the Premier by the Hon. Ulric Lee on the Reorganization of the Public Service, 1959.

Lewis Report – First Report of the Working Party on the Role and Status of the Civil Service in the Age of Independence (Chairman J. O'Neil Lewis), 1964.

List of Permanent Appointees of the Administrative/Professional/Technical Grade in the Ministry of Education for the Period 1985-90, Trinidad, Service Commissions Department.

Loan Contract between the Republic of Trinidad & Tobago and the Inter-American Development Bank. Primary Education Programme, 26 March 1987.

Major Achievements of the Organisation and Management Division of the Ministry of Finance & Planning 1956-86, 1986.

Natural gas. An Investor's Guide, 1985.

Public Administration for the 21st Century, Green Paper, 1997.

Public Sector Investment Programme, 1990.

Public Sector Participation in Industrial and Commercial Activities, White Paper, 1972 and 1975.

Report of the Commission of Enquiry into Subversive Activities in Trinidad & Tobago (The Mbanefo Report), 1965, House Paper No. 2 of 1965.

Second Five Year Plan 1964-68, 1963.

Ten-year Development Scheme for Trinidad & Tobago, 1946.

Third Five Year Plan 1969-73, 1968.

Towards a New Public Administration. A Policy Agenda for the Public Service of Trinidad and Tobago, Green Paper 1996.

Hansard

Cabinet Proposals on Education, Debates of the Legislative Council, 1960.

Pioneer Industries Programme, Debate of the House of Representatives, 1957.

Public Service Classification and Compensation Scheme, Debates of the Senate, 1966.

Sugar Areas Interim Development Programme, Debates of the Legislative Council, 1957.

Statement by the Prime Minister, the Honourable A.N.R. Robinson to the House of Representatives. August 19, 1988.

Tobago Development Programme, Debates of the Legislative Council, 1958.

Ministry of Industry (MOI)

Statement by the Hon. Errol Mahabir, Minister of Industry, On the opening of Industry Week, 21 September 1975.

T&T Industrial Development Corporation (T&TIDC)
Annual Reports, various years.
Change and the T&T Industrial Development Corporation, Statement by the General Manager of the Industrial Development Corporation, 1970.
Curriculum Vitae of Mr Eldon Warner, General Manager, Industrial Development Corporation, 1978.
Financial Statements of the T&T Industrial Development Corporation 1959 to 1991.
Private Investment Diagnostic Study, Trinidad & Tobago, 1991. Washington D.C., Inter-American Development Bank.
Record of Major Achievements of the IDC 1959-81, 1981.
Report on Small Business Consultation, Part I, IDC, 1979.
Report on the Second Five Year Development Programme 1964-68. October 1968.
Report on the Second Five Year Development Programme 1964-68. October 1968.
Scotland Report – Report of the Committee to Review the Operation of the IDC, 1985.
Statement to the Press, Steve de Castro, Economic Studies and Planning Division. 1 October 1969, Port of Spain.
The Role of the One Stop Shop and Impact Agencies, 1991.

Ministry of Education (MOE)
Draft Plan for Educational Development, 1967-83, 1967.
Framework for an education plan 1989-90. Towards an implementation Plan for Operationalizing the Education Sector in accord with the directions of the National Policy Guidelines and directions of the macro Planning Framework. 1988.
Maurice, H. Report, or, The Committee on General Education, 1959.
National Consultation on the Sectoral Plan for Education and Training, 1989.
Status report on the implementation of the 1985-90 Education Plan, 1988.
The Prime Minister's Proposals to Cabinet on Education 1975, 1975.
The Cabinet Proposals on Education 1960, 1960.
The Prime Minister's further Proposals on Education 1975, 1975.
UNESCO, Education Planning Mission to Trinidad & Tobago, 1964. Paris, UNESCO.
Verbatim Reports of the National Consultation on the 1968-83 Education Plan, 1969.
Verbatim Reports of the National Consultation on the 1985-90 Education Plan, 1985.

Ministry of Information (MOI)
Press Releases File for the period 1971-79.

UNIDO
Terminal Report on the T&T Industrial Sector Review, 1988. Vienna, United
   Nations Industrial Development Organization, UNIDO.

List of Interviews

Jamaica

April, 1992, Representative of the Private Sector Organization of Jamaica.
May, 1992, The Hon. Bruce Goulding, Deputy Political Leader of the Jamai-
   ca Labour Party.
May, 1992, Former JIDC Executive Manager 1976-79.
May, 1992, Former manager, JIDC.
May, 1992, Professor Norman Girvan.
May, 1992, Mr George Briggs, Permanent Secretary, Ministry of the Public
   Service.
May, 1992, Ms. Maurien Vernon-Stephenson, former Executive Officer,
   JIDC.
May, 1992, Former head of the Productivity and Industrial Services Divi-
   sion.
May, 1992, Ex-officers of JIDC subsidiaries, 1976-79.
May and June, 1992, The Hon. Robert Lightborne, former Minister of Indus-
   try and Commerce and founder of the JIDC.
June, 1992, Ms. Valerie Veira, Manager JIDC 1982-88.
June, 1992, Professor Errol Miller, University of the West Indies.
June, 1992, Ministry of Education Officials.
June, 1992, Mr Warren Woodham, former-General Manager JIDC 1982-88.
June, 1992, Mr Clan Anderson, Administrative Officer, Ministry of Industry
   & Commerce.
June, 1992, Former JIDC Board member 1976-77.
June, 1992, President of the Jamaica Teachers Association.
June, 1992, Board member, Cornwall Diary Board.

Trinidad & Tobago

January, 1992 Lennox Seales, Organization and Management Division, Office of the Prime Minister.
January-February, 1992, Mr G.H. Legall, former Permanent Secretary, Ministry of Petroleum and Mines.
February, 1992, Mr U. Forbes, Lecturer, University of the West Indies, Trinidad.

May and July, 1992, Ex-Government Ministers, 1976 Cabinet.

July, 1992, Representative, Trinidad & Tobago Manufacturers Association.

July, 1992, Mrs Eileen Douglas, former Small Business Representative on IDC Small Business Council.

July, 1992, Mr Lennox Seales, Organization and Management Officer, O&M Division.

July, 1992, Mr Roland Baptiste, Former Deputy Director, Central Training Unit and Chief Personnel Officer.

July, 1992, Chief Executive Officers of key parastatals, Agricultural Development Bank, Trinidad & Tobago Telephone Company, Public Transport Service Corporation, Water and Sewerage Authority.

July, 1992, Tobago House of Assembly Officials, Tobago.

August, 1992, Mr Jack Balkisson, Head, Small Business Division, Trinidad & Tobago Industrial Development Corporation.

August, 1992, Mr Waldron Emmanuel, retired Director of Planning, Ministry of Education.

August, 1992, Ministry of Education Officials.

August, 1992, Ms Liela Narinsingh, Loans Officer, Small Business Division, Trinidad & Tobago Industrial Development Corporation.

August, 1992 Maurice Chin Aleong, Planning Office, Ministry of Education.

August, 1992, Former Minister of Education, 1989.

August, 1992, Head, Principals Association of Trinidad & Tobago.

September, 1992, Former Loans Manager, Small Business Division, IDC.

September, 1992, Former Board Member, T&TIDC 1970 Board.

July 1997, Ex-Cabinet Ministers, Trinidad

Index